ITALIAN HIGH RENAISSANCE AND
BAROQUE SCULPTURE

AN INTRODUCTION
TO ITALIAN SCULPTURE

BY

JOHN POPE-HENNESSY

PART I

ITALIAN GOTHIC SCULPTURE

PART II

ITALIAN RENAISSANCE SCULPTURE

PART III

ITALIAN HIGH RENAISSANCE AND
BAROQUE SCULPTURE

IN THREE VOLUMES

JOHN POPE-HENNESSY

ITALIAN HIGH RENAISSANCE AND BAROQUE SCULPTURE

TEXT

PHAIDON PRESS

1963

MADE IN GREAT BRITAIN
PRINTED BY HUNT · BARNARD AND COMPANY LIMITED
AT THE SIGN OF THE DOLPHIN · AYLESBURY · BUCKS

CONTENTS

Plates

ITALIAN HIGH RENAISSANCE AND
BAROQUE SCULPTURE

ITALIAN HIGH RENAISSANCE AND
BAROQUE SCULPTURE

THE little that we know about the attitude of sculptors in the fifteenth century to the art of their own time comes from the *Commentaries* of Ghiberti. For the sixteenth century the sources are richer and more informative, but one of them transcends all others in importance, Vasari's *Lives*. Not only was Vasari on terms of friendship with most of the great sculptors of his day, but he supplies, in the prefaces to the three sections of the *Lives*, a precise account of the view which artists in the middle of the century took of the present and the past. For Vasari the history of Italian art falls into three sections, the first a pre-history running down to the end of the Trecento, the second the Early Renaissance – the period, that is, between the competition for the bronze doors of the Baptistry in Florence in 1400 and the emergence of Michelangelo – and the third 'the modern age'. It is the modern age, or High Renaissance, that is the subject of this book.

In sculpture the heroes of Vasari's three sections are Nicola Pisano, Donatello and Michelangelo, and his criterion of judgement is their relationship to the antique. Whereas Nicola was no more than an agent by whom the art of sculpture was improved, the works of Donatello 'are up to the level of the good antiques', while those of Michelangelo 'are in every respect much finer than the ancient ones'. This theory of continuous upward progress was fortified by the belief that a similar development had taken place in Greece, where the three phases were represented by Canachus, whose statues were lacking in vivacity and truth, Myron, who 'endowed his works with such excellent proportion and grace that they might be termed beautiful', and Polycletus, by whom 'absolute perfection' was attained.

In one respect Vasari recognised that this analogy might be misleading, in that the motive power behind Greek sculpture was self-generated, whereas Renaissance sculpture was a renewal, and its course was therefore influenced by the availability of antique sculptures. During the first phase 'the admirable sculptures . . . buried in the ruins of Italy remained hidden or unknown'; the second was one of discovery, though so exiguous were the remains that sculptors were necessarily guided by the light of nature rather than by that of the antique; in the third phase more and better sculptures became known. 'Some of the finest works mentioned by Pliny,' writes Vasari, 'were dug out of the earth, the Laocoon, the Hercules, the great torso of Belvedere, the Venus, the Cleopatra, the Apollo and countless others, which are copied in their softness and their hardness from the best living examples, with actions which do not distort them, but give them motion and display the utmost grace.' This made it possible for sculptors in Vasari's day to attain 'the zenith of design'. This view was not peculiar to Vasari; it was held universally, and is accountable for the main difference between Early and High Renaissance sculpture, that the background of the first is a sense

(1)

of struggle towards a distant goal, while that of the second is a feeling of achievement, the sense of life lived on a plateau from which the only advance possible is a descent. What Vasari, writing in 1550, could not foresee was that the revolution which was associated with the name of Michelangelo would be followed by two further stylistic revolutions led by Giovanni Bologna and Bernini, and that these later revolutions would also spring from the action of classical sculpture on the creative imaginations of great artists.

Growing familiarity with the antique, especially with Hellenistic sculpture, had the practical result that it led to changes in technique which are apparent initially in the work of Michelangelo. The best account of Michelangelo's technical procedure is given by Cellini in his *Treatise on Sculpture*. Michelangelo, Cellini tells us, was in the habit of drawing the principal view of his statue on the block, and of beginning the sculpture on this face as though it were in half-relief. Gradually the image, covered with its penultimate skin, was disclosed, and then, with a file and small-toothed chisel, this last skin was removed, leaving a figure modelled with the same veracity and freedom as an antique sculpture. The classic example of this technique is Michelangelo's unfinished statue of St. Matthew (Figs. 9, 10). Vasari stresses that technical advances in the sixteenth century enabled painters to turn out more and larger works; advances in technique also permitted sculptors to carve more rapidly and on a steadily expanding scale. The creative vistas that were opened up by this new technical facility can be gauged from the contract with Michelangelo for twelve more than life-size marble statues of Apostles to be delivered at the rate of one a year, and from the impractical first project for the tomb of Pope Julius II. According to Vasari, Michelangelo at first worked from a small model, but became a convert to the full-scale model while engaged on the Medici tombs. Full-scale models were invariably used by Giovanni Bologna. One advantage of employing them was that the execution of the marble could be entrusted to other hands. This contingency is first openly discussed in the case of Michelangelo, who was forced by circumstances to delegate the carving of certain statues for the Medici Chapel and the Julius tomb. In most of Giovanni Bologna's marble sculptures assistants played a material part. The use of full-scale models was pressed to its logical conclusion by Bernini in a number of large works – the monument of the Countess Matilda, the Fountain of the Four Rivers, the Chair of St. Peter, the tomb of Pope Alexander VII – in the execution of which he himself had practically no share. No exception was taken to this practice at the time – it was the prerequisite of superhuman productivity – but in judging the sculptures that resulted as works of art, a firm distinction must be drawn between the sculptor as designer and the sculptor as executant.

High Renaissance sculptors are distinguished from their predecessors by a concern with style, that is with the form in which their works are cast. In sixteenth-century art theory painting and sculpture are commonly presented as branches of *disegno* or design, and the prevailing faith in a style-concept applicable to both arts gave rise, at very beginning of the century, to the suggestion that the marble block from which Michelangelo subsequently carved the David should be made available to Leonardo, who had no experience of marble sculpture. This concern with form led to an unprecedented readiness to acknowledge the supremacy of the stylistic innovator, that is of the great artist. No sculptor in the fifteenth century enjoyed the god-like authority of Michelangelo. One of the epigrams written for his funeral describes his return to the celestial regions whence he had briefly descended upon Florence. Adaptations of Michelangelo's St. Peter's Pietà were carved during the sculptor's lifetime for Genoa and Florence; no sooner had the figures in the Medici Chapel been abandoned than reduced copies of them were made by Tribolo; casts of works by Michelangelo were known to Vincenzo Danti at Perugia and to Vittoria in Venice; and small bronzes were made after the Bacchus, the Moses and the Minerva Christ. As a result these works came to be looked upon as archetypes. But the style of a great artist arises from the demands of his own temperament, and when it is adapted as an academic discipline, it is transformed. This occurred in Florence with the style of Michelangelo, and contributed to the phenomenon which is known as Mannerism.

When this book was first announced, it was called *Italian Mannerist and Baroque Sculpture*. The epithet Mannerist has since been eliminated from its title, and the noun Mannerism has, so far as possible, been avoided in the text. Originally descriptive of a homogeneous style, the *maniera*, practised locally in Florence over a short period of time, the concept of Mannerism has been slowly extended to a point where it is little but a synonym for style during the sixteenth century. High Renaissance sculpture is of its nature meditated and sometimes artificial, but only by exception is it Mannerist, and the effect of applying this or any other descriptive label to it is to impose a spurious uniformity on a number of widely differing artists and works of art. In its legitimate historical sense, Mannerism is no more than a substyle of Renaissance sculpture, a brief parenthesis in a development that leads from the trial relief of Brunelleschi to the final dissolution of Renaissance ideals and Renaissance style in the mature sculptures of Bernini.

MICHELANGELO : THE EARLY WORKS

MICHELANGELO was the first artist in history to be recognised by his contemporaries as a genius in our modern sense. Canonised before his death, he has remained magnificent, formidable and remote. Some of the impediments to establishing close contact with his mind are inherent in his own uncompromising character; he was the greatest sculptor who ever lived, and the greatest sculptor is not necessarily the most approachable. But others are man-made, and when we turn for help to the books dealing with his work, only occasionally do the sculptures stand out from the pervasive Nietzschean mist.

Born in 1475, Michelangelo was brought up in the neighbourhood of Florence, and in 1488, when he was thirteen, was apprenticed to the painter Ghirlandaio. In later life he tended to play down the significance of this apprenticeship, mainly because of the terms in which he came to view himself and his own work. He had never, he claimed, been a professional painter or sculptor, by which he meant that he maintained no workshop, and he looked on his career as a break with the immemorial tradition of the artist as artificer and the work of art as artefact. Had events pursued their normal course he would have stayed with Ghirlandaio for three years, but he was rescued from that fate by Lorenzo de' Medici, who had established what was later known as the Medici Academy. This was not an academy in the sense of 1550 or of to-day; it was a loose arrangement whereby youths of exceptional talent were freed from routine duties, and set down under supervision to study the antiques in the Medici collection. It affected Michelangelo in two fundamental ways. It meant in the first place that he set off on his journey without the handicap of a conventional style or of an inculcated, an imposed technique; in both respects his attitude to sculpture was, from the first, empirical. It meant secondly that at fifteen he was imbued, through contact with the Medicean circle, with a conception of the visual arts as an exclusively intellectual activity. Years later, when he described the painter as working not with the brush but with the brain, and praised the sculptor's hand obedient to his intellect, he was pursuing trains of thought that must go back to this extremely early time.

Only one work dating from these years survives, the relief known as the Battle of the Centaurs in the Casa Buonarroti (Plate 2). From the life of Michelangelo written by his pupil Condivi in 1553 we learn that it was carved before the death of Lorenzo de' Medici, that is before April 1492, and was inspired by the humanist Politian. 'Michelangelo,' writes Condivi, 'gave himself up to his studies, showing every day some fruit of his labours to Lorenzo il Magnifico. In the same house lived Politian, who, perceiving Michelangelo to be a lofty spirit, conceived much affection for him, and used continually to spur him on in his studies, and was for ever interpreting and showing him some theme for his work. Among other things he proposed to him one day the rape of Dejanira, and the battle of the Centaurs, explaining the whole fable, passage by passage.' From a narrative standpoint the Battle of the Centaurs is ambiguous – a great many thousand words have been devoted to discussing exactly what it represents – and of all Michelangelo's multiple concerns when carving it, we should, on the evidence of our eyes alone, judge academic programme to have been least prominent. The importance of the relief is that it marks a revolutionary change of attitude to the morphology of the antique.

The Medici Academy was directed by the bronze sculptor Bertoldo, and we have one clue as to the methods of instruction he employed, for Vasari tells us that Michelangelo's co-pupil Torrigiani 'worked in the round in clay certain figures which had been given him by Bertoldo'. Michelangelo must have been trained in the same way. In London there is a Bertoldo statuette of Hercules on a little platform which is sunk into a later base. The platform indicates the point from which Bertoldo intended the figure to be seen, and the pose of the figure from this view (Fig. 1), with shoulders receding diagonally into space, neck tensed, head turned, and one knee thrust forward into a front plane, occurs again in a standing youth on the left of

Michelangelo's relief. Immediately to the right is a male figure seen from behind, and when we look at the back of Bertoldo's statuette (Fig. 2), it offers a precedent for this pose too. When, therefore, scholars tell us, as nowadays they sometimes do, that Michelangelo owed nothing to Bertoldo, and that the Medici Academy is a myth, we can answer that both propositions are wrong.

Bertoldo's interests extended from the single figure to the group. The main evidence for this is a bronze battle relief in the Bargello based on a classical sarcophagus (Vol. II, Figs. 138, 139). In the eyes of Renaissance sculptors Roman sarcophagus reliefs had one and only one defect, that they were inadequately organised. In Bertoldo's relief this is redressed by a number of devices of which one is specially significant, that of linking two figures so that they form a single unit within the scene. In the foreground, for example, a little to the right of centre, are two figures with backs turned, which have been linked together to establish a diagonal through the relief. This practice is taken over in the Battle of the Centaurs, where the male figure with back turned is joined to the female figure beneath him, and his left arm rests on a diagonal between the upper left and lower right corners of the figurated part of the relief. Michelangelo's employment of this compositional device is infinitely bolder than Bertoldo's (an example is the linked arms of the figures on the right, which establish a horizontal line parallel to the body of the woman beneath them and to the base of the relief), his command of movement is incomparably greater, and already, in the seated figure on the left, we sense the stirring of the divine compassion that inspired so many of his adult works. This exclusive, obsessive concentration on the human figure, not as representation but as language, this vocabulary of the nude is fundamental for all his later sculptures. In this sense the Battle of the Centaurs is a mirror which reflects the face not of the sixteen-year-old boy by whom it was carved, but of the ageing artist of the Medici tombs.

In another respect too the relief looks forward to the sculptor's later works: in that it is incomplete. In the fifteenth century unfinished marble sculptures are extremely rare; they exist, but they can be counted on the fingers of two hands. With Michelangelo, however, the number of works that were not finished far exceeds those that were. This fact is fundamental for an understanding of his work. A vast literature has grown up on Michelangelo and the unfinished, and the prevalence of unfinished sculptures has been explained in many different ways. There have been aesthetic explanations, and moral explanations, and metaphysical explanations, and distinctions have been drawn between what is called *innere* and *äussere Vollendung*, intrinsic and extrinsic finish, and between the unfinished and unfinishable, the *unvollendet* and the *unvollendbar*.

The first writer to discuss the problem was Vasari, who counted eleven completed statues. Since most of them were early works, he deduced that Michelangelo in youth had an ideal of completeness from which he retreated in later life. This diagnosis is not quite correct. The early works that are complete were one and all commissions, and the later sculptures that are finished were also works of whose utility there was no doubt; even the Moses remained unfinished in the sculptor's studio for almost thirty years until it was absolutely certain it would be required. The specific reasons why works were left unfinished are almost as numerous as the works themselves. Sometimes the sculptor was dissatisfied with the marble block, sometimes he lost his temper and damaged the block wantonly, sometimes he revolted against the patron for whom he was working, sometimes he reacted against the subject with which he had to deal. Just because the ostensible causes are so various, they can only be regarded as a projection of his creative nature, an expression of the kind of sculptor that he was. More than any other artist, Michelangelo worked at the limits of the possible. Each of his sculptures from the very first dealt with an artistic problem, and it seems that his interest in them waned once they were formulated to a point at which the solution was no longer in doubt. Michelangelo's concern lay with the problem, not with the completed work of art.

This had consequences that must be mentioned briefly here. The difficulties that beset his great commissions were inherent in his own psychology; his temperament made it preternaturally difficult for him to maintain a steady course. For this reason his influence on contemporary sculpture, great though it was, was infinitely less than it would otherwise have been. In the fifteen-eighties Francesco Bocchi, in his little eulogy of the St. George of Donatello, took it upon himself to express the academic critic's disapproval of the *bruttezza*, the ugliness, of Michelangelo's unfinished sculptures, and it was almost exclusively through finished or virtually finished works that the sculptor's influence was felt. But Michelangelo's unfinished works none the less introduced a new factor into art. They revealed the possibilities of the indefinite, and postulated a relationship between the work of art and the spectator, whereby the spectator was called on to invest with meaning forms whose exact meaning was not defined. The full significance of this transpired in the nineteenth century, when Michelangelo's lack of finish was acclaimed as an affirmation of individual liberty and as an intimation of the infinite, a realm superior to art. From there it was no more than a short step to the conviction that the unfinished works of Michelangelo were in fact complete. As an English writer on Michelangelo put it, 'they are complete to us'. But by objective standards these sculptures are not complete; they were not regarded by the sculptor as complete; in practically every case they were begun in the conviction that they would be finished; and they should be interpreted in terms of the completed sculptures they imply.

Between 1492, when Michelangelo left the Palazzo Medici, and 1494, when he visited Venice and Bologna, only one statue is recorded, an over-life-size Hercules. It remained in Florence till 1529, when it was sent to France, and there it disappeared leaving no trace. At this time Michelangelo embarked on the study of anatomy. We hear of his analysing corpses for the first time in Florence in 1492, and for the last time in Rome in the fifteen-forties, when he dissected the body of a Moor that had been given him by a physician friend. The scope of his studies was artistic and not medical – he despised the anatomical writings of Dürer because in them gesture and action were left unexplained – and they account for the preternatural confidence with which his earliest large sculptures are carved.

On his return to Florence in 1495 he carved two statues which have also vanished. One of them was a commission from Botticelli's patron, Lorenzo di Pierfrancesco de' Medici, for a Giovannino, and the other was a sleeping Cupid. The Cupid, which was based on a classical sleeping Cupid type and passed as an antique, was bought by Cardinal Riario, and in June 1496 Riario encouraged Michelangelo to move to Rome. Michelangelo went to Rome for purposes of study, and while there he depended upon the perceptiveness of private patrons, of whom the most important was Jacopo Galli, a rich collector of antiques. All his major sculptures at this time were either carved for Galli, or were contracted for with Galli as an intermediary, and if we knew more about Galli, we should understand more than we do about the early work of Michelangelo. For Galli he carved a second Cupid, which like the earlier Cupid has disappeared, and one work which has survived, the Bacchus in the Bargello (Plates 10, 11). Work on the Bacchus was probably begun at the end of 1496 or in the following year. About 1532 a drawing was made of the statue standing in Galli's garden, among his collection of antiques. The Bacchus was carved in Galli's house, and the classical carvings represented in the drawing may have been before the sculptor's eyes when it was made.

Like the Battle of the Centaurs, the Bacchus is based on the antique, but is constructed in a way peculiar to the fifteenth century. In Roman sculpture (Fig. 13) the subject of Bacchus and a Satyr is treated with a dominant view, usually with the two figures set flat across one plane. But in Florence the aesthetic of the free-standing statue had been developed in a contrary direction, first by Donatello, who devised a type of figure with four interdependent faces (Vol. II, Figs. 9–11), and then by Verrocchio, who in the Putto with a Fish (Vol. II, Plate 78) evolved a serpentine figure in which no view was predominant. In the Bacchus the corkscrew motion of the Satyr would be unthinkable without Verrocchio's experiments, and so would the slow spiral movement by which the Satyr is linked to the main figure, and the eye is carried upwards to the cup held in the right hand. One of the recurring preoccupations of Florentine Early Renaissance sculptors was with mobility, play of the features as well as movement of the frame. Donatello introduced this factor of mobility into the niche figure, so that the Prophets on the Campanile step forward as though about to speak, and both Desiderio da Settignano and Benedetto da Majano depict the Baptist advancing with parted lips. Hence Michelangelo's concern with the unstable stance of the drunken figure and with the loose movement of his lips. But there is nothing conventional in his perception of the human form, and nothing conventional in his technique. The form is apprehended not as surface only, but as a rational organism, and the means by which it is recorded derive from the antique. In the Bacchus Michelangelo proclaims his freedom from the fetters of technique; whatever problems faced him in the future, they could not arise from the rendering of the human figure in the round.

For religious sculpture the relevance of the antique was less direct, but its influence is manifest in Michelangelo's first sacred work. His arrival in Bologna in 1494 was timely, for the principal Bolognese sculptor, Niccolò dell'Arca, had died a few months earlier, while engaged upon the marble lid of the Arca of St. Dominic (Vol. I, Fig. 48). Two statuettes of Saints and one of a pair of candle-bearing angels were missing from the shrine, and responsibility for these was transferred to Michelangelo. Niccolò dell'Arca's roots were in Ferrara – his most intense experience was drawn from paintings by Cossa and Ercole de' Roberti – and his candle-bearing angel on the altar is elegant and fragile, and so lacking in tactility that from the front it looks as though its back were flat. Michelangelo made no attempt to imitate its style. He set his figure (Plate 1) not straight across the base, but with a slight diagonal emphasis in the extended leg, and posed the body so that the shoulders receded from the front plane. The principle of posture is that which underlies the figures in the Battle of the Centaurs, and the head is carved in precisely the same fashion as the head of Theseus in the relief. The points of juncture at the ankles, wrists and neck, and the attachment of the wings and shoulder blades, are articulated with amazing confidence. One of the most impressive features of this little figure is the way in which the candlestick acquires its own specific weight, and rests firmly on the pedestal of the knee and foot. The two Saints are less forward-looking, and the St. Petronius (Fig. 3) conforms in type to the statue of this Saint by Quercia above the doorway of San Petronio.

In 1498, in Rome, Michelangelo received his first commission for a major religious sculpture. There resulted one of his most famous works, the St. Peter's Pietà (Plate 6). We are prone to take the Pietà for granted, as we do all the greatest works of art, but if we could contrive for a moment to see it with fresh eyes, we should find it an entirely inexplicable sculpture on the counts of style, subject and typology. No large marble Pietà was carved anywhere in Italy in the whole fifteenth century, but in Florence about 1490 the subject became popular in painted altarpieces. The altarpieces are, however, self-contained – they show the Virgin mourning over the dead Christ – whereas the sculptured group is not – it shows the Virgin displaying the dead Christ to the onlooker. That this is the subject of the group is left in no doubt by the Virgin's extended hand, part of which has been restored, but where everything save possibly the index finger is in the position Michelangelo designed. The Virgin is a youthful figure. Many years later Michelangelo defended this break with conventional iconography, but it was not universally acceptable, and when a copy of the group was made for Genoa by Michelangelo's one-time assistant Montorsoli, this aspect of its imagery was modified.

The group is constructed with great deliberation as a pyramid. Christ's head is turned back in such a way as not to break the bounding line, and beneath his body the folds of the Virgin's cloak flood down like a waterfall. In the sculpture of the fifteenth century there is no motif at all like this, and for that reason parallels have been sought in the North among German Vesper-bildern and French sculptured Pietàs. The group was commissioned by a Frenchman, Cardinal Jean Villier de la Grolaie, who came from Auch and had been Abbot of Saint Denis, so it is not impossible that it was planned with a French Pietà in mind. But to admit that (and it is far from certain) is to recognise the transformation that has taken place. The jagged drapery has been rounded and ordered and filled out, a Hellenistic hero has been substituted for the doll-like

Figs. 1, 2. Bertoldo: HERCULES. Victoria & Albert Museum, London.

Fig. 3. Michelangelo: ST. PETRONIUS.
S. Domenico Maggiore, Bologna.

Fig. 4. Michelangelo: ST. PETER.
Duomo, Siena.

Figs. 5, 6. Michelangelo: THE TADDEI TONDO. Royal Academy of Arts, London.

Fig. 7. Michelangelo: THE DONI TONDO. Uffizi, Florence.
Fig. 8. Rustici: VIRGIN AND CHILD WITH THE YOUNG BAPTIST. Museo Nazionale, Florence.

Figs. 9, 10. Michelangelo: ST. MATTHEW. Accademia, Florence.

Fig. 11. Michelangelo: DRAWING FOR AN APOSTLE STATUE. British Museum, London.
Fig. 12. Michelangelo: DRAWING FOR THE BRUGES MADONNA. British Museum, London.

Fig. 13. Roman, first century A.D.: BACCHUS AND A SATYR. Museo delle Terme, Rome.
Fig. 14. Roman copy of a Greek original: PENELOPE. Museo Vaticano, Rome.

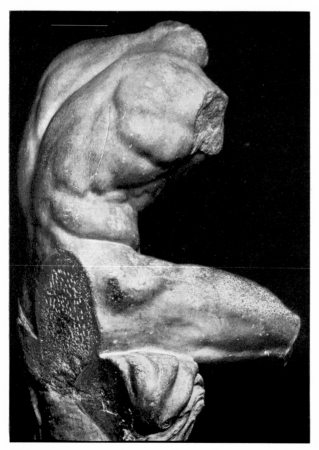

Fig. 15. Hellenistic, first century B.C.: THE BELVEDERE TORSO. Museo Vaticano, Rome.
Fig. 16. Rhodian, second century B.C.: LAOCOON. Museo Vaticano, Rome.

Christ, and the emotion on the Virgin's face is rendered with supremely classical restraint.

The Pietà can only have resulted from close intellectual application, but we have no way of reconstructing the ideas the sculptor sifted and dismissed. Some impression of the nature of his thought can none the less be gained from the only other work he produced of the same kind. This is the Madonna at Bruges (Plate 7), which was carved after he returned to Florence, probably in 1504 or 1505. Here, thanks to the survival of a number of preliminary drawings, we can watch Michelangelo's creative machinery at work. In what is presumably the earliest of the drawings, the Child is not shown standing, as in the completed group, but is supported on the Virgin's knee, with his head turned in right profile and his right leg outstretched. The Virgin in this version, like so many of her predecessors in the fifteenth century, is gazing down, and her feet, like the feet of so many fifteenth-century Madonnas, are set flat on the base. In another study the scheme is modified; the left foot of the Virgin is set higher than her right, and the Child stands between her legs. In a third sketch on the same sheet the relative positions of the two feet of the Virgin are preserved, but the Child is shown standing in front of her right knee, while in a fourth sketch (Fig. 12), in the British Museum, the Virgin gazes dispassionately outwards, as she does in the completed group. These preliminary drawings register a change of concept as well as form. The maternal motif on which fifteenth-century Madonnas almost without exception had been founded is progressively abandoned, and the resulting statue has the same relation to traditional Madonna groups that the Pietà has to the traditional Mourning over the dead Christ. In both the narrative element has been excised, and the Virgin is shown with her features frozen by suffering or by premonition, offering to the spectator the dead or living Christ. The effect is so meditated and withdrawn that at first sight we may be tempted to describe it as impersonal, but these are in fact the first examples of the highly personalised religious iconography which was to reach its climax in Michelangelo's late works.

In the spring of 1501 Michelangelo left Rome for Florence. Before he did so, negotiations were begun for the last of the commissions in which Jacopo Galli was involved, some statuettes for the Piccolomini altar in Siena Cathedral. The contract for them was signed in June 1501, and the four figures Michelangelo completed were finished by September 1504. The phrase the 'four figures Michelangelo completed' has an ominous ring. In Rome between 1496 and the first months of 1501 he finished three major works, but in Florence, between 1501 and March 1505 when he returned to Rome, the balance between his capacity and the demands made on it was for the first time disturbed. In 1501 it seemed that Michelangelo would complete a whole series of great sculptures; by 1505 some of the factors which would prevent his doing so were already making themselves felt. Michelangelo looked on the commission for Siena without enthusiasm; his figures were intended for a pre-existing setting, and on only one previous occasion, at Bologna, had he undertaken a commission of the kind. In the interval his stylistic will had grown increasingly intractable. The measure of the change can be judged if we contrast the St. Petronius at Bologna (Fig. 3), with its backward glances at Quercia and Niccolò dell'Arca, and the St. Peter at Siena (Plate 9, Fig. 4), where the pose is severely rational, and

each fold of drapery is calculated in relation to the total scheme. The St. Peter is almost twice
the size of the St. Petronius, but for the sculptor of the Bacchus and the Pietà its scale was still
too small to engage his whole mind or his whole heart.

Not so the Madonna relief. There are two of these, both carved after Michelangelo's return
to Florence. In the fifteenth century a large number of tombs included reliefs of the Virgin and
Child. For architectural reasons they were generally circular, so that the task of designing half-
length reliefs of the Virgin and Child inside a circular frame had been very fully explored. Their
emotional range is comparatively limited, since it was dictated by their function on the tomb,
and all of them are variations on one theme, that of the Virgin holding up the Child as he
blesses or absolves the figure on the bier below. The painted tondo, on the other hand, had no
structural function to perform; its imagery was self-contained, and its figures were depicted
in interior space. In Michelangelo's reliefs these two traditions fuse. Though they were carved
in marble, they were not planned in relation to a larger whole, but were intended as
autonomous, self-consistent works of art.

The earlier of the two reliefs, the Taddei Madonna in London (Plates 3, 5, Fig. 5), seems to
have been carved in 1503 or 1504, and must be almost exactly contemporary with the Doni
tondo in the Uffizi (Fig. 7), which Michelangelo painted between 1503 and 1505. In High
Renaissance theory a distinction was drawn between painting, which had the advantage of
internal light, and sculpture, which was lit externally. That thought occurs for the first time in
Leonardo da Vinci's *Paragone*, and in front of the Doni Madonna its significance becomes self-
evident, for the forms and their relationship to one another are defined by means of light; the
head of the Virgin is outlined against a pool of light on St. Joseph's cloak, the protruding arm
of the Child is outlined against the high light on the beard, and the Virgin's left arm and the
Child's right knee are isolated in precisely the same way. Were it not for the system of illumination, all these forms would inevitably coalesce. In the London relief Michelangelo investigates
the problem of a circular Madonna composition lit externally. The ideal of coherence is un-
changed, but it is achieved by means of a frieze-like scheme in which each element is invested
with the maximum lucidity. The Virgin faces to the left, with the upper part of her body
turned towards the spectator and her head turned slightly away, so that both contribute to
the spatial content of the scene. The Child is set diagonally on the relief surface, with head
turned back and the right leg, body and left arm in a continuous line. This motif was suggested
to Michelangelo by one of the children on a Medea sarcophagus, but it is here refined so that
the left, that is the further, leg of the Child is in a forward plane, and the right, that is the
forward leg, is at the back. On the left is the young Baptist holding a bird in his outstretched
hand. His head and heels are on the perimeter of the relief, and his left arm is parallel with
the base.

Whatever the reason, Michelangelo was dissatisfied with this relief, and a little, but only a
little, later he started work on a smaller Madonna relief, the Pitti tondo in the Bargello (Plate 4).
Here the expedient of the flat platform is done away with, and at the base the Virgin's cloak

conforms to the curved frame. The figure of the Virgin is set on a block protruding at an angle from the relief surface, and is tighter and more compressed than in the earlier relief, but the Child once more depends from the antique, this time – such is the continuity of Tuscan sculpture – from the Phaedra sarcophagus in the Campo Santo at Pisa (Vol. 1, Fig. 5), from which Nicola Pisano had drawn the figures for the Pisa pulpit two hundred and fifty years before. In the Pitti tondo only the head and throat of the Virgin have been worked up, and only the area behind the head of the Child is excavated to its intended depth. The Virgin was evidently to be shown on a concave ground in extremely deep relief, the Child in half relief, and the Baptist in lower relief still. In the London tondo the relief system is more uniform. A small area of background beside the Virgin's head has been smoothed off, and if that had been extended, the three figures would have been shown on a flat surface essentially in the same depth. If we look at the tondo from one side (Fig. 6), we can see that the full depth of the block is used throughout, and that the head and shoulders of the Virgin and St. John and the knees of St. John and the Child Christ all rest on a single plane.

What finished sculptures are implied in these reliefs? For the Pitti tondo we have an exact analogy, on almost the same scale, in the figure of St. Peter which was carved by Michelangelo under the terms of the Siena contract, and we can imagine the shoulder, sleeve and skirt of the seated Virgin finished off in rather the same way. The case of the Taddei tondo is more difficult, since parts of the relief are in a rudimentary and parts in a more highly finished state. The St. John, for example, is blocked out roughly, while the thighs, torso and head of Christ are more highly worked. It has been argued that the more highly finished parts were worked over by an assistant or by a later hand, but this is a misreading of the technique of the relief, and there can be no reasonable doubt that three separate technical stages, all of them autograph, are illustrated first by the head of Christ in the Pitti tondo, next by the head of Christ in the relief in London, and lastly by the head of Christ at Bruges. Certainly the Christ at Bruges would be inexplicable had it not been preceded by the technical phase recorded in the London relief. In the same way the drapery on the shoulder of the Taddei Virgin, where a claw tool is stroked across the surface till it produces a fine mesh of lines, is a prerequisite for the smooth folds of the Bruges Madonna.

The magnet that attracted Michelangelo to Florence in the spring of 1501 was the opportunity to carve a statue on a colossal scale. Forty odd years earlier the sculptor Agostino di Duccio had made a gigantic Hercules for the outside of the Cathedral, and in the summer of 1464 it was decided to commission a second figure from the same sculptor. The intention was that this should be made from four pieces of marble, but at the end of 1466 a block of exceptional size was quarried at Carrara, and it became apparent that the new statue, unlike the old, could be manufactured in one piece. Confronted with this block, Agostino di Duccio began to excavate the area between the legs, probably in such a way that its stability seemed to be impaired. But he left Florence shortly afterwards, and ten years later the mutilated block was offered to Antonio Rossellino. When Rossellino died in 1477, it was abandoned as what Vasari calls 'a dead thing'. The attitude of High Renaissance sculptors to size was very different from that of sculptors in the fifteenth century; and by 1501, only twenty-five years after it was pressed on the reluctant Rossellino, the block had ceased to be a liability, and was instead the focus of jealous eyes. Michelangelo had known it when he was in Florence, and seems at that time to have wished to carve a figure from it; Andrea Sansovino, in 1500 or 1501, petitioned for the block, guaranteeing that if pieces were added to it he could produce a statue; and Piero Soderini, as Gonfaloniere, contemplated giving it to Leonardo, who for the previous ten years had been occupied in Milan with the Sforza monument. However, it was to Michelangelo that the block was eventually awarded, and by January 1504 his statue was all but complete.

Paradoxically the David (Plates 12, 13) is a statue which nobody alive to-day has really seen. When it was finished, a committee of Florentine artists was convened to decide where it should be placed. Opinion was divided into two main camps: one that it should be shown in the Loggia dei Lanzi, because of the weathered condition of the stone, the other – a minority view which was in fact adopted – that it should replace Donatello's Judith outside the Palazzo Vecchio. Behind both views was implicit one assumption, that the statue should be shown before a flat wall surface in unrestricted space. But when in 1873 it was moved to the tribune of the Accademia, it was put in limited space, so that each of its component elements looks grotesquely large, and in a rotunda where the wall surface and mouldings destroy its silhouette.

The block was thin relatively to its width and height, and since the area between the legs was excavated, Michelangelo, when he started work, was committed to a pose that was both open and flat. In the nature of things the side views could never rival that from the front, and it was through contour that the figure must make its effect. In that respect the structure of the David is more classical than it might have been if Michelangelo had found himself, as a free agent, confronted by a deeper block. His source of inspiration was the colossal Horse Tamers on the Quirinal, which are within a few millimetres of the same height, but as Vasari claimed in 1550 it surpassed these and all the other colossal statues that were to be seen in Rome. What Vasari particularly praised about it is a quality that is no longer evident, its elegance, the contours of the legs, the smooth lines of the thighs, the grace of the conception and the sweetness of the pose. Vasari's words form a corrective to much that has been written on the statue in the last eighty years, for since 1873 writers on Michelangelo have seen it only as we see it now, and have been hypnotised, as we are, by the power of the conception and the magnitude of the detail. Vasari too must have looked up at the mat of hair that Michelangelo adapted from an Antinous, at its colossal pectoral muscles, and at its menacing eyes, but for him the merits of the figure were those of scale, not size.

As the David reached a stage of half completion early in 1503, one question assumed increasing urgency, to what could Michelangelo's energies be harnessed when the statue was complete? Soderini was alive to Michelangelo's potentialities; 'in his profession,' he wrote to his brother, the Cardinal of Volterra, in 1506, 'he is unique in Italy, perhaps even in the world.'

The plan he sponsored was unexpectedly ambitious, that Michelangelo should carve twelve more than life-size figures of Apostles for the nave of the Cathedral. What made this exceptional commission possible was the speed at which the sculptor worked. The St. Peter's Pietà was finished in one year or a little more, the David was begun in 1501 with the stipulation that it should be finished in three years, and in two and a half it was practically complete. So it seemed logical to the Consuls of the Arte della Lana, who were responsible for drawing up the contract, that Michelangelo should carve twelve statues of Apostles in twelve years. But they reckoned without Michelangelo's temperament and without the Pope.

At first all went well. The contract was signed in April 1503, and Michelangelo, still busy with the David, started to make drawings for the statues. There are three of them on a sheet in the British Museum. The most legible (Fig. 11) shows a figure with the left foot raised on a step or block, holding a book in his left hand, with his right hand pressed to his cheek. The drawing represents the side, not the front, view of the figure, and it leaves no doubt that the step and the projecting knee were alone to rest on the front plane of the block. On the basis of this and similar drawings five marble blocks were ordered from Carrara, and were quarried in the course of 1504, but in March 1505, before the blocks arrived in Florence, Michelangelo returned to Rome.

In practice he had no choice, since he was summoned by the Pope and was instructed by him to begin work on his tomb. But years later he seems to have looked back on the decision as a turning point, and considered that the path he chose was wrong. When the Pope sent for him, he wrote, he was busy with two great commissions, for the battle fresco in the Palazzo della Signoria and for the Apostle statues, and as a result of leaving Florence he completed neither work. His papal honeymoon was very short. He received his instructions from the Pope, spent eight months at Carrara procuring marble, returned to Rome in December and stayed there through the first months of 1506. But in the middle of April a crisis was reached. Starved of funds, suspicious of Bramante, frightened, angry and resentful, Michelangelo had recourse to flight. He fled to Florence, and remained there till November of that year. Instructions had been given that the Apostle contract should be cancelled, but the marble blocks lay there to hand, and Michelangelo returned to his old scheme. He was in a state of great emotional disturbance at the time – his grandiose projects for the tomb were thwarted, he had been treated by the Pope with what appeared to him to be contempt, and by precipitate action he had closed, it might be for good, the wide avenues of promise at the papal court – and all this is reflected in the statue of St. Matthew (Plate 14, Figs. 9, 10) on which he started work.

In the statue as it was carved the pose of the lower part was an inversion of that in the surviving drawing, and the protruding knee was brought across the figure, in such a way as to establish a continuous movement through the block. He had been cogitating the Apostle project spasmodically for three years, and many other sketches must have been made, but since the surviving drawing is our only point of reference, we must infer that the static composition of 1503 was invested in 1506 with a dynamism for which there was no parallel in any earlier work.

One reason for this was the discovery in January 1506 of the Laocoon. The Laocoon is not the basis of the St. Matthew in a formal sense – if the upper part has a precedent in the antique it is rather the statue known as the Pasquino, with which Michelangelo must have been familiar at least since 1501 – but without it the St. Matthew could not have been conceived. It was the Laocoon, with its sense of all-embracing effort, its disciplined emotional excess, that released in Michelangelo not only new formal rhythms and vastly enhanced tactility, but a state of self-immersion in his sculpture, whereby the statue was no longer something external to himself, but a projection of his total personality. Where his emotional condition came into play was in the speed and recklessness with which the work was carved. Precisely because its promise is so rich and its psychological horizons are so wide, it is in some respects more moving than the uncompleted later works. It is as though, after his rebuff in Rome, he had attacked the inert block in an effort to affirm to himself, not to the world, that he was indeed the supreme, the transcendent genius he supposed.

But suddenly his dream dissolved. The Pope's demands became increasingly insistent, in July he promised Michelangelo immunity if he returned, and Soderini, powerless to protect him, encouraged him to go, so in November he left Florence for Bologna, where the papal court then was.

MICHELANGELO : THE MEDICI CHAPEL

THE price of reconciliation with the Pope was that Michelangelo should make a more than life-size statue of the patron whom he feared in a medium he despised. Through the first half of 1507 the statue was modelled at Bologna, in the summer it was cast in bronze, and early in 1508 it was hoisted into its tabernacle high on the front of San Petronio, and Michelangelo was free to leave. As soon as the statue was finished, he returned to Florence to resume work on the Apostles, but he had been there only a few weeks when he received a new summons from the Pope. In April he left for Rome, where he signed the contract for the ceiling of the Sistine Chapel. The ceiling occupied him for over four years, to the exclusion of all other work, and on it the world of form opened up in the St. Matthew was first explored. Painting is a freer medium than sculpture, in that the figure is not fettered by a marble block, and in the Punishment of Haman on the ceiling Michelangelo develops the conception of the St. Matthew pictorially. But the nineteen genii on the body of the ceiling have the physical compression of marble statues, and the ideas investigated in them are fundamental for the artist's later style in sculpture.

Hardly was the ceiling finished than in 1513 Pope Julius II died, and fate conferred on Michelangelo the greatest benefit it could, the election of a Pope who did not really like his work. For the first three years of the new reign he was left in peace to work uninterruptedly on the tomb of the dead Pope, but in 1515 Pope Leo X visited Florence, and by the following year Michelangelo's peaceful concentration on the Julius tomb was at an end. The cause was the decision of the Pope and of his cousin Cardinal Giulio de' Medici to complete the Medici church of San Lorenzo. The first project was for a façade. It is easy to understand what attracted Michelangelo in this commission; it gave him the chance to create a major architectural work, and to devise a sculptural complex richer by far than that of the Apostles in the Cathedral. Early in 1517 the façade was to have ten statues, and soon afterwards the number was increased to twenty-four. In 1518 the contract was signed, but from then on enthusiasm – not on Michelangelo's part, but on that of his patrons – started to wane, and in March 1520 the contract was annulled. There were many reasons why work on the façade was not continued – its estimated cost had almost doubled in under twelve months – but the most important of them was that by 1519 interest had shifted to the building of a commemorative chapel.

From the very first San Lorenzo was designed as a Medicean place of burial. Giovanni and Piccarda de' Medici, the parents of Cosimo il Vecchio, were buried in the Old Sacristy, Cosimo himself was commemorated by a tomb slab in front of the high altar, and in the left transept was the tomb of his sons, Giovanni and Piero de' Medici. No monument had been erected to Lorenzo il Magnifico, because the Medici regime in Florence had collapsed soon after his death, and none had been put up to his brother Giuliano, who was killed in the Pazzi conspiracy in 1478. Since Lorenzo was the father of Pope Leo X, and Giuliano was the father of the future Pope Clement VII, both the Pope and Cardinal were interested in erecting a memorial. After Giovanni de' Medici was elected Pope in 1513, his younger brother, Giuliano de' Medici, Duc de Nemours, was appointed Captain of the Church, but three years later he died, and was succeeded by Lorenzo de' Medici, Duke of Urbino, his nephew, a grandson of Lorenzo il Magnifico. When Lorenzo in turn died in 1519, the commemorative project came to a head. The motive of the Pope and Cardinal was a double one, to commemorate Lorenzo il Magnifico and Giuliano de' Medici, who are referred to as the Magnifici, and the Dukes of Nemours and Urbino, who are referred to as the Capitani.

The earliest stage in the history of the Medici Chapel is totally undocumented. All we know is that the area adjacent to the right transept of the church, balancing Brunelleschi's Old Sacristy off the left transept, was a void, and that the new Chapel and the Old Sacristy were designed to correspond. Vasari tells us that Michelangelo planned the Chapel as an imitation of the Old Sacristy, but with another order of ornaments, and the meaning of that becomes plain if we examine the two schemes, for both are square, both have a small protruding choir or apse, and both are conceived in terms of the contrast between structural elements in pietra serena and the white wall surfaces. Stated in factual terms the difference between the structures sounds minimal; Michelangelo interpenetrated the pietra serena elements with marble, placed heavy pietra serena strips along the inner edge of the pilasters, filled the lunettes with tapering windows, and introduced beneath them an intermediate zone which divides them from the main register. On an aesthetic plane, however, it is very great. The Old Sacristy is a static architectural unit, whereas in the Chapel (Figs. 17, 18) everything conspires

to carry the eye upwards, first from the lower to the intermediate zone, then from the intermediate zone to the lunettes, and thence, through the dynamic placing of the windows, to
the cupola, which is based on the dome of the Pantheon. The Chapel, in other words,
gives a sense of physical ascent. That is an aesthetic phenomenon, but it lies at the root of a
good deal that has been written on the meaning of the tombs.

The little that we know about the tombs themselves during the planning stage depends
on one or two fragments of written evidence and on a number of drawings, and the
task is to reconcile what we read with what we see. One of the difficulties is that the projects
do not follow each other in an orderly fashion, as they would have done with other artists,
but were worked on simultaneously. One of them (which had no influence whatever on the
tombs as they were built) was for a free-standing central tomb. We first hear of it in a letter
written by Cardinal Giulio de' Medici to Michelangelo in 1520, and it collapsed when
the Cardinal suggested that the tomb should have the form of a four-faced triumphal
arch. A drawing made at this time (Fig. 19) shows a face of the free-standing tomb with two
mourning figures beside a sarcophagus. If these figures had been carried out, the genii on
the Sistine Ceiling would have been provided with a three-dimensional equivalent. Cal-
culations show that these figures were below life-size, and Michelangelo must have rejected
them without regret, since, in the space available in the Chapel, no centralised tomb could
offer proper scope for figure sculpture.

Simultaneously Michelangelo was turning over in his mind the possibility of placing
two monuments on each of the two lateral walls. This course involved two alternatives;
the first was to space out each pair of tombs so that they occupied the area now filled by
the doorways at each end, and the other was to link them together in the centre of the wall.
Michelangelo tried out both schemes, and in the drawings for the second (Fig. 20) we have
the first clear proof of his determination to augment the figure sculpture. Not only are
there mourners standing beside the podium, but on top of each sarcophagus is a reclining
figure on a much larger scale, and beneath the sarcophagus on the left is a River God. The
standing figures were omitted from the tombs as they were executed, but to the very end
the reclining figures on the lids and the River Gods remained part of the scheme. From the
proposal for linked monuments there grew the plan he actually adopted, to group two of
the tombs, those of the Magnifici, together on the third wall, leaving each of the side walls
free for a single tomb.

To discuss the drawings in this way is to suggest that they involved no more than the
placing of abstract forms in space. But the goal towards which Michelangelo was working
his way forward was the idea of the chapel, and not just the shape and size of the tombs. As
he finally planned it, the altar was reversed and faced towards the Chapel. The opposite
wall, therefore, was an altar wall separated from the altar by the whole depth of the room.
For that reason it was to contain not the tomb of the Magnifici only, but also a group of the
Virgin and Child with figures of the Medici patrons, SS. Cosmas and Damian, at her side.

Figs. 17, 18. THE MEDICI CHAPEL. S. Lorenzo, Florence.

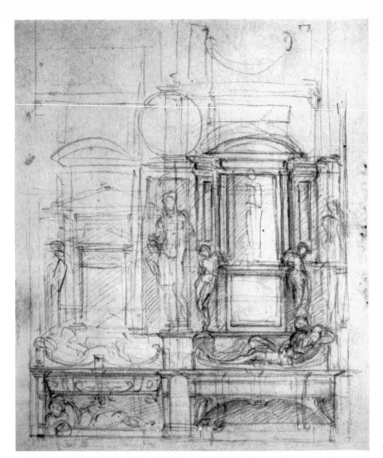

Fig. 19. Michelangelo: DRAWING FOR A CENTRALISED TOMB. British Museum, London.
Fig. 20. Michelangelo: DRAWING FOR TWO LINKED WALL MONUMENTS. British Museum, London.

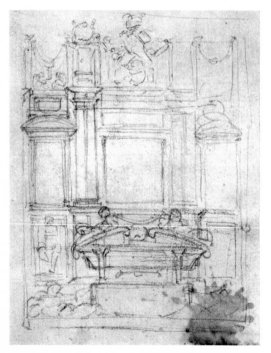

Fig. 21. Michelangelo: DRAWING FOR THE TOMB OF GIULIANO DE' MEDICI. British Museum, London.
Fig. 22. Michelangelo: DRAWING FOR THE TOMB OF GIULIANO DE' MEDICI. Ashmolean Museum, Oxford.

The focal point was naturally the altar, and it was from the altar that the complex of three tombs was intended to be seen. Seen from this position, the heads of the two Capitani gazed directly at the Virgin and Child.

Looking at the drawings, we might suppose that from the moment when work started on the tombs, Michelangelo had in his mind an inalterable scheme which he realised over the next fourteen years, but as soon as we approach the sculptures it transpires that that was not the case. The scheme, in quite important points as well as in detail, was constantly revised, and work on it was fraught with what, in any lesser sculptor, we should call uncertainty. Michelangelo in middle life treated the marble block almost as though it were a sketch-model, feeling his way forward, changing his direction, improvising, and in this same empirical spirit he approached the planning of the tombs.

We have a good deal of scattered information on the progress of work in the Chapel. The shell was under construction in March 1520, and by April of the following year it was completed up to the architrave. At this point Michelangelo visited Carrara and signed contracts with two stonecutters for marble blocks for figure sculptures. Some of these arrived in Florence in the summer of 1521, and by 1524 a quantity of marble had been quarried and shipped. An exception was the marble for the sarcophagus lids. The architecture of one of the two tombs was building by the summer of 1524, and the architecture of the other was begun in 1526. In practice work seems to have progressed less smoothly than these documentary references suggest, first because Leo X died in 1521, and his short-lived successor, Adrian VI, tried, probably successfully, to divert Michelangelo back on to the Julius tomb, and secondly because the quarrying presented unexpected difficulties. The marble for four figures was extracted in the summer and autumn of 1524, and Michelangelo, anxious to get down to work, added a block from his own studio in the Via Mozza, where the sculptures for the Julius tomb were carved. By October 1525 four figures had been begun, but they did not include the River Gods. In June 1526 Michelangelo proposed beginning what he refers to as 'the other Capitano', so one of the seated figures of the Capitani must have been blocked out before that time. The letter in which this statement occurs is very important for a study of the sculptures. What it says is this: 'The four figures on the tomb-chests, the four River Gods for the bottom of the tombs, the two Capitani and the Virgin and Child, those are the figures that I should like to carve with my own hand, and of them six are begun.' So already it was envisaged that some of the sculptures in the Chapel should be carved by other hands than Michelangelo's.

In 1527 work on the Chapel came to a halt. The Sack of Rome occurred in May, and at the end of the month a republican government was installed in Florence. A year later Michelangelo received an official commission for a colossal group of Samson and a Philistine which was to form a pendant to the David outside the Palazzo della Signoria, and soon after this he was forced to turn his mind to the task of fortifying Florence against attack. Through the summer of 1529 the situation became increasingly alarming, and in September he left

Florence, but returned in the second half of November, and was still in Florence in the summer of 1530 when the city surrendered to Pope Clement VII. The project for the Samson was put into abeyance, and Michelangelo resumed work in the Medici Chapel.

What had occurred in Florence was not simply that one government had been substituted for another, but that a regime which corresponded closely with Michelangelo's political ideals, and with which he was emotionally bound up, had been displaced by another, to which he was in principle opposed. As at other times during his life, this disillusionment was reflected in the rhythm of his work. At first he threw himself with unprecedented violence into the carving of the tombs. A letter of September 1531 tells us that he is overworking, eating little, sleeping badly, suffers from headaches, and is unlikely to live unless some steps are taken about his health; it recommends that he should be prevented from working in the Chapel through the winter. But suddenly his work slowed down. In April 1532 he went to Rome, returned briefly to Florence, and in August went back to Rome once more, staying there this time until the summer of 1533. He returned to Florence for four months, spent eight months in Rome, spent another three months in Florence, and in September 1534 left Florence never to return. The Pope, meanwhile, who was thoroughly familiar with the pattern of his conduct, became urgently concerned with the task of finishing the Chapel, and proposed that the physical labour of carving the outstanding statues should be entrusted to other hands. In 1533 the sculptor Tribolo, who was at Loreto working on the Holy House, was ordered to go at short notice to Florence to help carve the tombs, and use was also made of two other sculptors, Raffaello da Montelupo and Montorsoli. Before leaving Florence, Michelangelo installed the statues of the Capitani in the niches that had been designed for them, but the four Allegories were not put in position on the tombs. Soon after he reached Rome, Pope Clement VII died. For Michelangelo the Pope had been both a sympathetic patron and a bulwark against the newly installed Duke of Florence, the tyrannical Alessandro de' Medici, and without the Pope's protection he was, in common prudence, unable to return. Alessandro de' Medici at once diverted Tribolo and Raffaello da Montelupo to other tasks, and work in the Chapel was continued only after his murder in 1537, when his cousin and successor, Cosimo I, ordained that his body should be placed in the tomb of Lorenzo de' Medici, Duke of Urbino. Michelangelo was invited to return, but refused to do so, and in 1545 the four Allegories were placed by Tribolo on the sarcophagus lids. Fourteen years later the ugly pavement of the Chapel was laid down by Vasari, and the bodies of the Magnifici were interred beneath the site of their projected monument on the facing wall. Finally in 1562, when Michelangelo was on the threshold of the grave, Cosimo I made a last despairing effort to elicit his intentions for the Chapel, and his views on how it should be finished off. It is often difficult to follow the minds and motives of great artists, and at first sight nothing is stranger than that Michelangelo should have looked for the last time in 1534 at these great statues strewn about the Chapel floor, and then for thirty years refused not only to place them in position, but even to explain how he intended that they should be placed. But his reasons become more intelligible when we examine the individual sculptures.

Almost all of them are in some respect unfinished – the only fully completed figure is the Giuliano de' Medici – and Michelangelo must have worked on them concurrently. On one point he procrastinated through the entire period of work; he deferred until too late the moment at which the expressions of the two male figures had to be defined. None the less, there is one large caesura in the sculptures, and that is between the two pairs of Allegories. A letter of 1531 relates to the two female figures, and places them in order. The Night is described first, as though it had been in existence for some time, and the Dawn, the corresponding figure opposite, is mentioned without name. So on that fragile evidence the Night and Day would seem to be the earlier and the Morning and Evening to be the later pair. The same letter mentions the statue of Lorenzo de' Medici; Michelangelo could carve it this winter, it says. We know from other sources that one Capitano was well advanced before this time, so only one interpretation is permissible, that the statue of Giuliano de' Medici precedes that of Lorenzo on the tomb opposite. Whereas the Allegories on the tomb of Lorenzo de' Medici are moulded to the shape of the sarcophagus lid, the bases of the Allegories on the tomb opposite are almost flat. Augustus Hare, in an irreverent passage in *Walks in Florence*, describes them as slipping off the tomb, and that is what they seem to do. The distinction stands out very clearly if we look more closely at two of the figures. The pose of the Evening (Plate 32) on the Lorenzo tomb is ideally adjusted to the lid; one foot rests on the edge, and the extended leg is supported to a point rather below the knee. But with the Day (Plate 31) the legs and thighs are not supported, and the pose is unintelligible in relation to this sarcophagus. Perhaps it is worth while to emphasise the point by examining the figures from the back. In the Day (Fig. 26) the bottom of the block to all intents and purposes is flat, while in the Evening (Fig. 27) it is excavated. This difference has been explained in many different ways. It has been suggested, for example, that the Day and the companion figure of Night were originally intended not for the Giuliano tomb but for the monument of the Magnifici, in one version of which rather different tomb chests are shown. But the Night and Day and the Morning and Evening are counterparts, and it is inconceivable that they were not intended to stand opposite to one another, just as they do now. So we are bound to assume that when the Night and Day were carved the sarcophagus of the Giuliano tomb was to have had a different lid. Admittedly some early drawings for the tomb (Fig. 21) show the lid in its present form, but a later drawing (Fig. 22) also shows a sarcophagus with two flat sloping ends. There was, as we know, difficulty in procuring the marble from which the lids were made, and with Michelangelo nothing was settled until it was finally carved.

The figures also differ in size and scale – in size in that one of them, the Day, is carved from a somewhat shorter block than the remaining three, and in scale in that the Night is heavier and more monumental than the Morning and Evening, though it is carved from a block of almost the same size. If, therefore, we believe that the Dawn and Evening were carved before the Night and Day, we are committed to the view that Michelangelo developed from a less to a more monumental style, and if we invert the sequence we are committed to the opposite hypothesis. Luckily there are two securely datable works, one finished just before the Medici Chapel was begun, and the other begun just before it reached its final phase. The first is the Christ in Santa Maria sopra Minerva in Rome (Plate 23), which was delivered in 1521, and the second is a little figure of Apollo (Plate 22) carved for Baccio Valori in 1530 or 1531. The Christ is a version of an earlier statue which proved to have a flaw, and for Michelangelo is rather a weak work, but it has none the less the rigid, intractable quality of the Day, while the Apollo has the elegance and flexibility of the two figures opposite. The Day, then, was the first of the Allegories to be begun. The most striking confirmation of this is the fact that from the altar it reads extremely awkwardly. So clumsy is it that we might guess Michelangelo planned it in quotation marks, and that inference would be correct, for if we take the Belvedere torso (Fig. 15), which he unquestionably knew, and place it on its back, the source of the figure is not in the smallest doubt. It has been mentioned that in 1524 Michelangelo transferred to the Chapel a block from his studio in the Via Mozza. Since three of the Allegories on the tombs are carved from uniform blocks and one is exceptional, it is a reasonable inference that the exceptional figure, the Day, was carved from the exceptional block. It follows that in 1524, when work on this statue was started, the harmonious conception of the figures as we find it on the Lorenzo tomb did not exist even in embryo in the sculptor's mind. At that time the Allegories were conceived as four aggressive, classicising figures on angled sarcophagi, the two male figures like Roman River Gods.

For the corresponding female figure, the Night, Michelangelo also went back to the antique, to a Leda sarcophagus in Rome, now lost but recorded in a drawing made in the sixteenth century. Its scheme was changed in two significant respects, first that the further arm was brought across the body so that it conformed with the Day, and second that the near arm was eliminated. This second change was apparently due to a mischance, for we have near-contemporary evidence that the original left arm was spoiled, and that Michelangelo for that reason adopted the solution of concealing it. This is confirmed by the top of the mask beneath the shoulder, which would have been covered by the arm, and instead was left in the rough. In 1529 when Michelangelo turned to this same sarcophagus again for his lost painting of Leda for Alfonso d'Este, the complete left arm was shown. Perhaps the Night was impoverished by the change, but this casual occurrence had incalculable consequences, since the revised position of the arm meant that the front plane of the figure was no longer coterminous with the front plane of the block; a new tension was introduced into the pose, above all in the area of the waist, which rises slightly from the couch on which it rests. The emphatic diagonal movement of the Day and Night is rejected in the two Allegories opposite, and the off side of each figure is raised so that the whole surface of the body is exposed to the spectator, and the figure partakes of the nature both of a statue and of a relief.

Logically it can only have been at this point that the lids of the sarcophagi assumed their present form. How fundamental was this change of style becomes apparent as soon as we look at the Allegories from on top. From this view the earliest of the Allegories, the Day of 1524 (Fig. 28), is seen to be contained within its block as tightly as is the Minerva Christ, while in the latest of them, the Dawn of 1531 (Fig. 29), the open forms of Baroque art are clearly predicated.

In the seated statues of the Capitani the classicising imagery of the tombs reaches its peak. A large number of Roman commemorative statues were known in the sixteenth century; they comprised both seated and standing figures, and in a loose sense the Giuliano de' Medici (Plate 24) is an amalgam of the two types. Though the figure is shown wearing armour, the breasts and torso are depicted as though nude, and in this area the Belvedere torso once more served as a model, so that the figure of Giuliano de' Medici and the Day beneath depend from one and the same classical original. The corresponding area in the statue opposite is not worked up. In the Chapel the features of Lorenzo de' Medici (Plate 25) are in shadow. For that reason the figure was known in the eighteenth and nineteenth centuries as the Pensieroso, the meditative man, and a whole romantic literature grew up around the thoughts which were presumed to be passing through his head. Even Henry James 'lingered often in the sepulchral chapel of San Lorenzo, and watched Michelangelo's dim-visaged warrior sitting there like some awful Genius of Doubt and brooding behind his eternal mask upon the mysteries of life.' This figure was, however, also inspired by the antique, and the shadow on its face is nothing but an accident. The statue is slightly deeper than that on the Giuliano tomb, and in order to align the two front planes the wall was excavated so that it could be pushed back. If it were brought forward just a little, it would protrude (as do many other High Renaissance statues), but its ambiguity in relation to the second tomb and to the Madonna wall would be resolved.

The only other sculptures for the Capitani tombs the form of which we know are the River Gods, which were destined for the platforms beneath the sarcophagi. One of the four, for the left side of the Lorenzo tomb, is known through a model in the Accademia in Florence (Fig. 25), and a second, for the Giuliano tomb, is recorded in preliminary drawings. It has been inferred, probably correctly, that the model was made in 1524, that blocks were ordered on the basis of it, that the figures were then increased in size, and that new blocks were accordingly required. If this was so, the River Gods were subject to the same law of change as the other sculptures in the Chapel. It is extremely difficult to imagine what effect these sculptures would have made had they been set on the ground on a front plane, with the slightly smaller Allegories on the intermediate plane of the lid of the sarcophagus, and figures in the niches above. One of the few classical works known to Michelangelo which offers a parallel for this conception is the relief on the base of the column of Antoninus Pius, where a seated figure at the bottom, a diagonal nude figure above, and two portraits at the top are linked together in three superposed registers.

What, lastly, do the figures mean? If we trouble to collate what has been written about one of the four Allegories, the Dawn, we shall find that the results are most peculiar. Broadly the interpretations fall into two groups. First there are the optimists, who describe the figure as though she were Brünnhilde, in the third act of *Siegfried*, greeting the sun, and then there are the pessimists who believe she is reluctant to awake: 'Why, O my God, hast thou not made the night eternal,' are the words one of them puts into her parted lips. Obviously interpretations of this kind are subjective in the highest degree, and discussion of the meaning of the individual sculptures must be preceded by discussion of the programme of the chapel as a whole. The accounts that are given of the programme are, however, disconcertingly diverse. It has been explained theologically in terms of Ambrosian hymns, and politically as a Gladstonian anti-Medicean allegory. But in the last quarter of a century interpretations have settled into the rut of Neoplatonism. The subject of the tombs is a Neoplatonic apotheosis, and both represent ascent, from the zone of Hades symbolised by the River Gods, through a terrestrial sphere symbolised by the Allegories and the seated statues, to a celestial sphere symbolised by the thrones on the architraves of the two monuments and by the lunettes above. This explanation is susceptible of a number of refinements – that the seated statues show the two Dukes after death, or the antithesis between Nous and Psyche, the active and the contemplative life, that the niches beside them were intended to be filled with figures symbolising the contrasting souls of man, that the River Gods showed both the Rivers of Hades and the four elements or the fourfold aspect of matter as a source of potential evil, and that the Allegories depict the four humours as well as the times of day and transmit the conception of life on earth as a state of suffering through 'an impression of intense and incurable pain.'

Fundamental to all this is the notion of ascent. There is an objection to it, that we **know** the subjects of the projected figures for the niches of the Giuliano tomb. According to Vasari, they were to be carved by Tribolo from Michelangelo's models, and the models depicted Earth, crowned with cypress with hands outstretched and her head bowed, and Heaven, with a smiling countenance and both hands raised. It would be possible to claim that Vasari was mistaken, were it not for another piece of evidence which comes from Michelangelo. It occurs in a prose fragment with a dialogue between the figures of Night and Day on the Giuliano tomb, and in the form in which it is transcribed it reads simply, 'Heaven, Earth, Heaven, Earth.' As soon as we look at the sheet in the Archivio Buonarroti on which it occurs, however, its meaning becomes unambiguous, for the word Heaven (*Cielo*) occurs twice on the left, in the position of the left-hand niche on the monument, in the centre is a gap where the seated figure should be, on the right twice repeated is the word Earth (*Terra*), and below, running across the sheet in the position occupied by the Allegories, is a conversation between the Times of Day of the sarcophagus. If Heaven and Earth were represented horizontally in the same register on one of the two tombs, the whole idea of the tombs as an ascent falls to the ground. It appears as what it is, the philosophical rationalisation of a visual phenomenon.

There is no evidence at all that the River Gods represented Hades, but we have some reason to suppose that their significance was locative. It occurs in a poem by Gandolfo Porrini, which is quoted in the *Lezioni* of Varchi only fifteen years after Michelangelo left Florence. The tombs, complains Porrini, will await in vain the magnanimous rulers of Tiber and Arno. That could be disregarded, were it not for a tiny piece of confirmation that makes Porrini's testimony credible. In 1513, three years before his death, Giuliano de' Medici was invested in Rome as a patrician, and on the stage on which the ceremony was performed there were two River Gods, not the Rivers of Hades, but the Tiber on the right and the Arno on the left. So there is a presumption that this not very abstruse imagery was carried over to the tombs.

It is best to approach the seated figures from a tangent. One of the duties of the art historian is to explain what distinguishes the very greatest works from works of lower quality. This is an intricate and exacting task, and there is a temptation to evade it by explaining the difference in terms of the ideas implicit in the work rather than through the work itself. In 1544, for example, Cosimo I commissioned from Bandinelli a statue of his father Giovanni dalle Bande Nere (Fig. 120), which is still outside the church of San Lorenzo. It shows Giovanni dalle Bande Nere seated in classical military costume, and because it is an inferior statue no one has ever doubted that it is what it appears to be, an idealised commemorative portrait conceived in the style of the antique. Michelangelo was a much greater sculptor than Bandinelli, and whereas the Giovanni dalle Bande Nere is a sterile work, the Giuliano de' Medici has the enhanced communicative power of all transcendent works of art. But the reason for that is not that it represents a different idea from Bandinelli's statue; it represents the same idea on a different level of creativity.

With Michelangelo we are dealing with a sculptor who could not help carving expressively. The most conventional ornament takes on a personal inflection at his hands. Whether it be the swags above the Giuliano tomb with sacrificial ewers over them, or the funerary emblems on the ends of the sarcophagus under this same tomb (Plate 26), or the face on the corselet of the seated figure, or the extraordinary frieze of grimacing masks, or the bat head beneath the elbow of Lorenzo de' Medici (Plate 27), the effect is so personal that we instinctively ask ourselves, 'What does this mean?' The right answer to that question is that in terms of logic it means nothing at all, or rather that it means no more than ordinary ornament would mean in the hands of a pedestrian sculptor. If we insist on rationalising these intuitive projections of the sculptor's personality, we debar ourselves from entering fully into his fantastically rich imaginative world.

Historically there is one useful step that we can take, and that is to put into the witness box some of Michelangelo's contemporaries, and ask them what they think the Chapel signifies. The first witness is Condivi, Michelangelo's biographer and friend. The Night and Day, Condivi tells us, signify Time, which consumes all things. Michelangelo, he adds, had intended to portray Time as a mouse, and left a piece of the block for that purpose, but was prevented (*impedito*) from using it. The next witness is the Vasari of the 1550 Life of Michelangelo. Michelangelo, he declares, considered that the earth alone was not enough to give the Captains the honoured burial they merited, and wished that all parts of the world should be present in the Chapel. The antithesis in this passage is between *terra* and *mondo*, the earth and the natural world. For that reason he put the figures of Night and Day, and Morning and Evening on the tombs. The Dawn is 'a naked woman who is such as to awaken melancholy in the soul. In her attitude may be seen her effort, as she rises, heavy with sleep, and raises herself from her downy bed; and it seems that in awakening, she has found the eyes of the great Duke closed in death, so that she writhes with bitterness, lamenting her continued beauty in token of her great sorrow.' As for the Night, 'in her may be seen not only the stillness of one sleeping, but the grief and melancholy of one who has lost a great and honoured possession.' So far as concerns the seated statues, it does not enter Vasari's head that anything save their ostensible subject is shown. These statues are described in a letter of 1544 by Niccolò Martelli, who explains that Michelangelo did not represent the Capitani as they were in nature, but gave them a grandeur, a proportion, a decorum which would earn them greater praise; a thousand years hence, Michelangelo observed, nobody would realise that they did not look quite as he had shown them on their monuments. The fourth witness is Benedetto Varchi, whose account is vaguer than Vasari's, but who maintains the same antithesis between earth and world, though with a slightly different emphasis. The fifth witness is Michelangelo, who testifies through two manuscripts in his own hand. The first of them, written about 1520, occurs on a sheet for the Magnifici tomb in the British Museum (Fig. 23), and reads as follows: 'Fame holds the epitaphs; it neither advances nor retreats, because they are dead, and their work is at an end.' The second was written about 1526, and is the dialogue between Night and Day already referred to: 'Day and Night are speaking, and they say: With our speedy course, we have led Duke Giuliano to his death; and it is right that he should take revenge for this as he has done. The revenge is this: that just as we have killed him so he in death has deprived us of our light, and with his closed eyes has closed our eyes, which no longer shine upon the earth. What then would he have done with us, while he was still alive?' Quite a number of scholars refer to the Allegories as incarnations of the times of day. That is an awkward term when one is speaking about marble statues, and Michelangelo's words suggest that he considered them the opposite – living figures turned to stone.

There are differences between these interpretations, but they have much in common, first of all in the things that are not mentioned – the Rivers of Hades, the four humours, the four elements, the three zones and the twin souls of man – and secondly in the things that are mentioned, or more strictly in the assumptions that lie behind them. That the iconography of the tombs was concerned with Fame, that is with immortalising the official personae of the two Dukes as patricians and Captains of the Church, and was therefore orthodox; that the portraits are portraits, albeit idealised; and that the Times of Day are shown in a state of deep

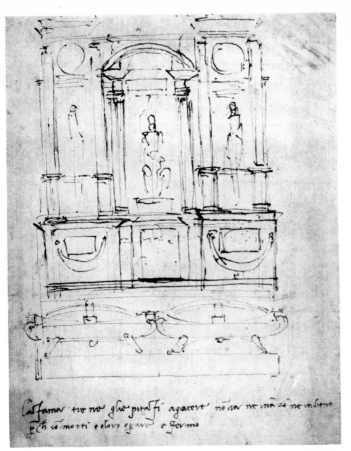

Fig. 23. Michelangelo: DRAWING FOR THE MAGNIFICI MONUMENT. British Museum, London.
Fig. 24. After Michelangelo: DRAWING FOR THE MAGNIFICI MONUMENT. Ashmolean Museum, Oxford.

Fig. 25. Michelangelo: MODEL OF A RIVER GOD. Accademia, Florence.

Fig. 26. Michelangelo: BACK OF THE DAY. Medici Chapel, Florence.

Fig. 27. Michelangelo: BACK OF THE EVENING. Medici Chapel, Florence.

Fig. 28. Michelangelo: VIEW OF THE DAY FROM ABOVE. Medici Chapel, Florence.

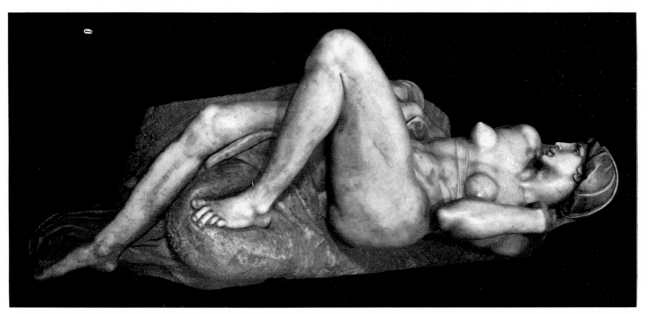

Fig. 29. Michelangelo: VIEW OF THE DAWN FROM ABOVE. Medici Chapel, Florence.

Fig. 30. Michelangelo: THE TOMB OF POPE JULIUS II. S. Pietro in Vincoli, Rome.

and incurable grief, not of deep and incurable pain. To this we can apply a simple test of probability, for not only do we know many letters from Michelangelo, but we have as well two transcripts of discussions in which he took part. Everything we learn from these sources about his mental processes suggests that the imagery of the Chapel is likely to have been comparatively simple, intensely apprehended, and based on the principle of direct plastic communication, not on some elaborate intellectual theorem. Indeed the vagueness of his intentions, the indefiniteness of his objective, the fact that by temperament he was an artist not an expositor, may have been among the reasons why he lacked the impulse to complete the tombs.

The least finished, earliest and most anomalous of the sculptures in the Chapel is the Virgin and Child (Plate 20). It is the only figure in which an element of movement is introduced, not gentle movement, but violent movement that seems a little irreverent in the still complex of the tombs. The pose of the Virgin, seated on a rectangular plinth, with her right hand at her side and her left leg crossed over her right knee, derives from a Roman copy of a fifth-century Greek statue of Penelope (Fig. 14). The employment of this model is surprising, because we know that the tomb of the Magnifici was to have in the centre a rectangular tabernacle corresponding with those of the Capitani tombs. The Capitani are centralised, with both knees on a single plane, but the Madonna is inherently unsuited to a tabernacle of the kind. Moreover, it can be established both from copies and autograph drawings that Michelangelo, when he planned the tomb of the Magnifici, conceived a group (Figs. 23, 24) of a rather different kind, with a symmetrical figure of the Virgin looking down at the Child between her knees. We have then a figure which was suited to the Chapel but was not carved, and a figure which was carved but was not suited to the Chapel. Through the whole period of work in the Chapel Michelangelo had a second contractual obligation for the tomb of Pope Julius II, and between 1521 and 1523 he was actively at work on sculptures for a revised version of this tomb. There is proof that the possibility of exchanging sculptures for the tomb and sculptures for the Chapel was entertained, and one of the figures now on the tomb seems indeed to have been carved for a niche on the monument of Lorenzo de' Medici in Florence. The most likely explanation of the Virgin and Child is that the opposite occurred, that it was carved for the 1519 version of the tomb and was later diverted to the Chapel. The focus of the Virgin's gaze, therefore, may not, as we might now suppose, be an arbitrary point in the middle of the Chapel floor, but the dead body of the Pope.

MICHELANGELO : THE TOMB OF POPE JULIUS II

OF all great works of art the tomb of Pope Julius II in San Pietro in Vincoli in Rome (Fig. 30) is the most dispiriting. The first thing we notice as we look at it is the incongruity of the architecture of the upper and the lower parts. So divergent are they that we might infer either (and this would be wrong) that they were by two different artists, or (and this would be

correct) that they were designed by the same artist at different points in time. The great
statue of Moses in the centre is not integrated in the tomb, and is discrepant both in style and
size from the figures in the niches at the sides, while the side figures, though they are consistent with the figures in the upper register, differ from them in quality. Strangest of all,
it appears that no space was left for the figure of the Pope, which is placed on a sarcophagus
spanning the centre of the tomb. From a sculptural point of view this figure, and the Virgin
and Child in the niche behind it, are far the worst and puniest pieces of the monument. On a
superficial level the story of the Julius II monument is the story of how this tomb came to be
built; on a deeper level it is the story of Michelangelo's development over exactly forty
years.

In March 1505 he was summoned to the papal court. According to Condivi, some months
passed before the tomb was formally commissioned, but the time that elapsed cannot in
practice have been very long, for that summer Michelangelo was at Carrara procuring the
marble for the monument. Given this short interval, it is reasonable to suppose that the
tomb had been discussed before Michelangelo arrived in Rome, and that in at least two respects its form was dictated by the Pope. The contract for it is lost, but it was to cost the
enormous sum of ten thousand ducats. The reason for this becomes clear from two sub-
contracts which Michelangelo signed at Carrara in the winter of 1505, providing for the
quarrying of unprecedented quantities of marble and their despatch by sea to Rome. In
January 1506 Michelangelo was back in Rome, impatiently waiting for the marble to arrive.
When it did so, a financial crisis broke, and the Pope, instigated by Bramante, began to retreat from the whole scheme. Michelangelo endeavoured to see him, but was turned away
by a chamberlain, and he thereupon despatched a letter of protest to the Pope. 'Most Holy
Father,' ran this letter, 'I was this morning chased out of the palace on the instructions of
your Holiness. I wish to intimate that if from henceforth you require me, you must seek me
elsewhere than in Rome.' That is the first phase in the history of the monument.

We have only one means of telling what Michelangelo intended, and that is by analysing
the account which he himself, almost half a century later, gave to his biographer Condivi.
There are other written sources for the tomb (Vasari for example), but they are of secondary
importance compared to this. According to Condivi, Michelangelo planned a free-standing
tomb, not a wall monument, with two longer and two shorter sides. The long sides measured eighteen braccia and the short sides measured twelve, so that the ratio of the longer to the
shorter sides was three to two, and the ground plan of the tomb was a square and a half.
The tomb was designed to be set endwise, with the short sides forming the back and front.
It consisted of a lower section at eye level, of a kind of platform on top with figures seated
on it, and of an upper section which Condivi does not fully describe. The lower section
contained niches with statues, and between them were terms, against which stood figures
of bound captives symbolising the Liberal Arts. Above the niches ran a unifying cornice,
and on top of this, on the platform, were 'four great statues' one of which represented

Moses. Inside the tomb was 'a chamber in the form of a little temple, in the midst of which was a sarcophagus in marble wherein the Pope was to be buried,' and at the extreme top were two angels holding up what Condivi describes as an *arca* (presumably a symbolic tomb chest), one of whom appeared to laugh 'as though rejoicing that the soul of the Pope should be received among the blessed spirits,' while the other appeared to weep 'as though mourning that the world should be deprived of such a man.'

Pope Julius II, as Cardinal Giulio della Rovere, had been responsible for the tomb of his uncle Pope Sixtus IV (Vol. II, Fig. 72). This tomb also was free-standing, and it is likely that the impulse towards a free-standing monument came from the Pope and not from Michelangelo. At all events when the Pope died, this aspect of the tomb was modified. The Sixtus IV tomb was installed in the middle of a specially constructed chapel, but the new tomb was far more cumbersome. The joint egotism of a great Pope and a great artist conspired to produce a monument which would have covered about eight hundred square feet of floor space, was extremely high, and included, in addition to bronze reliefs of scenes from the Pope's life, more than forty marble statues. At first it was suggested, it seems by Giuliano da Sangallo, that the choir of St. Peter's, which was still unfinished, should be roofed over to receive it, and from this proposal there grew the project for the complete rebuilding of St. Peter's by Bramante. On this point the dates speak for themselves; the form of the tomb was settled by the summer of 1505, and in November of that year we first hear of the centralised plan that Bramante had worked out for the church. Though one scheme touched off the other, it is not the case that the centralised church was devised as a setting for the tomb. The two projects were in competition and the commission to Bramante for the church was the death warrant of the monument.

Two drawings in Berlin enable us to put some flesh on the dry bones of Condivi's account of the bottom of the tomb. There is no absolute proof that the lower register in these two drawings (Fig. 33) relates to the scheme of 1505 rather than that of 1513, when work on the tomb was resumed, but it is likely that this is so. Certainly it corresponds with Condivi's account in so far as it shows niches, and terms, with figures in front of them in the form of prisoners, and a platform on top. It has been suggested that this scheme may have been inspired by classical sarcophagi with figures of prisoners, of a class of which an example is in the Vatican; we should have only to transfer the prisoners on this sarcophagus from the sides of the columns to the front, and reproduce them at the ends, to obtain a scheme that would be generally similar to that of the base of the tomb. There are, moreover, other reasons to suppose that Michelangelo thought along these or somewhat similar lines. Years later, on a drawing by Zanobi Lastricati in Milan, there occurs a mysterious sentence to the effect that Michelangelo, for the first project of the tomb, planned 'a free-standing rectangular catafalque shaped like that of Septimius Severus near the Antoniane'. A number of drawings by Giovanni Battista da Sangallo also show reconstituted classical sepulchral monuments. One of the prisoners on the Berlin drawings corresponds in rather a suggestive way with a classical statue of

Narcissus in the Louvre. These, it must be reiterated, are not the specific models used by Michelangelo, but give some indication of the kind of thinking that lay behind the first version of the tomb.

Condivi does not mention the subjects of the niche figures, and Vasari's account of the bottom of the monument is exceedingly confused. He says, for example, that the prisoners represented not the Liberal Arts, but the provinces subjugated by Pope Julius II; this cannot be correct, because in 1505 no provinces had yet been subjugated. But he also mentions Virtues, and not only would we expect to find Virtues on a papal tomb – they and the Liberal Arts occur on the tomb of Pope Sixtus IV – but the female figures in the niches of the drawings in Berlin can hardly be explained in any other way. These particular figures must have had some sort of actuality, perhaps in the form of models, since years later, about 1540, a protégé of Michelangelo, the Florentine sculptor Ammanati, made use of one of them for the Nari monument in the church of the Annunziata in Florence (Plate 73).

We know much less about the two sections above, and the interest of the attempts that have been made to reconstruct them on the basis of our present evidence is purely dialectical. Condivi tells us that on the platform there were 'four great statues, one of which, namely the Moses, is to be seen in San Piero ad Vincula,' and Vasari, in addition to the Moses, mentions three other statues, a St. Paul and figures of the Active and the Contemplative Life. The juxtaposition of Moses and St. Paul is Neoplatonic – Pico della Mirandola describes them as types of intellectual and intuitive cognition – as are the Active and the Contemplative Life, so there is a strong probability that the first version of the tomb, unlike the Medici Chapel, had a Neoplatonic programme, or at least a programme with a strong Neoplatonic accent, for which Michelangelo, however, was not necessarily responsible. According to Vasari, the smiling and lamenting figures in the topmost section represented Heaven and Earth, and that is quite possibly correct; figures of Heaven and Earth were to be included in the Giuliano de' Medici monument, and Michelangelo, with his limited interest in formal iconography, may have transferred this idea from the earlier to the later tomb. Otherwise the wording of Condivi's and Vasari's descriptions is extremely vague. Neither source mentions a statue of the Pope, though that must certainly have been included in the monument. Two theories have been advanced, that the Pope was represented in a death effigy or in a life statue. The balance of evidence is that a life image was employed. In the summer of 1508 a stonemason at Carrara was busy blocking out the papal statue, and this piece of marble seems to have remained in Michelangelo's studio for the remainder of his life. Eventually, in 1602, it was used by Niccolò Cordieri for a statue of St. Gregory the Great in San Gregorio al Celio (Fig. 153). It is very doubtful if any of the carving in this figure in its present form is due to Michelangelo, but the pose cannot have been radically changed, and we shall not go far astray if we imagine a statue of this general type at the apex of the tomb.

When he returned to Rome in 1508, Michelangelo's preoccupations were with the Sistine ceiling, which was unveiled in October 1512. A few months later the Pope died, but before his death his mind reverted to the monument, and as soon as his successor was elected steps were taken to resume work on the tomb. In May 1513 the late Pope's executors signed a new contract with Michelangelo. Under its terms the work was to be finished in seven years, that is by 1520, and Michelangelo was to receive a further thirteen thousand ducats. At the same time the scheme of the monument was modified. It was no longer to be free-standing, but it was not thought out afresh as a conventional wall monument; instead it was conceived as a free-standing monument with one end attached, in a more or less arbitrary fashion, to the wall. The width of the exposed end was a little less than in the scheme of 1505, and the long sides were less long, but even so the depth of the sides contiguous to the wall was very nearly double the width of the front. There were two niches on the front and two on each of the two sides, six niches in all, filled with two-figure groups, one figure standing on the other as in the scheme of 1505. Each of the niches was flanked by pilasters with figures placed in front of them, so that round the bottom there were six two-figure groups and twelve single figures. The tomb was also to include three large reliefs. The fact that the monument was now to be set against the wall made it necessary to replan the upper part. On the platform was a tomb-chest supported by four figures which were roughly double life-size, and round its edges were six seated figures on the same scale. At the back, against the wall, was a structure described as a *cappelletta*, a little chapel, which seems from the contract to have been a kind of altar piece. It was to be extremely tall – its height above the platform was equal to the total depth of the tomb – and it was to contain five further figures, one in the centre, two on the sides and two on the returns against the wall, all of them larger than the double life-size figures since they were further from the eye.

The scheme of 1513 has been described as an enlargement and as a reduction of the scheme of 1505, and both statements are true. It was an enlargement in so far as it was much higher, and the size of the figure sculptures was greater than it had been before. It was a reduction in so far as the number of figures, on a quantitative count, was slightly reduced. We can get some impression of how the upper part of the tomb, the *cappelletta*, might have looked from a section added to the top of the drawing in Berlin (Fig. 31). Though the subjects of the figures are not mentioned in the contract – they are never mentioned in any of the later contracts for the matter of that – it is generally assumed that the central feature of the *cappelletta* was, as in this drawing, a Virgin and Child. By combining the contract and the drawing, we can reach a tentative reconstruction of the 1513 monument, and once we do so it becomes obvious that a great deal more was changed than the shape of the tomb. In 1505, apart from the Moses and the conjectural St. Paul, the tomb contained no religious imagery. Now it is presided over by the Virgin and Child, and probably by four standing Saints as well. In 1505 the statue of the Pope was a life portrait, now a death effigy is shown. In 1505 the four figures on the platform were seated at the corners of a central architectural structure, now they, and the sarcophagus, and the four figures supporting it, are grouped together as elements in an immense sculptural tableau, and are posed in an almost pictorial fashion against the high niche behind. This can be deduced from the insistence in the contract that the further figures should be larger than the nearer figures with a view to keeping them in scale.

The touchstone of this scheme is the Moses (Plate 15), which was carved not for the niche that it now occupies, but for the right hand corner of the platform of the 1513 tomb. The figure was designed to be looked at from below, and what is now its front is its least favourable aspect, since the point of vision it presumes was from the centre of the 1513 tomb, that is about ten feet to the left of its present niche. Its secondary function was to link the front and sides, or turn the corner of the tomb, and this it achieves with complete success by means of the withdrawn left leg. Its present placing violates not only its structure, but its meaning too. Viewed at such close proximity the pose takes on an active character; one German critic claims that Moses is gazing in anger at the Golden Calf. But at its proper height the effect of this majestic figure, staring outwards into space, would have been less menacing and less theatrical, and its meaning has been interpreted correctly in the light of a passage from Pico della Mirandola: 'With this vision Moses and Paul and many others among the elect saw the face of God, and this vision is the vision that our theologians call intellectual or intuitive cognition.'

Speaking of the tomb of 1505, Condivi tells us that the figures in front of the pilasters round the base represented the Liberal Arts, and that by them Michelangelo 'sought to denote that all the Virtues had become with Pope Julius prisoners of Death, since they would never find anyone by whom they would be so favoured and nourished as they were by him.' In 1505, with the Pope alive and the prospect of a ten-year pontificate ahead, that was a permissible conceit. Retrospectively, however, it was meaningless, since it was abundantly apparent that the Liberal Arts had not died with the Pope, and that the Pope's reign opened a period of patronage that would continue through that of his successor. For this reason we must eliminate the idea of death when we look at the two figures of the Liberal Arts which Michelangelo carved between 1513 and 1516 for the 1513 tomb. These are the Dying Slave (Plate 16B) and the Rebellious Slave (Plate 16A) now in the Louvre. Many people would, of course, deny that these statues represent the Liberal Arts at all. In 1898 Ollendorf dismissed the explanation as *lächerlich*, and declared that instead they must portray the human soul on earth as though in prison. More recently they have been thought to represent 'the human soul enslaved by matter.' In Roman art prisoners were prisoners, and nothing more, and when the prisoner motif was taken over in Renaissance sculpture, it was often employed in the same restricted way. But Michelangelo's figures are symbolical. Whether they represent the soul enslaved by matter or the Liberal Arts in bondage, a convention from Roman sculpture is used as the means of conveying an idea which was not implicit in it from the start. So when it is argued that the personification of the Liberal Arts as slaves is opposed to the traditional use of the slave in art, or conversely that it is inconsistent with the traditional personification of the Liberal Arts, neither argument need be taken into serious ac-

count. We, moreover, like the Slaves, are bound – not by fetters but by evidence. There is
no evidence at all that the Slaves represent the soul, but there is evidence that they represent
the Liberal Arts, for on one there appears a roughly carved ape, and on the other there is a
lump which might be a second embryonic ape. The likelihood therefore, is that the two
figures depict 'art the ape of nature,' and that the Dying and Rebellious Slaves are symbols
respectively of the arts of Painting and Sculpture. Even if that is granted, what they are
doing is not altogether clear. The Dying Slave is said in the great romantic Michelangelo
biography of Grimm to portray 'the moment of death,' but it could equally portray the
moment of awakening, and it is probable that the figures together represent what we might
expect personifications of the Liberal Arts on a posthumous tomb of Julius II to represent,
the resurgence of the Visual Arts.

In the seven years that intervene between the first and second versions of the tomb,
Michelangelo's thoughts had naturally revolved from time to time round the problem of the
Slaves. We know that from a sheet at Oxford (Fig. 32) which contains six studies for
Prisoners, along with a large sketch for the Libyan Sibyl on the Sistine ceiling, and which
must therefore have been made after the first project for the tomb had collapsed and before
the second had been begun. The studies are for two angle figures, shown with knees raised
in profile to left and right, and four frontal figures to be placed against the flat pilasters on
the inside of each niche. These two categories of figure are also represented by the statues in
the Louvre; one of them has the strong profile of an angle figure, and the other has the
unemphatic profile of a figure intended to be seen only from the front. The Rebellious Slave
is generally photographed as though it were facing to the left, but any study of its structure
must lead one to the opposite conclusion, that it faced to the right, and stood immediately
beneath the Moses on the right corner of the tomb. The Dying Slave is much more highly
worked; part of the body is taken almost to the same state of completion as the Moses, and
the transitions between the planes are less abrupt. The motif of the raised arm is one with
which Michelangelo had experimented on the Sistine ceiling, but the planes in the statue recede
less sharply, and the treatment of its contour is more mellifluous. This figure was intended
to be seen against the flat pilaster to the left of the centre of the tomb, and the system on which
it is composed depends from the David, where the thinness of the block had forced the sculptor to fall back upon a linear scheme. But the fact of the pilaster precluded the employment
of an open scheme like that used for the David, so that the figure is closed in on itself. On
one side the curved line of the leg is balanced by the unbroken contour of the torso, and on
the other the straight line of the leg is balanced by the curved line of the waist, while above
the two forearms are posed on corresponding diagonals.

One last point must be made about the 1513 scheme. Vasari tells us in parenthesis that
Michelangelo made 'one side of the work in many pieces complete in every detail,' and a
drawing of the base of the tomb, probably of about 1516, includes a statement in the sculptor's
hand that all of the decorative carvings in it were complete, some of them in Florence and

some in Rome. The style of the decorative carvings on the bottom of the present tomb must logically belong to this and to no later phase, so we may guess that the bottom of the monument that was completed in 1545 was in large part identical with the bottom of the monument carved in 1513. If, therefore, we imagine the base of the monument as it now stands in San Pietro in Vincoli (Fig. 30) with the volutes removed from the pilasters, the Rebellious Slave on the right side and a corresponding figure on the left, the Dying Slave and a companion figure on the inside of each niche, and the Moses and a St. Paul at the ends of the platform at the top, we shall have a reasonably faithful picture of Michelangelo's visual intentions in the 1513 tomb.

In 1516 the whole scheme was once more thrown into the melting pot, and a new contract was drawn up. According to Michelangelo himself, the reason was that Pope Leo X diverted him against his will on to a new project, the façade of San Lorenzo. But a simplification of the tomb and a deferment of its terminal date must have been welcome on general grounds, since the 1513 tomb was due to be completed by 1520, and no more than three of its thirty-eight figures had been carved. Moreover, and one cannot help feeling this motive may have been predominant, by 1516 Michelangelo had outgrown the architectural conceptions embodied in the first two versions of the tomb. The new contract bound him to complete his task in nine years, that is by 1525, and it transformed the tomb into a true wall monument. The lower part of the structure was now to protrude from the wall by no more than one bay, that is by the depth of a niche flanked by two supporting Prisoners, and the platform on top was thereby eliminated. The front of the upper structure was therefore brought forward, and aligned with the front of the structure beneath, and the six figures on the platform were reduced to two, which were set between pilasters at either side. In the centre there was no longer room for the tomb chest in depth with its end to the spectator and four figures round it, and it was replaced by a seated figure of the Pope (possibly the statue which was blocked out in 1508) supported by two other figures, perhaps with a tomb-chest placed lengthwise with its long side towards the front of the tomb. This involved both a simplification and a revision of the earlier scheme. The forty odd figures were reduced to twenty, and instead of the pictorial disposition of the sculptures before an architectural background which had been intended three years earlier, the sculpture was completely integrated in the architecture of the tomb.

New blocks were ordered for the new scheme, but work was irregular and slow. The façade project was partly responsible for that, but it transpires from the letters written to and by Michelangelo at this time that there were other obstacles, part artistic and part psychological. In the Medici Chapel the conceptions of the monuments and of the individual sculptures change shape and size seemingly of their own accord, and the same fate overtakes the Julius tomb. For a great part of the three years that followed the signature of the new contract Michelangelo was at Pietrasanta and Carrara, in daily communion with the medium through which he worked, and it would be contrary to everything we know of his

Fig. 31. After Michelangelo: UPPER PART OF A STUDY FOR THE TOMB OF POPE JULIUS II. Kupferstichkabinett, Berlin.
Fig. 32. Michelangelo: STUDIES FOR THE SLAVES ON THE TOMB OF POPE JULIUS II. Ashmolean Museum, Oxford.

Fig. 33. After Michelangelo: LOWER PART OF A STUDY FOR THE TOMB OF POPE JULIUS II.
Kupferstichkabinett, Berlin.

Fig. 34. Michelangelo: HERCULES AND CACUS (?). Casa Buonarroti, Florence.
Fig. 35. Michelangelo: THE DEPOSITION. Duomo, Florence.

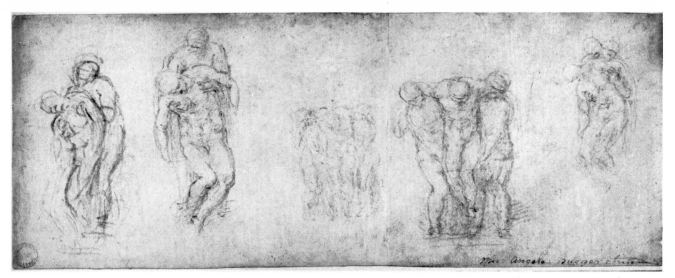

Fig. 36. Michelangelo: STUDIES FOR THE RONDANINI PIETA. Ashmolean Museum, Oxford.

Fig. 37. Michelangelo: THE RONDANINI PIETA. Museo del Castello Sforzesco, Milan.
Fig. 38. Michelangelo: STUDY FOR A CRUCIFIXION. British Museum, London.

Fig. 39. Rustici: THE PREACHING OF THE BAPTIST. Baptistry, Florence.

Fig. 40. Danti: THE EXECUTION OF ST. JOHN BAPTIST. Baptistry, Florence.

creative processes if, while he was isolated with his scheme, the scheme itself remained un-changed. The main evidence that it did not is afforded by the four unfinished Slaves (Plates 17A, 17B, 18, 19) in the Accademia in Florence.

In 1519, when the dead Pope's executors were exerting all possible pressure to compel Michelangelo to complete the tomb, there is a reference to four figures on which he pro-posed to work during the summer of that year, and it is very difficult to escape the conclusion that those four figures are the Slaves. If they are, a second conclusion follows, that Michel-angelo in 1519 proposed to revise the whole of the bottom of the tomb. Whereas the Prisoners he had left behind in Rome – the Slaves in the Louvre – are roughly seven feet high, the four Slaves in the Accademia are roughly eight, and are carved from deeper blocks. At this time, in other words, he concluded that the old figures had to be abandoned since they were too slender and too small to marry with the superstructure of the 1516 tomb, and that new figures and a new base must be supplied. The four Slaves in Florence remained unfinished because he had neither the time, nor the heart, nor the physical resilience to push this vast revision through.

All unfinished sculptures present us with interpretative problems, and none more so than these. For some students they are among the most valuable figures by Michelangelo that we possess. Through them, as through no other works, we plumb the depths of his vast reservoir of creative vitality; they are a physical embodiment of the romantic concept of the spirit struggling to escape from the prison of the block. For others – a very small minority – they are figures blocked out from the master's models in the quarry or the studio, in which he himself had, manually speaking, scarcely any part. The realism of the second view is more acceptable than the romanticism of the first, though it cannot be adopted in so crude a form. Taking, for example, the figure known as the Awakening Slave (Plate 19), we find in the area of the left shoulder and the raised left arm forms that are not only rudimentary, but are so empty and distended and unfunctional that they could well be executed by a studio hand. This is true also of the more highly worked right calf. But as soon as we approach the area of the torso and the waist and the right thigh, Michelangelo's miraculous chisel can be seen at work, shaping, refining, toughening the flaccid forms. This line of analysis can be pursued through the companion figures. Whichever of the two views we adopt, the statues are no more than potential works of art.

The contrast with the Louvre Slaves is so great that at first sight it might appear that Fafner and Fasolt supplanted Mars and Apollo on the front of the tomb. But this is not in the least what occurred, for two of the figures are direct substitutions for the two Slaves in the Louvre. One of them is the figure known as the Young Slave (Plate 17A), where the raised left elbow and the bent left knee are taken over from the Dying Slave, but are treated with stronger plastic emphasis, so that the figure appears to support an upper structure and not simply to rest against the flat plane of the wall. Plastically it is still conceived as a relief, but a relief forcibly wrenching itself from its ground. The thick limbs would, of course, have been thinned down. This figure, like the Dying Slave, was destined for the second pilaster from the left, and on the second pilaster from the right was its counterpart, the figure known as the Bearded Slave (Plate 18). On the extreme right, in the position occupied by the Rebellious Slave, there would have stood its substitute, the figure known as the Atlas Slave (Plate 17B), a much superior work in which the surface treatment is exactly consonant with that of the Day in the Medici Chapel. Once more the transitions are more violent and abrupt than in the earlier statue. Michelangelo's intention at this time was not just that the importance of the architecture vis-à-vis the sculpture should be increased, but that the supporting figures should establish a causative connection between the two. The Prisoners – whether or not they still represented the Liberal Arts we do not know, even Michelangelo may have been uncertain – were to have a functional relationship to the whole monument.

There were six niches in the scheme of 1513 and four in the scheme of 1516, and all of them were to contain two-figure groups. Only one group was carved, the Victory in the Palazzo Vecchio in Florence (Plate 21), where the hair is decorated with the oak leaves of the Della Rovere. Its height is almost exactly the same as that of the Accademia Slaves, and since it is unfinished, we should have reason on our side if we supposed that it was unfinished for the same reason, that it was made for the revised lower section of the tomb. The treatment of the torso contrasts at many points with the male nudes in the Medici Chapel, and there is a possibility that it was reworked later in the sixteenth century. When allowances are made for that, it is plain that its affinities are with the earlier Allegories in the Chapel, not with the more fluid forms of the Evening and the Dawn, and that it must date from the two mysterious years between the death of Leo X and the election of Clement VII, when the Della Rovere obtained the support of Pope Adrian VI, and Michelangelo was diverted back from the Chapel to the tomb. There are two main theories about the corresponding group for the niche opposite. The first, and less convincing, is that we have a model for it in the Casa Buonarroti (Fig. 34), and the second, and more persuasive, is that the model for it is recorded in a statue by another artist. Its subject is Honour triumphant over Falsehood (Plate 77), and it was carved in the early fifteen-sixties by an admirer of Michelangelo, Vincenzo Danti. One reason for supposing that this group was planned as a counterpart to the Victory is that the torso slopes away diagonally in the opposite sense, so that the relationship of the two figures is broadly analogous to that of the two unfinished slaves destined for the centre of the 1519 tomb.

One of Julius II's executors died in 1520, and the whole matter of the tomb was raised by the surviving executor at the end of 1523. With the terminal date of the 1516 contract little more than a year away, Michelangelo was asked to produce a statement of the sums that had been paid to him and the work that had been done. He replied that he needed eight thousand ducats more to finish off the tomb. This was presumably because the architecture of the lower part, into which the Prisoners were to be fitted, had to be carved afresh. The Cardinal on his side seems to have felt that the main impediment was not financial, and he made what, on the face of it, was an extremely fair suggestion, that the tomb should be completed by Jacopo Sansovino and other artists, and should incorporate Michelangelo's sculptures, among them a Virgin and Child. In the autumn Michelangelo turned his proposal down, declaring that he would rather repay the money he had received than allow the tomb to be completed in that way. At this time and later he was resentful of the criticism to which he had exposed himself through his delays over the tomb. The impression left by the correspondence of his representatives in Rome is a little disingenuous, but that was not Michelangelo's own attitude. In the face of his commitment he felt a sort of sublime helplessness. No one was more alive to the nature of moral obligation than he, but he was no longer master of his destiny. From the letters of his representatives in Rome two aims stand out, still further to diminish the size of the tomb, and to entrust some of the sculptures to other hands. In October 1526 he prepared a reduced scheme, but the Pope's heirs rejected it. This was a counsel of despair. His mind was filled with the reality of the Medici Chapel, and for the first time we sense that the tomb is no longer a positive achievement borne forward on the creative wings of his own genius, but a negative duty to be carried out. It is contrary to probability to suppose that any of the major sculptures for the tomb were conceived after this time.

The negotiations were resumed in 1531, when Michelangelo, in a state of mounting frenzy, was working in the Medici Chapel. This time the spokesman for the heirs was Francesco Maria della Rovere, Duke of Urbino, but the decisive influence was that of the Pope, who regarded the completion of the tomb as a psychological necessity for Michelangelo. It was not essential, he suggested, for Michelangelo to admit to the Duke that the tomb would be finished by other sculptors; it would suffice if he prepared the models and tacitly allowed that to occur. There was, he insisted, already too much autograph sculpture in the monument. Suddenly, at the end of the year, the Duke of Urbino bowed to the inevitable, and accepted the proposal for a reduced tomb, so in April 1532 a new contract was signed. By its terms the number of sculptures was again cut down – they were now to consist of six by Michelangelo and five by other artists – and the tomb was transferred from St. Peter's to San Pietro in Vincoli, where, in 1533, work on the foundations began. The six sculptures by Michelangelo probably included the Dying and Rebellious Slaves, and excluded the unfinished sculptures carved for the 1516 tomb, the Prisoners in Florence and the Victory.

A letter to Michelangelo written by Sebastiano del Piombo from Rome at the end of 1531 reports an interview with the Pope, in which it was proposed that the sculptures carved for the tomb should be made available for use in the Medici Chapel. Then, said Sebastiano del Piombo, if any of them pleased His Holiness, His Holiness could say, 'I want this or that.' But His Holiness expressed some scruple about this, and declared that he would not touch a single stone destined for the tomb. There is no further written evidence, but the matter cannot have ended precisely at that point, since one of the figures used for the tomb, the Active Life (Plate 34), was very probably carved in the first instance for the Chapel. In practice the applicability of the tomb sculptures to the Chapel was extremely limited. The

Slaves could have no part in the scheme, and neither could the Moses nor the Victory. There was indeed only one major iconographical feature of the tomb that was common to the Chapel, and that was the Virgin and Child. Not only does the statue in the Chapel differ from the group that Michelangelo planned, but it is related, in form, condition and technique, to the Victory from the Julius tomb, and must have been carved at the same time. In the circumstances there is a strong case for supposing that it was made for the tomb not for the Chapel, as part of a revision of the upper section of the monument.

The beginning of work in San Pietro in Vincoli proved premature, for in 1534 Clement VII died, and was succeeded as Pope by Paul III, who was less indulgent than his predecessor towards the tomb. For him it was simply an impediment in the way of a new project, the fresco of the Last Judgement. The cartoon of the Last Judgement was prepared in September 1535, and work on it continued till the autumn of 1541. In 1538 Francesco Maria della Rovere died, and his successor as Duke of Urbino, Guidobaldo, had no alternative but to acquiesce in the completion of the fresco, but when it was finished the Pope at once diverted Michelangelo to a new task, the painting of the Cappella Paolina. A campaign was started to bludgeon the Duke of Urbino into accepting even less favourable terms than those that had previously been agreed upon. 'Michelangelo,' explains one letter, 'is obliged to paint the Pauline Chapel, and will be unable to work further on the tomb. He is old, and is resolved, when the chapel is finished in three or four years time, if he lives so long, to undertake no further work.' Some other arrangement for the completion of the tomb must therefore be made. The only difference, ran this insidious argument, was that the six statues supplied by Michelangelo, instead of being autograph sculptures, would be made from his designs. Possibly they might include something which he had carved or at least sketched out, but even that was uncertain, because the Pope thought the sculptures unsuited to the tomb but well adapted to his own chapel. To his credit the Duke of Urbino stood firm; there must be three completely autograph finished statues, he insisted, and one of them must be the Moses.

The Moses (Plate 15) in the twenty odd years of its existence had suffered rather a peculiar fate. The first indication we have of that occurs during a visit paid by Pope Paul III to Michelangelo's studio probably in 1535. He was accompanied by the Cardinal of Mantua, who caught sight of the statue, and exclaimed: 'This statue alone is amply sufficient to do honour to the tomb of Pope Julius.' By 1535 the Neoplatonic programme of the 1513 tomb was of small account, and the historical significance of Julius II's pontificate was open to no doubt. So the militant figure of Moses presented itself in a new light; it came to be regarded as an allegory of the pontificate and of the Pope. That idea lay at the base of the final revision of the tomb, was resuscitated in the nineteenth century – the figure is interpreted in that way, for example, by Gregorovius – and affects most of us when we look at it to-day. As the meaning of the Moses swelled, the effigy destined for the tomb shrivelled into its present insignificance.

The solution proposed by the Duke of Urbino was agreeable to Michelangelo, and in

1542 he agreed to supply three figures carved from his models by Raffaello da Montelupo, a Virgin and Child, a Prophet and a Sibyl, and three figures of his own which were almost complete, the Moses and the Dying and Rebellious Slaves. But he personally thought the Slaves unsuited for the niches on the reduced tomb – the reasons for that must have been part formal and part iconographical – and he preferred to substitute two other statues, one of which was already under way, of the Active and the Contemplative Life (Plates 34, 35). The Duke of Urbino delayed ratifying the new contract, but work went ahead. The bottom storey of the tomb of 1513 was completed and installed, the upper storey of 1516 was put on top of it, the Prisoners were replaced by volutes, the Moses was set in the centre of the tomb with smaller figures of the Active and the Contemplative Life on either side, and above were four workshop statues, a Prophet and Sibyl, an effigy and the Virgin and Child. By 1545 all this resulted in the monument we know to-day (Fig. 30). When it was finished, the surplus sculptures were dispersed. The Dying and Rebellious Slaves of 1513 were given to Ruberto Strozzi, and found their way to France. The Victory, discovered after the sculptor's death in the studio in Florence, was first provisionally allocated in his tomb, and was then installed by Vasari in the Salone dei Cinquecento of the Palazzo Vecchio. The four Prisoners were taken over by Cosimo I, and eventually were built by Buontalenti into a grotto in the Boboli Gardens, from which they were rescued as recently as 1908. Michelangelo's artistic conscience may have been weighed down by the enormity of what had happened, but his moral conscience was absolved.

The tragedy of the tomb – that famous expression is Condivi's – was not simply a tragedy of compromise, a great artistic concept trimmed by fate or by expediency; it was the tragedy of a work rooted in deep artistic convictions that was completed by a man to whom artistic considerations were in themselves no longer of great consequence. In 1542, the year of the final contract for the tomb, the Inquisition was introduced in Italy, the Council of Trent had already been convened, and the Counter-Reformation, which had cast its shadow over the preceding decade, was fully launched. In the life of Michelangelo reason was expelled, and dark contemplation took its place. This was the period of his spiritual intimacy with Vittoria Colonna, and of the mystical poems that have pride of place in his poetic works. Between the latest of the statues carved for the 1516 tomb, the Victory, and the new statues carved for the monument of 1542, there intervene the mysterious figures in the Pauline Chapel and the visionary images of the Last Judgement, in which painting is treated as a vehicle for the transmission of mystical experience. The bottom of the Julius monument is not just a union of figures of different dates, but the meeting point of two irreconcilable attitudes to sculpture. In the statue of the Contemplative Life the postulates that underpin the Moses are denied. The essential medievalism of this figure was apparent even to Condivi, who relates it and its companion figure to the Divine Comedy. It represents, he writes, 'a woman of rare beauty with head and hands turned towards heaven, which in all its parts breathes love.'

In 1541, in the course of the negotiations for the building of the tomb, it had been intimated that Michelangelo would undertake no further work, and after the monument was finished he adhered to that so far as sculptural commissions were concerned. But in those nineteen years – he died in 1564 – he was tormented by the urge to create a sculptural equivalent for the style of the Pauline Chapel and of the Last Judgement. Before 1550 he started work on a group destined for his own tomb (Plates 36, 37, Fig. 35). It represented the active subject of the Deposition, not, like the early sculpture in St. Peter's, the passive subject of the Pietà. The mask of classicism has been torn away, and mother and son are participants in a real scene. Vasari describes the figures as shown in momentary action, the Virgin 'overcome by grief, failing in strength and not able to uphold Him,' and Nicodemus bending forward to assist her 'planted firmly on his feet in a forceful attitude,' while Christ 'sinking with the limbs hanging limp, lies in an attitude wholly different not only from that of any other work by Michelangelo, but from that of any other figure that was ever made.' Of conscious refinement of the sculpture as a work of art – as we meet it in the sculptures of the Medici Chapel and the Victory – there is no longer the least trace, and the communicative power of the whole group is inseparable from the brutal directness of its form. But the figures, though depicted in momentary action, are also symbols, and the head of Nicodemus expresses the compassion not of one onlooker, but of mankind.

Michelangelo, in the Hollanda Dialogues, declares that ideally the religious artist should be a saint, and in conformity with that belief the Deposition is conceived as a form of visual prayer. 'O flesh, O blood, O wood, O extreme suffering' exclaims Michelangelo in one of his later poems, 'through you may my sin be atoned,' and in a moving poem, also dating from the period of the marble group, he protests at the veil of ice by which his innermost being is encased, and begs Christ to break down the hard wall that prevents the light of grace from penetrating to his heart. The status of the group as a summation of these poems seems to have been accepted by Michelangelo's contemporaries, and in 1564 the head of Nicodemus was already looked upon as an idealised self-portrait.

In 1554 this group – the most subjective and most overtly emotional that has ever been produced – was defaced by the sculptor in a moment of exasperation, and was worked up by a studio hand into the state in which we see it now. This affected especially the kneeling figure on the left hand side, which is smaller than the Virgin and is so incompetently carved that its function is not immediately evident. Condivi, however, tells us that the figure was conceived by Michelangelo as 'performing for Christ the office which his mother could not undertake,' that is the cleansing of the corpse. The block-like simplicity of the Virgin, for which Michelangelo was responsible, stands in sharp contrast to the artificial disposition of the figure opposite. At the side and back the figure of the Virgin is rounded in a way which is consistent only with the view that the group was intended for a niche, and in a containing space its effect would be even more pictorial than it is to-day. In the Hollanda Dialogues Michelangelo insists that 'amongst men there is but one single art or science, and that is drawing or painting, all others being members proceeding therefrom.' The primacy of painting is maintained visually in the

Deposition group. The linking of the three main figures in a single visual unit with a strong vertical emphasis is a device that was repeatedly employed by Michelangelo in the Last Judgement, and the Virgin and Nicodemus can indeed be looked upon as figures from the fresco invested with physical instead of notional tactility. Though the group was cast aside, the expressive problem it presented could not be so easily dismissed, and from this time there survive a number of drawings for a Crucifixion, conceived in the same style as the Pauline Chapel frescoes but projected as a marble group. Sometimes the three figures coalesce, as they do in the marble Deposition; sometimes they are spaced apart (Fig. 38) as three inter-dependent statues; and sometimes they are so lightly indicated that they seem to float below the level of the sculptor's consciousness. On the back of one of them there is an indication of the block from which, had the group become an actuality, the Christ would have been carved. It did not become an actuality, perhaps because the image was inherently unsculptural, perhaps because it was so charged with meaning that Michelangelo could not reconcile himself to reducing it to finite terms. There remained one last project for a sculpture of a subject he had treated in his youth, the Pietà. It appears first on a sheet at Oxford for a Virgin supporting the Dead Christ (Fig. 36). This eventually became the pathetic relic of the Rondanini Pietà (Fig. 37), where Michelangelo, in the last weeks of his life, hacked away the marble till nothing but a skeleton survived.

Seen in relation to his ambitions and to his own interior life, the career of Michelangelo the sculptor was one of failure, ending in a symbolic act of suicide. Seen in relation to the outer world, it was one of unparalleled success, for his contemporaries without exception recognised that he had raised the art of sculpture to an expressive level that had never been conceived before and could never be surpassed.

THE HIGH RENAISSANCE STATUE

AT the very beginning of the sixteenth century attention in Florence was once more directed to the Baptistry, the building on which it had been focused a hundred years before. The centre of interest was no longer the doors (which continued to excite the admiration that had been felt for them throughout the fifteenth century) but the register above them, which was filled by three decaying marble groups. Carved in the shop of Tino di Camaino, the three groups had one peculiarity, that they were narrative scenes composed of large-scale sculptures. Over the north door was St. John the Baptist preaching to a Levite and a Pharisee, over the south door was the Baptism of Christ, and over the east door, above the Porta de Paradiso, was the Baptist with figures of the Virtues and St. Michael. From the few fragments of them that survive we know that the individual figures were soft, immobile and bland. Vasari describes them as *goffe* (awkward or clumsy), and very primitive they must have looked in 1483 when Verrocchio's Christ and St. Thomas, which also depicted a large-scale narrative scene, was installed on Or San Michele. No steps to replace the statues were taken, however, before 1502, when it was decided by the Arte de' Mercanti that marble figures of Christ and the Baptist should be commissioned to replace Tino di Camaino's Baptism, and be installed over the east, not the south, door. The figures were entrusted to Andrea Sansovino, who had established himself a short time earlier – with the Corbinelli altar in Santo Spirito and two still unfinished statues of the Virgin and Child (Plate 42) and St. John the Baptist for Genoa Cathedral – as the principal classicising sculptor of his time. Work on them was broken off in 1505, when Sansovino moved to Rome. In the winter of the following year a second large group was commissioned to replace the Preaching of the Baptist over the north door. The medium of the new group was bronze, and it was allotted to Giovanni Francesco Rustici, who completed it in 1511. A third group, the Decollation of the Baptist, was commissioned for the south door almost sixty years later from Vincenzo Danti.

It might be supposed that two groups designed for the same building in the same term of years would be stylistically uniform. But Andrea Sansovino's Baptism of Christ (Plate 43) and Rustici's Preaching of the Baptist (Fig. 39) have in common nothing save the architectural expedient by which they are united to the fabric of the church. The wall of the Baptistry above the entrances was covered with polychrome arcading, and the height of the statues was determined by the height of the arcade. The wall surface made it impossible to build external niches which would isolate the groups, and instead it was decided, in the case of the Baptism of Christ, to construct a simple tabernacle, comprising an entablature supported on two columns, planned as a background not as a containing niche. This scheme, in a somewhat different form, was used again by Rustici.

The contrast between the Baptism of Christ and the Preaching of the Baptist is not only one between a group in marble and a group in bronze. It is also the contrast between an artist whose predilections were strongly classical, and an artist whose concern was with expression and who for that reason disregarded the antique. The first group has a key place in the history of Renaissance sculpture, while the second stands alone, and for that reason it may be well to look at the later of the two groups first. The Preaching of the Baptist consists of three figures on circular bases disposed symmetrically against the tabernacle. In the centre, framed by columns, is the preaching Saint, and to the right and left there stand his auditors, a bald-headed Levite and a Pharisee. Though the statues are set on a single plane and widely spaced, they none the less form a dramatic unit; each is linked psychologically to the next. None of the three figures could be explained without reference to the other two; the auditors presuppose a preacher, and the preacher postulates an audience. There is no precedent in sculpture for a composition of this kind, but it had a parallel in painting, in the fresco of the Last Supper where Leonardo makes use of a very similar narrative device. This is significant, because the sources one and all link Leonardo's name with Rustici's at the time he was working on the group.

Though they are set in line, the three figures are posed in rather a peculiar way. The Baptist is shown with the left shoulder retracted and the right advanced, and with his right knee thrust forward and his left leg drawn back. The spiral implications of the pose are underscored by a cloak which falls from the right shoulder and by the sharp turn of the head. The posture of the Levite (Plate 38) is still more complex: the left elbow is pushed forward and the right shoulder is held back, while below the rhythm is reversed and the right foot is crossed over the left. This opposition between the shoulders and the knees is found again in an inverted form in the figure of the Pharisee. Vasari, who refers to the group twice, tells us first, in his life of Rustici, that the sculptor was assisted by Leonardo, who never left him during the modelling of the figures, and second, in his life of Leonardo, that the figures were planned by Leonardo but made by Rustici. There is no documentary confirmation that this was so, but the three figures certainly establish a formal pattern that is typical of Leonardo and of no other artist, and this relationship can be confirmed from numberless details – the Levite's head, which so closely recalls the caricature heads by Leonardo, the crossed legs, which make use of a motif explored by Leonardo in his early studies for an Adoration of the Shepherds, and the Medusa-like hair shirt of St. John. An extraordinary feature is the extent to which the group preserves the spontaneity of modelled sculpture; one of the devices employed in it, the use of drilling in the cavities between the wild locks on the Baptist's head (Plate 39) and in the unruly tufts of his hair shirt, may also be ascribable to Leonardo's pictorial consciousness.

By contrast Sansovino's Baptism of Christ (Plate 43) is a work of great restraint. The hands of Christ are folded on his chest, and his shoulders are parallel with the wall. The Baptist is also posed frontally, with his head turned in profile towards Christ and his right arm raised above Christ's head. The effect is here made not by abrupt changes of plane, but by smooth transitions within a continuous silhouette. This and the pyramidal design also suggest analogies with painting – not with Leonardo, who was engaged upon his battle fresco in the Palazzo della Signoria while Sansovino was working on the group, but with Raphael, who arrived in Florence when the figures were already far advanced, in 1504. Unluckily this splendid group, which might have exercised a beneficial influence in Florence, was not finished, and only in 1569 was it set up on the Baptistry.

The reason why the group was left unfinished was that the eddies of Sansovino's reputation reached the papal court, and in 1505, seduced by the same prospects that had tempted Michelangelo before him, he moved to Rome. There, as the Baptism of Christ might lead us to expect, he rapidly aligned himself not with Michelangelo, but with the orthodox classicism of Bramante, and after 1508 with Raphael. Initially he was employed on two wall monuments for Bramante's choir of Santa Maria del Popolo, and when in 1510 or 1511 he was allotted the commission for a free-standing statue this was associated with a work by Raphael. Completed in 1512, it owed its origin to a native of Luxembourg, Johann Goritz, who formed the centre of a humanist circle in Rome. On the feast of St. Anne, Goritz habitually entertained his friends – Sadoleto, Bembo, Castiglione and Giovio among them –

at his villa, and he determined to give his devotion to this Saint permanent expression in Sant'
Agostino. In the monument he planned painting and sculpture were combined. Above was
a fresco by Raphael of the Prophet Isaiah, bearing a Greek dedication to St. Anne, and below
it was a group of the Virgin and Child with St. Anne by Sansovino (Plate 48).

Goritz was not only a distinguished humanist, but a man of strong artistic views. With his
approval Raphael's fresco was revised in the light of the Prophets on the Sistine ceiling, and it
may have been at his request that Sansovino took as his starting point a work by Leonardo.
From Sansovino's years in Florence one event must have stood out with special clarity –
the exhibition, in 1501, of the cartoon of the Virgin and Child with St. Anne prepared by
Leonardo for the high altarpiece of the Annunziata. 'When it was finished,' Vasari tells us,
'men and women, young and old, continued for two days to crowd into the room where it
was shown, as if attending a solemn festival.' Leonardo's cartoon has disappeared, but elements of the composition are recorded in a second cartoon in London and in a painting in
the Louvre. In the London cartoon the Virgin is shown seated on St. Anne's right thigh.
This motif of one figure supported on the other was unsuited to sculpture, and was unclassical,
and Sansovino for this reason represents the figures seated side by side. The right foot of
each of Leonardo's figures is set lower than the left. This too Sansovino modified, placing
his figures on two different levels and showing St. Anne gazing at the Child. At the same
time he changed the axis of the group. He did this because his subject differed both from that
of the cartoon (where the Child is shown blessing the young St. John) and from that of the
painting in the Louvre (where the Child plays with a lamb). If there were no lamb and no
St. John, the Child need no longer be stretched across the composition from left to right, but
could instead be set across the Virgin's body from right to left. In this way Sansovino evolved
a closed, flattened composition, in which Leonardo's scheme was classicised.

The intellectual mastery of this group stands out most clearly if we compare it with a
group of the same subject (Plate 56) which Francesco da Sangallo completed for the altar
of St. Anne in Or San Michele in Florence fourteen years later, in 1526. Sangallo must also
have been familiar with Leonardo's scheme, and from it he took over the motif that
Sansovino had avoided with such care, the Virgin seated on St. Anne's right thigh. To achieve
this he set the right leg of St. Anne on the rear plane of the block, and treated the front
plane as a triangle, with the Virgin's left knee as its apex and her right leg and the left leg of
St. Anne as the two sides. Not only is this composition laboured and inelegant, but it is
lacking in the human content, the equipoise of form and subject, that is the crowning glory
of Sansovino's group.

The opposition to Michelangelo that is implicit in this statue becomes explicit in the work
of Andrea's namesake and disciple, Jacopo Sansovino. Jacopo left Florence for Rome in
1505, and may have been present in 1506 when Michelangelo and Giuliano and Francesco
da Sangallo identified the newly found Laocoon. Soon afterwards he made a wax copy of
it, which brought him to the notice of Raphael and Bramante. Returning to Florence about

1511, he began work on his first important marble statue, the Bacchus (Plate 50), commissioned by Giovanni Bartolini, later owned by Cosimo de' Medici and now in a sadly damaged state in the Bargello. Bartolini's palace at Gualfonda was designed by Baccio d'Agnolo, and there, in a courtyard or loggia, on a red and white marble base by Benedetto da Rovezzano, Sansovino's statue stood. When he designed it, he must have been thoroughly familiar with Michelangelo's Bacchus in Rome. Trained as he was in the orbit of Andrea Sansovino and of Raphael, he perceived what we too see today, that Michelangelo imposed upon his Bacchus a continuous spiral movement that was essentially unclassical. In Sansovino's Bacchus an attempt is made to revive the antique on its own terms. The realism of Michelangelo is replaced by a strain of idyllic poetry, and the figure, though it rests on a circular base, is planned with one main and three subsidiary views like a statue in the fifteenth century.

The contest between Sansovino and Michelangelo was fought out on a larger field in the Cathedral. All hope that Michelangelo would execute twelve more than life-size statues of Apostles for the Duomo was finally abandoned in 1508, when he began work on the Sistine ceiling. For three years the scheme was in abeyance, and then, in the first half of 1511, it was decided to allot the statues separately to such sculptors as were available. In June the first commission, for the St. James (Plate 51), was awarded to Sansovino. In the second half of 1512, after a vain attempt to induce Andrea Sansovino to undertake two statues, a figure of St. John was commissioned from Benedetto da Rovezzano, who completed it, with great expedition, in twelve months, and at about the same time a St. Andrew was commissioned from Andrea Ferrucci. In 1514 Ferrucci was unsuccessfully invited to carve a second statue, a St. Peter, and when he refused, this was entrusted, early in 1515, to a young and unproved protégé of Giuliano de' Medici, Baccio Bandinelli.

The four statues are of unequal merit. The least successful is the St. John of Benedetto da Rovezzano (Fig. 43), who was accustomed to working in relief, and whose figure reveals in every fold the limitations of a small-scale artist. Ferrucci's St. Andrew (Fig. 42) is more accomplished, though the elaborate drapery and the Michelangelesque motif of the left hand held heroically against the body are insufficient to redeem the inertia of its pose. Bandinelli's St. Peter (Fig. 41) is the victim not of slack sculptural thinking but of perfunctory technique, and its boldly contrived design is smothered in inanimate detail. The St. James is a sculpture of a very different class. In 1511, when Sansovino started work on it, the only basis of comparison was Michelangelo's St. Matthew. The challenge of this figure was the more real in that Sansovino was making use of a block quarried for Michelangelo. Moreover, he must have been familiar not only with Michelangelo's unfinished statue, but with the creative stages through which it had passed. He would, for example, have been aware of the importance that Michelangelo from the beginning attached to violent contrasts within the pose and of the emphasis that rested on the knee, protruding arrogantly from the block. In Sansovino's statue of St. James each of the propositions implied in the St. Matthew is contradicted by its opposite.

Plastic contrasts are replaced by a system of smooth articulation. A careful equilibrium is established between the planes of the shoulders and the knees, and a great fold of drapery softens the transition from the forward leg to that behind. One hand is raised, the other lowered, and the smooth drapery along the legs is balanced against broken drapery above, the two separated from each other by heavily scored folds of cloak held round the hips. The head is treated not with the visionary intensity of the St. Matthew but with classical restraint. Sansovino's point of departure in this work was the statue of the Baptist carved by Andrea Sansovino for Genoa, but its simple contours are overlaid by the influence of two other artists, one of them Ghiberti, whose statues of Apostles on Or San Michele were stylistically of far greater importance for the sixteenth century than for the fifteenth, and whose work still fascinated Sansovino at a much later time, and the other Raphael.

In 1518, when the St. James was finished, Jacopo Sansovino returned to Rome, and three years later began work on a group of the Virgin and Child for Sant'Agostino (Plate 49), where the Virgin and Child with St. Anne of Andrea Sansovino already stood. The relation of the later to the earlier group is that of the St. James in Florence to Andrea Sansovino's Baptist at Genoa. The core of classicism is unchanged, but the surface contrasts have been heightened and there is a new animation in the drapery. Where the robes in Andrea's group are spread tightly across the knees in repeated curves like a wave pattern in a Chinese painting, the robe of the Madonna del Parto is draped in heavy folds. The Virgin's lap is treated not as an indeterminate receding area, but as a solid platform for the Child, and the two free arms are not disposed on planes parallel with the body, but establish a circular movement which invests the group with greater amplitude. The figures have emerged from their cerebral cocoon, and in the posture of the Child there is an illusion of movement that is deeply Raphaelesque.

Sansovino's Virgin and Child is indeed more authentically Raphaelesque than the only statue Raphael himself designed, the Jonah (Fig. 44) in the Chigi Chapel in Santa Maria del Popolo, where his cartoon – and very beautiful it must have been – was blurred and weakened by the sculptor Lorenzetto. This is one of the few sculptures in the world whose true merits transpire more clearly from plaster casts than from the original.

In 1527, after the Sack of Rome, Jacopo Sansovino moved to Venice, and two years later Andrea Sansovino died at Loreto, where he had been at work since 1512. From this point on, Rome as a sculptural centre yields to Florence, where the accession of Alessandro de' Medici in 1530 opened a long period of stable patronage. For four years Michelangelo dominated the artistic scene, but in 1534 he left Florence never to return, and the leadership of Florentine sculpture passed, by default, to his rival Baccio Bandinelli. The hostility of the two sculptors centred upon a single work, or rather on the block of marble from which that work was to be carved. The David had been set in place outside the Palazzo della Signoria in 1504, and not long after it was proposed that Michelangelo should carve a two-figure companion group. A colossal block of marble was ordered by the Gonfaloniere, Piero Soderini, for his use, but by 1525 the sculpture had not been begun, and Pope Clement VII, in defiance of the wishes of the Signoria, withdrew the block and allotted it afresh to Bandinelli. Boasting of his intention to surpass the David, Bandinelli made two models for a group of the same subject as Michelangelo's projected group, Hercules and Cacus, and the Pope personally opted for one of them. In 1527 carving began. But a year later the Medici were once more expelled, and the block was withdrawn by the popular government from Bandinelli and reallotted to Michelangelo, who started work on a project for a group of Samson and two Philistines. With the return of the Medici this project collapsed. Michelangelo was instructed to continue his work in the Medici Chapel, and Bandinelli resumed the carving of his Hercules and Cacus, which was completed in 1534. The group was much criticised when it was unveiled, and the authors of some of the lampoons directed at it were imprisoned by Alessandro de' Medici. This criticism was both artistic and political; the group from the beginning had been sponsored by the Medici, and was the first emphatic statement of Medicean High Renaissance taste.

In approaching the Hercules and Cacus (Plate 64), we must resist the temptation to compare it with the David, as Bandinelli intended, or with the model for the Samson and two Philistines, as his contemporaries would have done. The group is a product of the same academic-classicist mind as the St. Peter in the Cathedral. At first Bandinelli planned an active group showing Hercules 'holding the head of Cacus with one knee between two rocks and squeezing him with his left arm, pressing him between his legs in a painful attitude,' and Cacus 'suffering from the violence of Hercules with every muscle strained.' This scheme is recorded in a model in Berlin. Luckily for Bandinelli, it proved unsuited to the block, and he fell back instead on a static composition from which the element of movement was excised. From the first it was destined for a corner position on the steps of the Palazzo della Signoria near the Loggia dei Lanzi, and this affected its design; the rectangular base was aligned with the wall of the palace and the front of the platform and the figures were set diagonally across it. The dominant view is from the corner, not from the front of the base, and is established by the shoulders of Hercules and by a diagonal running from the right knee of this figure through the left shoulder of Cacus. On its own academic level, the group is a remarkable work, but its interest is structural, and nowhere does it rise above the level of an arid intellectual theorem. On a large scale Bandinelli was at once a coarse and timid sculptor, and we cannot but feel a pang of sympathy at his predicament, as he attempted, after the statue had been set in place, to strengthen its weak modelling by excavating it in greater depth.

In his own lifetime sympathy was an emotion Bandinelli did not commonly arouse, least of all in the mind of Benvenuto Cellini, who from the time of his return from France in 1545 emerged as Bandinelli's principal competitor. Cellini, in a poem, complains of Bandinelli's 'arrogant voice', and when Cellini's Perseus was unveiled, Bandinelli in turn wrote a lampoon on it which begins *Corpo di vecchio, gambe di fanciulla*. Cellini thought that Bandinelli was spiteful and ungenerous, and Bandinelli complained of the malignancy of *questo pessimo mostro di natura*. But art and vice, he wrote, smugly recalling a dictum of Michelangelo, do not go hand in hand. A good deal of the hostility between Bandinelli and Cellini was professional, but it involved principle as well. Where Cellini by training and temperament was a sculptor craftsman, Bandinelli was an artist from whose composition the element of craftsmanship had been left out. For Cellini, who had gate-crashed into sculpture at the age of forty-two, Bandinelli, a fast worker, felt the scorn of the professional for the amateur, while Cellini seems to have sensed that the reach-me-down system of geometrical forms on which Bandinelli's groups were artificially built up was deeply at variance with the traditions of Florentine sculpture.

The first fissure appeared in August 1545, when Cosimo I awarded Cellini the commission for the Perseus (Plate 70). For Cellini this commission to add one more to the little group of statues in front of the Palazzo Vecchio was of immense significance. At the north corner of the building, on the platform that was later destroyed to make way for Ammanati's fountain, stood the Marzocco of Donatello. To the left of the entrance was Michelangelo's David, to the right of the entrance on the south-east corner stood Bandinelli's Hercules and Cacus, and in the westernmost of the three arches of the Loggia dei Lanzi, in the position now occupied by the Rape of the Sabines, was Donatello's Judith. The Perseus from the first was destined for the corresponding arch on the east side of the entrance, so for Cellini it offered a challenge on every count. He was to supply a bronze pendant to one of Donatello's greatest statues, in full view of the David of Michelangelo and adjacent to the Hercules and Cacus by the sculptor he intended to expose.

In looking at the Perseus there is one misconception that must be cleared away. Cellini is sometimes credited with what is called a kinetic view of sculpture, a conception of the statue as an infinite number of continuous, ceaselessly merging views. There is, admittedly, a poem in which, in a moment of not untypical hyperbole, he seems to state that statues have a thousand views. But in a letter which he contributed in 1549, while the Perseus was still in progress, to the *Lezioni* of Benedetto Varchi, he does not express himself in that fashion at all. 'I affirm,' he says, 'that the art of sculpture is seven times greater than any of the other arts depending on design, because a sculptured statue must have eight views, and all must be of equal excellence.' Another tell-tale passage occurs in the *Vita*, where he describes how Cosimo I, confronted with his model for the Neptune fountain, 'walked all round it, stopping at each of the four points of view exactly as the ripest experts would have done.' So Cellini's theory of statuary, if the written sources are to be trusted, belonged to the late fifteenth century, and was only a little more elaborate than the theory behind the Judith itself.

That conclusion receives ample confirmation from the statue. When it was designed, indeed, Cellini must have had the Judith (Vol. II, Plate 31) constantly in mind, for not only is the figure, like the Judith, planned in relation to a rectangular base, but the rectangle is once more established by a cushion, over which there hangs the Medusa's right arm. Curiously enough this return to Donatello was not part of the original conception, for in the earlier of the two surviving sketches, a wax model in the Bargello (Fig. 45), the figure stands on a circular base with the Medusa draped around it – a goldsmith's image which was difficult to realise on a colossal scale. Only in a later sketch, a bronze model also in the Bargello (Plate 46), is a cushion, smaller and thicker than Donatello's, introduced. It is as though the artist were appealing for guidance to the past. From this it was no more than a short step to the wider, thinner cushion on which the body of Medusa in the final version rests.

The development of the figure of Perseus follows that of the base. In the wax model Perseus is a lithe, elegant, lightly balanced figure represented picking his way over the corpse with his face turned to one side and the Medusa head held outwards to his left. The posture is consolidated in the bronze model, where the Medusa head is represented frontally, the left knee is more sharply bent, and the torso is treated with greater emphasis. In making these changes, Cellini seems to have been influenced by one of the few great Florentine bronze nudes he can have known, the David of Donatello. The implications of movement are less in the bronze model than in the wax, and least of all in the large statue, where *maniera* reigns supreme. It is not just that the modelling is more carefully worked out, but that the whole scheme has been frozen and rationalised. The sword is no longer, as in the model, turned at an angle from the figure pointing down, but is poised horizontally parallel with the ground, and the body of Medusa is not a crumpled heap, but is placed diagonally across the base, with the lower legs set along the edges of the cushion. As we should expect from a goldsmith of Cellini's stature, the detail is notably expressive; the helmet in particular is treated with great imagination and vivacity, and the Medusa head (Plate 71) shows an astonishing command of nuances of form. But it is by the huge nude Perseus that the group must stand or fall, and this, if not a strikingly original invention, is none the less a work of great vitality. The Judith, fortunately for Cellini, no longer stands in the Loggia dei Lanzi, but the relationship between the Perseus and the Hercules and Cacus is still that which he intended. There is no doubt which statue is the greater work of art.

The whole of Florentine sculpture in the second quarter of the century is not comprised in the names of Cellini and Bandinelli; beside them there worked two less aspiring sculptors whose minds operated on a smaller scale, Tribolo and his pupil Pierino da Vinci. Tribolo had worked in Rome in his twenties on the tomb of Pope Adrian VI in Santa Maria dell'Anima (Fig. 61) in the legendary period before the Sack, was employed at Loreto after the death of Andrea Sansovino, and in 1546 was responsible for installing Michelangelo's sculptures in the Medici Chapel. These three commissions brought him into contact with all that was most fertile in the sculpture of his time. His stylistic convictions – and they must have been extremely strong – never found expression in a major statue (to judge from the account of his character given by Cellini, the inhibitions were psychological), but they inspired a number of distinguished garden sculptures, notably the fountains at Castello, and some small bronzes, and found consummate expression in the work of his pupil Pierino. The place of Pierino da Vinci in the Florentine cinquecento is not unlike that of Desiderio da Settignano a century before: he was precocious (he first appears as a youth of fifteen executing independent carvings in Tribolo's shop), he was shortlived (the whole of his activity is comprised in the eight years between 1546 and 1554), and he was a hypersensitive marble sculptor. Pierino's sensuous apprehension of the possibilities of his material are apparent in the beautiful figure of a River God in the Louvre (Plate 63), which was carved for Luca Martini about 1548. The affinities of this enchantingly elegant work are not with Cellini or Bandinelli, but with Michelangelo, and though the tone is more intimate and the idiom more feminine, it is clear that the Apollo (Plate 22) was the source of inspiration of the group.

By the middle of the sixteenth century Bandinelli's Hercules and Cacus must have been widely recognised for what it was, a negation of all those principles which underlay Michelangelo's two-figure groups. In Rome in 1548 Pierino extended his knowledge of Michelangelo's sculptures, and when he returned to Tuscany he began work on a statue which had as its subject a theme associated with Michelangelo, was loosely based on Michelangelo's designs, and was an essay in Michelangelo's sculptural technique. These three points are stressed in Vasari's description of the group: 'Luca (Martini) next sent to Carrara for a marble block five braccia by three for Vinci to make two statues of five braccia on the subject of Samson slaying the Philistine with the jawbone of an ass, for which he had seen a design by Michelangelo. Before the marble arrived, Vinci busied himself by making models all different from each other. At length he settled on one, and when the block came, he set to work at once, imitating Michelangelo in gradually developing his idea from the block, without impairing it or making mistakes. He made the perforations with great facility.' This group (Plate 62) is now in the courtyard of the Palazzo Vecchio.

Unlike Bandinelli, Pierino da Vinci recognised the limits of his own capacity. He had no experience of carving a multi-facial action group fully in the round. The Samson is therefore planned as an exceptionally deep relief; it presents a single view to the spectator, and from this alone can it be read. The ultimate source of the design is Michelangelo's model for the Hercules and Cacus (Fig. 34), but divested of those features which lend it an effect of circularity. The pose of the Philistine follows the Cacus, but the left arm is hidden and the right leg and thigh are aligned on the front plane of the base, while the Samson is posed frontally, with his left knee on his opponent's neck and his head in profile to the right. Despite these changes the two figures retain much of their pristine force. The forms are tactile and three-dimensional, the idiom is broadly naturalistic, and there is a splendid intimation of movement in the tense torso of the standing nude. More important still, the head of Samson is treated with a gravity and earnestness which is at the opposite pole of creative endeavour to the grimacing automata of Bandinelli. Pierino da Vinci's Samson and a Philistine inaugurates a long series of two-figure action groups. When the Perugian sculptor Vincenzo Danti determined, about 1561, to prove himself in marble sculpture, his subject was Honour triumphant over Falsehood (Plate 77); Ammanati included a Victory (Plate 73) in one of

Fig. 41. Bandinelli: ST. PETER. Duomo, Florence.

Fig. 42. Ferrucci: ST. ANDREW. Duomo, Florence.

Fig. 43. Benedetto da Rovezzano: ST. JOHN EVANGELIST.
Duomo, Florence.

Fig. 44. Lorenzetto: JONAH. S. Maria del Popolo, Rome.

Fig. 45. Cellini: WAX MODEL FOR THE PERSEUS. Museo Nazionale, Florence.
Fig. 46. Cellini: BRONZE MODEL FOR THE PERSEUS. Museo Nazionale, Florence.

Fig. 47. Cellini: JUPITER. Loggia dei Lanzi, Florence.

Fig. 48. Cellini: ATHENA. Loggia dei Lanzi, Florence.

Fig. 49. Giovanni Bologna: WAX MODEL FOR FLORENCE TRIUMPHANT OVER PISA.
Victoria & Albert Museum, London.
Fig. 50. Giovanni Bologna: GESSO MODEL FOR FLORENCE TRIUMPHANT OVER PISA. Accademia, Florence.

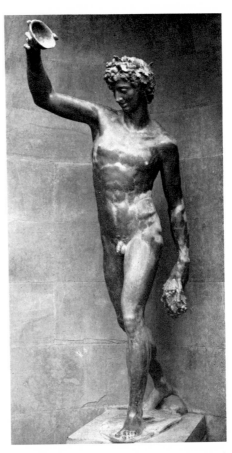

Fig. 51. Giovanni Bologna: FLORENCE TRIUMPHANT OVER PISA. Museo Nazionale, Florence.
Fig. 52. Giovanni Bologna: BACCHUS. Borgo San Jacopo, Florence.

Fig. 54. Giovanni Bologna:
WAX MODEL FOR THE RAPE OF THE SABINES.
Victoria & Albert Museum, London.

Fig. 53. Giovanni Bologna:
WAX MODEL FOR THE RAPE OF THE SABINES.
Victoria & Albert Museum, London.

Fig. 55. Giovanni Bologna: THE RAPE OF A SABINE WOMAN. Museo Nazionale di Capodimonte, Naples.
Fig. 56. Hellenistic, second century B.C.: THE FARNESE BULL. Museo Nazionale, Naples.

his first works in Florence, the Nari monument in the Annunziata; and facility in handling the two-figure action group set the seal on the Florentine reputation of Giovanni Bologna. A climax was reached in 1564, when, at the obsequies of Michelangelo, the catafalque was surrounded by four two-figure groups.

In 1554, when the Perseus was set in place, it appeared to Cellini that he was destined to cast or carve a long series of major works. The death of Pierino in this year must have fortified him in that view. But never again did he receive an official commission for a major work of sculpture. One reason no doubt was his egotism and conceit, and another was that in the middle of the fifteen-fifties the climate of Florentine sculpture became more competitive. In 1555, after the death of Pope Julius III, Ammanati moved from Rome to Florence. His reputation had been made in Padua, and in Rome he had collaborated with Vasari on the splendid Del Monte monuments in San Pietro in Montorio. Two years later there arrived Vincenzo Danti, who had established himself by the forceful statue of Pope Julius III outside the Cathedral at Perugia, and in about 1560 he was followed by Vincenzo de' Rossi, who had completed the Cesi Chapel in Santa Maria della Pace. The style of Vincenzo de' Rossi was a projection of Bandinelli's; he was a coarse, ungainly sculptor who, in a series of large-scale statues of the Labours of Hercules executed after 1568 for the Palazzo Vecchio (Fig. 59), attempted vainly to reconcile a zest for violent action with a perverted brand of formal ingenuity. The importance of Ammanati, a more considerable artist, lies in his contribution to the tomb and fountain rather than to the statue. Vincenzo Danti, on the other hand, applied himself to the problems of the statue with the same seriousness as Pierino, and from a standpoint that was not entirely dissimilar, since his main article of faith was belief in Michelangelo.

The postulate that Michelangelo, as sculptor, painter and architect, surpassed all modern and perhaps all ancient artists forms the opening premise of the *Trattato delle perfette proporzioni*, which Danti published in 1567. But his devotion to Michelangelo was diluted by tendencies that were essentially unMichelangelesque. The proof of this is the group of Honour triumphant over Falsehood in the Museo Nazionale (Plate 77). Its status is not altogether clear. Either it is a synthesis of two separate works by Michelangelo, the Victory and the model for the Hercules and Cacus, or (and this explanation is more probable) it depends from a lost drawing or model by the master for a counterpart to the Victory intended for the Julius tomb. In favour of this second view is the fact that structurally the group is an inversion of the Victory. Where Pierino da Vinci, in the Samson and a Philistine, proves himself familiar with Michelangelo's technique, Danti's handling of his material is crisp and dry; his forms are linear and lacking in plasticity. The sense of organic growth which Michelangelo imposed upon the Victory was far beyond his reach, and though his intentions, in the back and exposed arm of Falsehood, were broadly realistic, he did not possess the means of translating them from theory into fact. He apprehended form as outline, and the point of reference for his group is not Michelangelo's own works, but the linear schemata based on

Michelangelo which were incorporated by Bronzino in his frescoes in the Palazzo Vecchio.

In Florence, the future lay not with Vincenzo Danti, nor Ammanati, nor Vincenzo de' Rossi, but with a young Fleming, Giovanni Bologna. He had been born in Mons in 1529, was trained locally in the studio of an Italianising sculptor, Jacques Dubroeucq, and in the fifteen-fifties, like so many Flemish artists, went to Rome. He went there to study, not to practise as a sculptor, and worked assiduously for two years, 'copying all the celebrated figures in clay and wax'. About 1556 he packed his bags, and taking his small models with him left for home. Heading northwards, he arrived in Florence, and there, by some stroke of inspired good fortune, his work came to the notice of Bernardo Vecchietti. Vecchietti, a collector and connoisseur, was so much impressed with the young artist's models that he volunteered to support him while he continued his studies in Florence. In making this offer Vecchietti changed the course of art, for instead of returning to Flanders, Giovanni Bologna remained in Florence for just over half a century, became the greatest sculptor of his time, and coined a language that flowed outwards in space from Tuscany to Vienna and Paris and Madrid, and onwards in time from the sixteenth century to the end of the eighteenth.

There was nothing meteoric about his career. In Florence he established himself slowly, participating unsuccessfully in 1560 in the competition for the Fountain of Neptune in the Piazza della Signoria. Leone Leoni, who was in Florence at the time, implies in a letter that if Giovanni Bologna had had heavier backing he, not Ammanati, might have been victorious. His failure, however, was short-lived, and three years later opportunity knocked once more, bringing him the commission for the Fountain of Neptune at Bologna, in which his plans for the Florentine fountain could be put to use. The successful progress of work on the Bologna fountain was one factor that contributed to his career in Florence. The other was the deaths in 1560 of Bandinelli and in 1564 of Michelangelo. Bandinelli's death removed the main obstructive force in Florentine sculpture. But when this was followed by the death of Michelangelo, joy was succeeded by remorse, for Florence was filled with works by Bandinelli, while in his native city so much by Michelangelo was might-have-been, and so little was fact. This reacted in a positive way on Giovanni Bologna. Years later, in 1581, an agent wrote to the Duke of Urbino, who had wished for some works by Giovanni Bologna, explaining what kind of artist he was. 'He is the best person one can imagine,' runs the letter, 'entirely unmercenary, as his poverty proves, and dedicated only to glory. His dearest ambition is to equal Michelangelo, and in the view of many connoisseurs, he has already done so, and may surpass him if he lives. This is the Grand-Duke's view.' The Grand-Duke in 1581 was Francesco de' Medici, and it was Francesco de' Medici who was responsible, in 1565, for awarding Giovanni Bologna the two commissions which set him on this path. They were for two-figure groups, one of them a pendant to the Victory and the other a recreation of the Samson and a Philistine.

After Michelangelo died, the Victory (Plate 21), which had been presented to Cosimo I, was installed by Vasari in the Palazzo Vecchio, and for the marriage festivities of Francesco de' Medici in 1565 Giovanni Bologna was commissioned to make a companion group of Florence triumphant over Pisa. As a counterpart, it was to represent a female figure, and was to reverse the axis of the Victory. That is the point from which Giovanni Bologna took off, in the only wax sketch-model for the group that has survived (Fig. 49). The model is constructed with a strong vertical accent on the right side (corresponding with the vertical accent on the left side of the Victory), and opposite the crouching figure is broadened out so that the visual unit becomes a half-pyramid. The Victory, like all Michelangelo's sculptures, proclaims the integrity of the marble block, but in Giovanni Bologna's model that is denied. The two figures touch only at one point, and the whole scheme is punctuated by voids, between the left leg of the female figure and the captive, between her left arm and her body, and between the captive's head and thigh. This compositional technique is drawn from Hellenistic sculpture, and probably from one specific work, the Farnese Bull, which had been excavated in the Baths of Caracalla in 1546, not long before Giovanni Bologna arrived in Rome.

The next stage in the Florence triumphant over Pisa is represented by the full-scale gesso model (Fig. 50) which was shown in 1565 in the Palazzo Vecchio. Some of the changes introduced in this are practical – for reasons of stability the two figures coalesce more closely than before – but others are stylistic. The left leg of the captive is now wound round the left leg of the female figure, so that the pose of the captive from the front reads as a triangle, and the hard line down the right side of the woman, which had been imitated from the Victory, is replaced by sinuous curves. There was a delay in translating this model into a permanent medium, and only in 1570 was the marble carved. But in this final version (Fig. 51) further changes were made, and all the apertures from the first model were reintroduced.

When the gesso model was finished Giovanni Bologna began work on the Samson and a Philistine (Plate 82), which was virtually completed in 1567. It was based on the same model that had been available to Pierino da Vinci and to Vincenzo Danti, that for the Hercules and Cacus (Fig. 34), amplified by bronze reductions of the lost models for the Samson and two Philistines (Fig. 128). The stages by which Giovanni Bologna first combined and then adapted Michelangelo's designs must have run parallel to those in the Florence triumphant over Pisa, but in this case no model and no full-scale gesso is preserved. When the group was contrasted, as it must have been, with Danti's Honour triumphant over Falsehood, it would have seemed pre-eminent in three respects. The first was its design; it was planned fully in the round, and was indeed, outside the work of Michelangelo and Donatello, the first multi-facial two-figure action group. The second was its musculature, which had had no equal since the Medici Chapel, and which was combined with a continuity of movement that recalled that of the Victory itself. The third was its expressiveness. The solemn head of Samson is based on the Evening in the Medici Chapel, and the dramatic range of the conception extends to the cowering Philistine. As we look at Samson gazing reflectively downwards at his victim, and the Philistine, his frightened face turned upwards to his executioner, our

minds go back to the Judith and the Abraham and Isaac on the Campanile, where Donatello had imposed on bronze and marble the same overpowering humanity.

Not for ten years did Giovanni Bologna again apply the whole of his technical and intellectual resources to a marble group. In the interval he had matured, his self-confidence
had grown, his propensity towards experiment had sharpened, and the spectre of Michelangelo had receded imperceptibly into the past. The result was the Rape of the Sabines
(Plate 86), which occupied him from 1579 till 1583. In Raffaello Borghini's *Riposo*, published
in 1584, there is a famous account of how the group came to be made. Giovanni Bologna, we
learn, wished to prove that he could carve not only ordinary marble figures, but groups
comprising a number of figures in the most difficult poses that could be devised. So, solely
to show his skill, he carved a proud youth seizing a girl of great beauty from a weak old
man. When the group was almost finished, the Grand-Duke decided to instal it in the Loggia
dei Lanzi, opposite Cellini's Perseus, in the place then occupied by Donatello's Judith. In
1583 no statue could be exhibited without a title, and Giovanni Bologna therefore sought
for an invention that could be attached to it. At first it was suggested that the subject should
be assimilated to the Perseus statue, but this reasoning was rejected, and the title the Rape of
the Sabines was chosen instead.

One writer describes this attitude as a *l'art pour l'art Standpunkt*, but the definition is
not a very happy one. The fact is not that the group has no subject, but that it represents the
highest common factor in a number of alternative scenes. Its meaning was from the first
self-evident; only its context was in doubt. Nowadays, in our modern art-historical writing,
we use the terms 'subject' and 'programme' as though they were interchangeable, but we
must distinguish between them here. Giovanni Bologna's was a reaction against the concept
of programme, and the reason for it was that he took the concept of subject so seriously. Like
the Samson and a Philistine, the new group posed an expressive problem; it involved three
figures participating in different and contrasting fashions in one event. The dual relationship
between the Samson and the Philistine was superseded by a triple relationship between the
zestful youth, the distraught girl, and the cowed old man from whom she has been borne
away. In 1579 there was nothing exceptional about large figure sculptures whose meaning
was clear but whose subjects were uncertain, but they were all of them antique. Giovanni
Bologna's intention was to add one more to the great narrative groups of Hellenistic art. In
the marble this is freely admitted; the head of the female figure seems to have been inspired
by a figure of the class of the Niobe in the Uffizi – the Niobe group was not discovered until
583 and became available in casts in Florence only in 1588 – and the motif of the outstretched
arms is also classical, while the torsion of the body of the girl and the stance of the youth originate
in the Farnese Bull (Fig. 56), and the head of the old man looks back to the Laocoon (Fig. 16).

The sculptor's intention was not to equal but to surpass. In the repertory of classical art
as it was known to him there was no lifting group. There were figures of Hercules and
Antaeus, of the child Dionysus raised on a satyr's shoulder, and of Ganymede caught up by

the eagle, and there were groups which showed a standing figure supporting the inert weight of a second figure slumped in front of him. But even Pliny gave no account of any lifting group. The Rape of the Sabines, therefore, was an extension of the principles of Hellenistic sculpture. Technically, too, it was superior to the multi-figure groups Giovanni Bologna can have known. Pliny repeatedly refers to the technical prowess by which the great classical groups were carved from single blocks. *Ex eodem lapide*, he says of the Farnese Bull; *ex uno lapide*, he says of the Laocoon. But Giovanni Bologna was fully aware that neither group was carved from a single block. On a technical plane, therefore, the Rape of the Sabines represents an antique aspiration that was not realised in antiquity.

Our first reference to the group is in a letter from the sculptor to Ottavio Farnese in 1579, in which he alludes to a two-figure bronze group that can be interpreted as the Rape of Helen, or the Rape of Proserpine, or the Rape of a Sabine Woman, 'a subject chosen to give scope to artistic ability and skill.' This bronze (Fig. 55) is now in Naples, and a very curious work it is. The male figure stands with the right knee flexed and the left turned slightly outwards holding the female figure with both arms. What the bronze illustrates is the extreme difficulty of the subject which the sculptor set himself; it represents a Pas-de-Deux and not a Rape. If a group of the kind were to be carved in marble, the poses had clearly to be consolidated. The first stage in this process is shown in a small wax model (Fig. 54) for the torsos of the two main figures. In this the female figure is transferred from the right side of the male figure to the left. Her weight rests on his left shoulder and left arm, and she is held in place by his right arm, which crosses her body horizontally with the hand on her left hip. This scheme was rejected probably because it was too flat; from the front both figures were seen frontally, and they appeared in profile from the sides. Moreover, it had a second disadvantage, that the heads were in two separate planes, so that the male figure was represented looking backwards across his shoulder at the head of the woman above. In the second and later of the surviving models (Fig. 53) the youth and girl are represented with their bodies at right angles to one another, with the third figure threaded through beneath, and through a number of in themselves trivial devices a spiral movement is introduced into the group, while the interconnection of the heads is made simpler and less strained. As with the Florence triumphant over Pisa, so here the next phase is a full-scale gesso model from which the marble was carved.

Like the Samson and a Philistine, the Rape of the Sabines has a rectangular base. But where the Samson presents a number of merging views, and has a clearly defined back and front, the Rape of the Sabines is serpentine. It has no preponderant view, and is indeed the first multi-figure group in European sculpture that was so planned. In that respect its neo-Hellenism differs from the neo-Hellenism of the young Bernini, who adhered, as Giovanni Bologna in one later work appears to do, to the classical principle of a dominant view. But to one aspect of Hellenistic sculpture Bernini was alive and Giovanni Bologna seems to have been blind, and that was the wealth of its illusionistic technique. The right hand of the youth in the Rape of the Sabines presses into the soft flesh of the thigh with the same physical insistence as does the right hand of Bernini's Pluto into that of Proserpine, but the texture of the two bodies is not differentiated. The cause of this is not that Giovanni Bologna rejected the factor of illusionism in Hellenistic art, but that he entered this Hellenistic phase with a technique that was already formed.

Giovanni Bologna produced one other major marble sculpture, the Hercules and the Centaur in the Loggia dei Lanzi (Plate 91). The subject filled his mind for nearly a quarter of a century. It is first mentioned in 1576 when he made a silver cast. In 1587 he struck a medal which had the subject of Hercules and the Centaur on its reverse, and seven years later, in 1594, he set to work on the marble group, which occupied him for five years. The genesis of the Hercules and the Centaur, therefore, spans the whole of the period in which the vital change in Giovanni Bologna's style recorded in the Rape of the Sabines took place. His point of departure was the Hercules and the Centaur by Vincenzo de' Rossi (Fig. 59), which was finished in 1568. In this the Centaur is shown with one flank on the ground. The only wax model of the subject by Giovanni Bologna that survives also shows the Centaur in this way. Predictably, however, the design is a much tighter one; the action of Hercules is reversed and the body of the Centaur is twisted back. By 1587 this scheme had been revised, and on the medal the Centaur is shown standing with its weight transferred from the hind quarters to the front legs.

From time to time Giovanni Bologna was involved in the restoration of antiques, and in one undated letter he refers to the projected reconstruction of a 'Centauro detto Cilla in Roma'. Ferdinando de' Medici, too, owned a fragmentary Hercules and the Centaur, which was completed by Giovanni Caccini in 1595. One or other of these figures may have inspired the marble group. The Hercules and the Centaur is a less spectacular work than the Rape of the Sabines, but it is the artist's masterpiece. The physical stresses are treated with great freedom, and a splendid intimation of movement is conveyed by the Centaur's wildly curling tail and powerful rear legs. To compare its bursting forms with the tight pyramid of the Samson of thirty years before is to recognise that Giovanni Bologna, the alien in Florence, had single-handed brought about a revolution which would decide the future of Italian art.

THE HIGH RENAISSANCE TOMB

WHILE Michelangelo was planning the tomb of Pope Julius II, there died in Rome an old rival of the Pope, Cardinal Ascanio Sforza. A brother of Lodovico il Moro, Sforza had been taken prisoner by the French and the Venetians in 1500, and was permitted to return to Rome only after Giuliano della Rovere's election to the papacy. In the last months of his life he and the new Pope were reconciled, and when he died in the early summer of 1505 the building of his tomb was undertaken by the Pope. According to the epitaph at the bottom of the monument, the Pope's motive was magnanimity born of respect for Sforza's conduct in adversity. But he had an aesthetic motive as well, for the choir of Santa Maria del Popolo, for which the tomb was destined, was in course of reconstruction by Bramante. Standing behind the high altar against the left wall, Ascanio Sforza's tomb (Fig. 57) was one of the main features of a decorative scheme that included frescoes by Pinturricchio and windows by Guillaume de Marcillat. For the wall opposite the Pope commissioned a companion monument (Fig. 58) to Cardinal Girolamo Basso della Rovere, a son of the sister of Pope Sixtus IV and a cousin of Julius II, who died two years after Sforza, in 1507. Since the tombs are fully integrated in the choir, we might guess that they were due to the same architect, and there is some reason for supposing that they were indeed planned by Bramante. But the name that appears on them is that of the sculptor by whom they were carved, Andrea Sansovino.

The architecture of the monuments is much more complex than that employed in any quattrocento tomb. In the centre is a high triumphal arch, at each side on a forward plane is a niche flanked by decorated columns, and beneath is a deep base with a recessed epitaph. The effigy is represented sleeping, with the head supported on the arm (a motif that is reproduced in countless later cinquecento tombs), in the niches are statuettes of Virtues, and above are figures of Faith and Hope seated between candelabra, while at the top on an elaborate volute is God the Father in benediction flanked by two acolytes. The acolytes are the only features explicitly related to Sansovino's earlier work in Florence; they appear in the Corbinelli altar in Santo Spirito (Fig. 82), on which he must have been engaged before he carved the Baptism of Christ. Elsewhere the tombs offer irrefutable proof of the speed and the success with which Sansovino assumed the modes of thinking current in his new environment. In Rome a tradition of classicising carving had been established by the Lombard Andrea Bregno, and it is Bregno's idiom, not that of the Corbinelli altar, that Sansovino employs in the decorative portions of the tombs. In Rome, too, the niche figures on sepulchral monuments habitually assumed a strongly classicising form; Isaia da Pisa's Temperance on the Chiaves monument in St. John Lateran (Vol. II Fig. 108), is, for example, shown with bared breasts and with her lower limbs swathed in diaphanous drapery. In Andrea Sansovino's Temperance on the Basso monument (Plate 44) the same style is employed, and though the treatment of the pose is subtler and the handling of the drapery is more sophisticated, it is possible that a common model lies behind both statuettes. But the language of Sansovino's Virtues is more consistent and more meaningful than that of earlier Roman sculptures. For the seated Hope of the Sforza monument (Plate 45) there is a parallel in a beautiful preparatory study by Raphael for the Poetry on the ceiling of the Stanza della Segnatura, and the values implicit in the Stanze are implicit also in Sansovino's tombs.

Precisely because they are so unemphatic and so undemonstrative, the Sforza and the Basso tombs are easy works to underrate. But their sovereign merits emerge clearly enough if we compare them with the monuments produced in Rome in the third decade of the century. One of these, the tomb planned by the architect Peruzzi for Pope Adrian VI in

Santa Maria dell'Anima (Fig. 61), also includes statuettes of Virtues and a reclining figure of the Pope on a sarcophagus, but the statuettes are heavy and pedantic, and the effigy is clumsy and inelegant. Another, Jacopo Sansovino's Sant'Angelo monument in San Marcello (Fig. 62), is a more distinguished work, but here the delicate balance between the architecture and the figure sculpture is disrupted, and the Virtues are replaced by St. Peter and St. Paul gazing ferociously across the tomb. Raphael, on the other hand, planning the tomb of Agostino Chigi for Santa Maria del Popolo, designed it as an architectural unit, and made provision only for reliefs.

In Naples there was no Bramante to set the High Renaissance tomb upon its course, and the first important sixteenth-century sepulchral monument owes its appeal solely to its imagery. This is the tomb of the poet Sannazaro in Santa Maria del Parto (Fig. 63), which was carved at Pisa and Carrara in or soon after 1536 by a Florentine, Montorsoli, assisted by a younger artist, Ammanati. The church derived its title from Sannazaro's poem, *De Partu Virginis*, and on the tomb is the inscription:

DA SACRO CINERI FLORES. HIC ILLE MARONI
SINCERUS MUSA PROXIMUS UT TUMULO.

As the reference to Virgil's tomb might lead us to expect, the subject matter is classical. At the sides, under the sarcophagus, are seated figures of Apollo and Minerva, in the centre is a mythological relief with Pan, Marsyas, Euterpe, Neptune and Amphitrite, and at the top is the laureated bust of Sannazaro between two putti balanced on the lid of the sarcophagus. This programme is one to which the Jacopo Sansovino of the Bartolini Bacchus could alone have brought a concomitant of visual poetry; Montorsoli, for all his vigour, was an earth-bound artist, and Ammanati, destined to become one of the most distinguished sculptors of his time, was still hesitant and immature. Both artists worked under the spell of Michelangelo, whose statue of Giuliano de' Medici was adopted by Ammanati as the basis of the Apollo on the tomb. Montorsoli's two genii on the sarcophagus, each with its outer arm thrown expansively across the body, also stem from Michelangelo. The bust was worked up by Montorsoli from a cast of the poet's face and skull.

In 1524, in a celebrated letter written to Marcantonio Michiel in Venice, the humanist Summonte names the artists working in Naples, and among them a young sculptor Giovanni da Nola, from whom Sannazaro had commissioned a wooden Nativity group for Santa Maria del Parto. The influence of this humanist circle on Giovanni da Nola was reflected in the classicising effigy of Antonia Gaudino of 1530 in Santa Chiara and in a lost group of Medea slaying her Children. Talented and sensitive, his object was to charm not to exalt, but from first to last his work, like that of his contemporary and disciple Girolamo Santacroce (Plate 53), is saved from facility by a vein of classicism still evident in the latest of his tombs, the cenotaph of Don Pedro da Toledo in San Giacomo degli Spagnuoli (Fig. 64, Plate 52). By Roman standards the cenotaph is strikingly unorthodox. It consists of a square platform, with the figures of the Viceroy and his wife at the front corners kneeling in prayer. On the

Fig. 58. Andrea Sansovino: THE BASSO MONUMENT.
S. Maria del Popolo, Rome.

Fig. 57. Andrea Sansovino: THE SFORZA MONUMENT.
S. Maria del Popolo, Rome.

Fig. 59. Vincenzo de' Rossi: HERCULES AND THE CENTAUR. Palazzo Vecchio, Florence.
Fig. 60. Giovanni Bandini and Pietro Tacca: MONUMENT OF FERDINAND I. Piazza della Darsena, Leghorn.

Fig. 61. Peruzzi: MONUMENT OF POPE ADRIAN VI. S. Maria dell'Anima, Rome.
Fig. 62. Jacopo Sansovino: MONUMENT OF THE CARDINAL OF SANT' ANGELO. S. Marcello, Rome.

faces of the platform are the epitaph and three scenes from the Viceroy's life, and beneath is a second platform at the corners of which are projecting consoles with four statues of Virtues. Vasari tells us that the tomb was to be despatched to Spain (like an earlier monument by Giovanni da Nola, which is at Bellpuig), and though there is some doubt whether this is correct – it was erected in Naples only in 1570 by Don Garzia da Toledo – there can be no doubt that Spain is its source of inspiration. Through the first quarter of the sixteenth century Spanish sculptors were at work in Naples, and the most important work they left behind them, the altar by Ordoñez in the Caracciolo di Vico chapel in San Giovanni a Carbonara, is a Spanish variation on a conventional Italian form. The tomb of Don Pedro da Toledo is the opposite, a Spanish form filtered through the mind of a cultivated local artist.

In the early stages of work on the Medici Chapel in Florence, Cardinal Giulio de' Medici expressed the wish to be buried there, and after he was elected Pope, a plan was considered for erecting his tomb and that of Pope Leo X either in the Chapel itself or in a room adjacent to the Old Sacristy of San Lorenzo. As late as September 1526 Michelangelo was urged to speed up his work in the Chapel, so as to leave himself free to execute the papal tombs. But in the last years of his life the Pope's principal concern was to ensure the completion of the Chapel, and he was compelled to look elsewhere for an artist for the papal monuments. To judge from a surviving drawing, Andrea Sansovino was a candidate for the commission, and before the Pope's death in 1534 Bandinelli also made models for the monuments. Michelangelo's drawings for the tombs were, however, in existence, and when the Pope died, it was decided by Cardinal Ippolito de' Medici that they should be realised in Santa Maria sopra Minerva in Rome by an Emilian sculptor, Alfonso Lombardi. Basing himself on the drawings, Lombardi prepared a wax model and would have carried out the monument, had the Cardinal not died and the commission been transferred, through the good offices of Donna Lucrezia Salviati, the sister of Pope Leo X, to Bandinelli. According to Vasari, Bandinelli obtained the commission through intrigue. Bandinelli's own account, in his *Memoriale*, is rather different. Pope Clement VII, he tells us, used to say that if the sculptor outlived him, he must prepare his tomb, and knowing this the Pope's executors gave him a free hand in the planning of the monument. At a late stage he received from Michelangelo a note containing his own proposals for the tombs, and these, he adds with the egotism that earned him the dislike of most of his contemporaries, 'were not far removed from mine'. The latitude that the Pope's executors allowed to Bandinelli amounted to considerably less than a free hand, for they mistrusted, as well they might, his capacity as a designer, and solicited from Antonio da Sangallo a plan for the architecture of the tombs. Cast in the conventional form of a triumphal arch, each shows in the centre a seated statue of the Pope and in the lateral niches two standing Saints (Fig. 65). In the attic are three large reliefs, one in the centre with a scene from the Pope's life, and two at the sides with scenes from the lives of the Saints standing in the niches underneath. Vasari complained that this iconography was profane and sycophantic, because the statues of the Popes were displayed more prominently than the statues of the Saints, and because the scenes from the Popes' lives were double the width of the religious scenes at either side. But in justice to Bandinelli it must be recognised, first that a historical scene had been included in the tomb of Adrian VI in Santa Maria dell'Anima, and second that Sangallo's scheme, with its wide central niche and its small niches at the sides, was, from a sculptural standpoint, rather specially intractable. Probably the task of devising a statue which would fill the central niche, and of carving reliefs which would be legible in the top register of the two monuments, would have defeated a better sculptor than Bandinelli, and in the event the only parts of the monuments that merit serious attention are the four lateral Saints, in two of which he again makes use of the diagonal posture with which he had experimented in the Hercules and Cacus a few years before. For contemporaries these desiccated statues evidently had some interest, and one of them was reproduced by Vincenzo de' Rossi on the façade of the Cesi Chapel in Santa Maria della Pace (Fig. 68).

On one other occasion Bandinelli was again involved with a sepulchral monument. The tomb this time was his own, and it was set up in 1559 in a chapel in the Annunziata in Florence, which was ceded to him by the Pazzi at the request of Eleanora of Toledo. Bandin-elli's motives were seldom pure, and the initial impulse behind this work was jealousy, for in 1554 news reached him that Michelangelo in Rome had begun to carve a marble Pietà intended for his monument. Bandinelli's son Clemente, before his death in 1555, started work on a group of the Dead Christ supported by Nicodemus, apparently from a model by his father, in which the head of Nicodemus was an ideal likeness of Bandinelli; and Bandinelli determined to complete it as part of his own tomb. Despite its chequered origins, the group (Plate 65), in the form in which it was erected on the altar of the Bandinelli Chapel, is a moving work. As always with Bandinelli, the scheme is cerebral and self-conscious – the two figures are cast in the form of a right-angled triangle, with the body of Christ supported by the knee of Nicodemus and by a block placed providentially beneath the thigh – but the conception is noble and serious, and the handling is exceptionally consistent and precise.

Bandinelli's group in turn impinged on the commemorative plans of Benvenuto Cellini. In 1539 Cellini had been imprisoned in Rome in the Castel Sant'Angelo, and there, despair-ing of human succour, he invoked the aid of God, praying that he might see the sun. The prayer to which he had recourse is given in the Vita: 'Ah, very son of God, I pray thee by thy birth, by thy death upon the Cross, and by thy glorious Resurrection, that thou wilt deign to let me see the sun, if not otherwise, at least in dreams.' Early one morning Cellini's prayer was granted. Bareheaded and dressed in a white shirt, he found himself walking be-side an angel along a street illuminated by the sun, from which he climbed a stairway to a point where the whole sphere of the sun, 'a bath of purest molten gold,' was visible. As he watched, there emerged from the gold surface a crucified Christ, a Virgin and two angels, and a priest, St. Peter, pleading Cellini's cause with Christ. Subsequently in the prison Cellini was supplied with wax, modelling tools and paper, and with these he made a little wax model of the Crucified Christ as the vision had revealed him. This model was still in his possession years later, in 1555, when he was planning his own tomb in Santa Maria Novella, and in one of his many wills he asked that it should be preserved in a glass tabernacle in the church. The monument was to include two other features, one a marble Crucifix, and the other a marble relief showing the Virgin and Child enthroned, with on the left a little simulacrum of the Crucifix, below it a smiling angel, and on the right St. Peter interceding with Christ. The marble relief was to be surrounded with gold rays. So all of the elements of the tomb derived from Cellini's vision of sixteen years before.

The only part of the tomb to be completed was the Crucifix (Fig. 66, Plate 72). Originally Cellini intended that it should be carved from his model by a professional marble sculptor, and in a will of 1555 he made provision for this, but with the prudent reservation that the sons, pupils and kinsmen of Bandinelli should be ineligible for the task. Ultimately he decided to carve the Crucifix himself, and by 1562 he had completed both the white marble Christ and the black marble cross from which it hangs. At first the tomb was to be in Santa Maria Novella, and the Crucifix was to be placed in the right transept, as a counterpart to Brunelleschi's wooden Crucifix in the transept opposite. Later the plan for the monument was switched to the Annunziata (where, however, it was anticipated by Bandinelli's monument), and then in some mysterious fashion the tomb and Crucifix became detached from one another, and in 1559 the Crucifix was offered as a gift to Eleanora of Toledo. Had it been accepted, it might have been installed in the place for which it was stylistically most suitable, Bronzino's chapel in the Palazzo Vecchio. But unfortunately this proposal came to nothing, and it found a home at last in the Escorial. Though it is a personal testament, the Crucifix has the same meditated quality as the Perseus, and its relationship to the wax model of 1539 must in all essentials have been that of the Perseus to the first of the two models that are preserved. In the head Cellini for the first time successfully transfers to marble the full modelling, the rhythmical eyes and the loose, sensual mouth of the Medusa head in the Loggia dei Lanzi, and if the figure were shown, as he intended, without a loin-cloth, the long containing line would reveal it as what it is, the supreme achievement of Florentine mannerist sculpture.

In 1550 Giovan Maria del Monte was elected Pope as Julius III. Previously he had been legate in Bologna, where he was visited by the painter Vasari, and as he passed through Florence on his journey to the conclave, he and the artist met again. 'I am going to Rome,' said the Cardinal to Vasari, 'and I shall be elected Pope. As soon as you receive the news, come to Rome without awaiting any further summons.' Vasari did as he was bid, and on the day of his arrival hastened to kiss the new Pope's feet. He was not by any means unknown in Rome – under Pope Paul III he had carried out the sprawling frescoes in the Sala Paolina of the Palazzo della Cancelleria – but in the commission he received from Pope Julius III soon after his coronation he was employed in a new role, as architect and not as painter. The commission was for a commemorative chapel in San Pietro in Montorio to house the tombs of the Pope's uncle Cardinal Antonio del Monte and his great-uncle Fabiano del Monte. In the planning of the chapel Vasari's hands were tied, for the Pope's artistic mentor was Michelangelo. At first Vasari proposed employing Simone Mosca, who had been responsible for the elaborate reliefs with classicistic ornament on the façade and in the interior of the Cesi Chapel in Santa Maria della Pace (Fig. 68). His plan was submitted by the Pope to Michelangelo, who observed that decorative carvings, though they might enrich the surface, would confuse the figures. 'Figures,' announced Michelangelo, 'do not like reliefs round them.' The plan for employing Simone Mosca in the chapel, and the ornate classicistic decoration which would have resulted, were therefore dropped. It was also intended by Vasari that the figure sculpture of the tombs should be entrusted to Raffaello da Montelupo, but this too was vetoed by Michelangelo, who preferred the work of a much younger artist, Bartolommeo Ammanati. This decision meant that the conception of the figure sculptures was also fundamentally revised. Finally, Michelangelo must have intervened in the architecture of the chapel, imposing on it the harmonious proportions that it retains to-day (Fig. 69).

Michelangelo also kept a watchful eye upon the figure sculptures. Visiting Ammanati in his studio not long after the sculptures were begun, he reported that 'he works with faith and love, and is a splendid boy, and so good-natured that he may be called Bartolommeo the angel.' The reputation of *l'angelo Bartolommeo* at this time rested mainly on a single work, the Benavides monument at Padua (1564), the only Tuscan tomb in the second quarter of the century outside the Medici chapel in which a serious attempt was made to weld sculpture and architecture into an aesthetic unity. The figure sculpture of the Benavides monument reflects, albeit obliquely, that of Sansovino. With the effigy of Antonio del Monte (Plate 75), however, Ammanati moves once more towards Michelangelo. In everything save the flattened legs and the forward movement of the head it depends from the Evening in the Medici Chapel, and we can well believe that when the model for it was prepared, Michelangelo was himself standing at Ammanati's side. In the same way the four pairs of putti on the balustrade are a recreation in three dimensions of the pairs of painted putti on the ceiling of the Sistine Chapel. The presence of Vasari is most clearly felt in the statues of Justice and Religion above the tombs. In the Sala Paolina the large frescoes are punctuated by allegorical figures in rectangular niches, and these formed the basis of the figures over the Del Monte monuments, though both the Justice, represented with her dress blown out by an imaginary gust of wind, and the Religion, wearing a cloak which hangs free of her body and is deeply undercut, are presented as lapidary statements cleansed of the looseness and the rhetoric that mar their painted counterparts.

A few years later Michelangelo's shadow again fell over the tomb. This was in 1560, when Pope Pius IV determined to erect a monument in Milan Cathedral to his brother, Gian Giacomo de' Medici, Marquess of Marignano (Fig. 70). With Michelangelo's approval, the contract was awarded to his friend and admirer, Leone Leoni, and according to Vasari Michelangelo himself prepared a drawing for the tomb. Architecturally it is a most distinguished work. A triple division of the lower register is effected by four variegated marble columns

Fig. 63. Montorsoli and Ammanati: THE SANNAZARO MONUMENT.
S. Maria del Parto, Naples.

Fig. 64. Giovanni da Nola: MONUMENT OF DON PEDRO DA TOLEDO. S. Giacomo degli Spagnuoli, Naples.

Fig. 65. Bandinelli: MONUMENT OF POPE LEO X.
S. Maria sopra Minerva, Rome.

Fig. 66. Cellini: CRUCIFIX. Escorial.

Fig. 67. Vasari: THE MICHELANGELO MONUMENT.
S. Croce, Florence.

Fig. 68. Vincenzo de' Rossi: ST. PAUL.
S. Maria della Pace, Rome.

Fig. 69. Ammanati: THE DEL MONTE CHAPEL. S. Pietro in Montorio, Rome.

Fig. 70. Leone Leoni: THE MEDICI MONUMENT. Duomo, Milan.

Fig. 71. Montorsoli: HIGH ALTAR. S. Maria dei Servi, Bologna.

Fig. 72. Ammanati: THE BUONCOMPAGNI
MONUMENT. Camposanto, Pisa.

Fig. 73. Giovanni Bologna: THE ALTAR OF LIBERTY.
Duomo, Lucca.

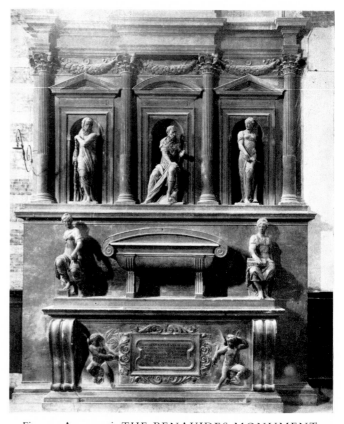

Fig. 74. Ammanati: THE BENAVIDES MONUMENT.
Eremitani, Padua.

which were sent from Rome for Leoni's use, and the intervening spaces are filled with a standing statue of Gian Giacomo de' Medici (Plate 103) and seated figures of Peace and Military Virtue gazing mournfully at the ground. The pyramidal disposition of the statues, the rectangular niche of the main figure, and the poetical concept of Virtues mourning a military leader, take us back to the world of the Medici Chapel. But Leoni was a modeller and a specialist in bronze casting, and the contrast in his monument between bronze statues, the white marble ground on which they are set, and the coloured marble columns, would have been condemned by Michelangelo as indefensibly pictorial.

None the less a truer understanding of Michelangelo's creative intentions is evinced by Leoni's monument in Milan than by the tomb which Vasari installed in Santa Croce in Florence after the sculptor's death in 1564 (Fig. 67). In 1563 the Grand-Duke Cosimo I had accepted a proposal, of which Vasari was the sponsor, for the creation of a Florentine Academy, and after Michelangelo died the Academy, as one of its first tasks, assumed responsibility for a commemorative service in San Lorenzo. The Academy was a restrictive body – its dogma sprang from prejudice, and its unifying bond was a determination to evade the challenge of a living art – and its official veneration of Michelangelo concealed a latent antagonism to the aesthetic values he exemplified. As we read the list of artists who prepared the decorations of the catafalque for this funeral festivity, it seems that no secondary sculptor was left unemployed. Once the ceremony was disposed of, there arose the problem of a permanent memorial. In Michelangelo's studio in Florence there were a number of rejected statues for the Julius tomb, among them the Victory and the four unfinished Slaves. The first suggestion, originating with Michelangelo's nephew Lionardo and his pupil Daniele da Volterra, was that these sculptures should be built into a monument. From the first Vasari was hostile to this plan – he was personally concerned with a project for installing the Victory in the Palazzo Vecchio – and Cosimo I, while ostensibly accepting it, made a counter-suggestion, that the damaged Deposition should instead be used for the purpose for which it was originally carved. The objection to this was that the Deposition was owned by Pierantonio Bandini, and that Bandini refused to part with it. None the less, Lionardo Buonarroti, in response to what was tantamount to a command, forewent the Victory and the Slaves, which were offered as a gift to Cosimo I, and there is no further mention of the use on the tomb of works by Michelangelo. At this point a new voice is heard, that of Vincenzo Borghini, the Prior of the Innocenti, one of the arbiters of taste in Florence, whose mistaken ingenuity doomed so many projects to sterility. Let Vasari design the tomb, was the gist of Borghini's advice, but in order to distribute the work fairly, let the sculptures be entrusted to young artists. Three names were mentioned, Battista Lorenzi, a pupil of Bandinelli, Giovanni Bandini, another Bandinelli pupil, and Battista, a pupil of Ammanati. This plan was adhered to, save that Ammanati refused to release his pupil and the third statue was accordingly commissioned from Valerio Cioli. Vasari's sarcophagus is an undistinguished travesty of the tomb-chests in the Medici Chapel, and in looking at the statues of Painting, Sculpture and Architecture (Plate 67) seated underneath it, we must remember that abler and more experienced sculptors were, by the terms of the commission, automatically ruled out. None the less there is something ironical in the fact that Michelangelo, in his native town, should be commemorated in this mean and unimaginative manner by the spiritual heirs of Bandinelli.

The monument was finished in a healthier climate than that in which it was begun, for in 1578, in the very year in which Naldini painted the fresco of the Pietà that marked the completion of the tomb, Giovanni Bologna was at work on the first of his great religious commissions, the Altar of Liberty in Lucca Cathedral (Fig. 73), and three years later he started work on the shrine of Sant'Antonino in San Marco. In the lower register of the Altar of Liberty is a statue of the Risen Christ with figures of Saints Peter and Paulinus at the sides. This iconography is a product of the Counter-Reformation. In 1565 a Tuscan sculptor active in Venice, Danese Cattaneo, had completed for Sant'Anastasia at Verona an altar of the kind (Fig. 106), and two such works were known to Giovanni Bologna; one of them was in the Camposanto at Pisa, where in 1572 Ammanati was engaged upon the Buoncompagni monument (Fig. 72), which has a central niche housing a Risen Christ, and the other was the high altar of the Servi at Bologna (Fig. 71), which had been commissioned from Montorsoli in 1558. Montorsoli's Christ is a wretchedly stolid, inexpressive work, but it formed the point from which Giovanni Bologna took off. He was cogitating the Rape of the Sabines at the time, and his Christ (Plate 84) is shown in movement with head upturned and right arm raised. The pose has the same upward thrust as that of the youth in the large group, and the expression of momentary rapture in the features is handled in precisely the same way, while in the stance there is a marvellous illusion of lightness and incorporeality. This same lively imagination was brought to play on the Chapel of Sant'Antonino (Fig. 75). Round the walls are six niches with marble figures, all of them carved by Francavilla, two on the facing wall from models by Giovanni Bologna, above them are six bronze reliefs with scenes from the Saint's life, and over the altar are two bronze putti and an angel pointing with one arm towards heaven and extending the other towards the tomb (Plate 89). In 1580 Giovanni Bologna had cast the Medici Mercury which is now in the Bargello, and in the angel the principles that lie behind it are transferred to a religious theme. The Chapel as an active unit hinged on a sarcophagus beneath the altar, and this sarcophagus (which is now in the sacristy of the church) is the most inspired and most carefully planned feature of the shrine. It is in black marble and has a precedent in Flanders in a work Giovanni Bologna must have known, the De Croy monument of Jacques Dubroeucq at Saint-Omer. On top of it is a bronze effigy (Plate 92). Tranquil and compact, this flattened figure has no precedent in Florence in the sixteenth century, and when he designed it Giovanni Bologna may have had in mind an earlier Dominican bronze effigy, the Dati tomb-slab of Ghiberti.

The Chapel of Sant'Antonino is not a satisfactory whole, first because Giovanni Bologna was an indifferent architect, and second because provision was made for frescoes, and Florentine painting was at its lowest ebb. For this reason it is less effective than the Niccolini

Chapel in Santa Croce (Fig. 76), which was designed by Giovanni Antonio Dosio, and where there are no frescoes on the walls. The appeal of the Niccolini Chapel is exercised in part through its polychromy. In the centre of the lateral walls are tomb-chests with tabernacles over them, each containing a seated figure, on one side Aaron and on the other Moses (Plate 94). Two of the three Virtues beside them are signed by Francavilla, Giovanni Bologna's assistant on the Rape of the Sabines and the Altar of Liberty, and there is a presumption that Francavilla also carved the seated figures. The relation of the Moses to the Moses of Michelangelo is essentially the same as that of Giovanni Bologna's Samson and a Philistine to Michelangelo's projects for this group. The position of the knees has been reversed, and the head, turned over the right shoulder, is balanced by a book resting on the left thigh. While Francavilla's Moses lacks the solidity of Michelangelo's, it has a gravity and weight of meaning of which Michelangelo could not but have approved.

Before his death the Grand-Duke Cosimo I, obsessed with the consolidation of his dynasty, conceived a plan for building in San Lorenzo a third sacristy to house his own monument, and those of his wife, parents and descendants. A model for this was prepared by Vasari. Cosimo's successor, Francesco I, began to collect semi-precious stones – chalcedony, sardonyx, agate and jasper – for the adornment of the Chapel, but when he died in 1587 the sacristy had still not been begun. With the accession of Ferdinand I, however, a start was made, and plans were drawn up by Buontalenti, Giorgio Vasari il Giovane and the Grand-Duke's brother, Don Giovanni de' Medici. Buontalenti's scheme must have been much superior to the other two, but Don Giovanni de' Medici's was preferred. This was not due solely to sentiment – though the idea of a Medici mausoleum planned by a Medici was an inherently appealing one – but to the fact that Buontalenti's scheme divided the area of the sacristy into separate chapels, whereas in Don Giovanni de' Medici's all the tombs could be seen simultaneously (Fig. 77). The ground plan was based on that of the Baptistry in Florence, but the preconceptions in the light of which it was revised were those which had been sketched out by Vignola in the church of the Gesù in Rome twenty years before.

As grand-ducal sculptor, Giovanni Bologna was naturally involved in the project for the tombs. Initially the effigies were thought of as marble statues ten feet high, with, in the case of the tomb of Ferdinand I, two huge allegorical supporting figures. But the commissioning of tombs would have been premature if the building to house them had not been started, and only in 1604 was the erection of the chapel, 'superior in price to the golden house of Nero and to the palace of King Cyrus', actually begun. In 1613 the semi-precious stones, which had been carefully amassed over more than thirty years, were set into the walls, and in 1626 Giovanni Bologna's successor as grand-ducal sculptor, Pietro Tacca, was commissioned to prepare two gesso models of the Grand-Dukes Ferdinand I and Cosimo II. In the quarter of a century that had elapsed since Giovanni Bologna was involved in the scheme, the figures had grown – they were now roughly fifteen feet high – but it was still intended that they should be carved not cast. According to Baldinucci, the change of medium from marble to bronze was

effected at Tacca's insistence, but it may also have been influenced by the news which filtered
through to Florence of the most splendid commemorative project of the kind, the great
bronze statues of the Emperor Charles V and Philip II of Spain with their families by Pompeo
Leoni in the Escorial (Plate 107). A pupil of Giovanni Bologna, Tacca reacted against his
master's style, preferring bronze to marble because of the greater liberty that it allowed
him. His stylistic sympathies can be judged from one of his earliest independent works, the
monument of the Grand-Duke Ferdinand I at Leghorn (Fig. 60), of which the statue was
carved in 1599 by Giovanni Bandini and the bronze Slaves (Plate 96) round the base were
added by Tacca in the sixteen-twenties. Bandini's statue is a typical product of its time, tight and
self-contained, but the Slaves (which to this day remain Tacca's most popular works) are set
freely round the plinth, so that they pull away from the corners of the monument. Tacca was
an emotional artist, and the bulging bodies of the Slaves are modelled with strong dramatic
sense. The strain of journalism in his temperament caused him difficulty in the Cappella dei
Principi, where he was criticised not, as we might assume, for the caricature head of the Grand-
Duke Cosimo II – one of the most unflattering portraits that has ever been inserted in a commemorative sculpture – but for the statue of Ferdinand I. Buontalenti's intention was to place
the statues on brackets, so that to one observer they looked as though they were walking in a
garden, and Tacca, moving in the same direction, originally proposed to show the Grand-
Duke Ferdinand I in contemporary costume with one thigh exposed, like a St. Roch. But this
defect was quickly remedied, and instead the Grand-Duke was presented in a likeness (Plate
97) that appeared, by seventeenth-century standards of decorum, to be more dignified.
Nowadays the Cappella dei Principi is regarded merely as a means of access to the Medici
Chapel, but if we make the imaginative effort of isolating Tacca's tombs from their lugu-
brious setting, and of seeing them as they were when they were new, with light refracted from
their gilded surfaces and with the crowns in the centre of the gilded cushions on the tomb-
chests studded with precious stones, we shall find no difficulty in accepting them as the first
great Florentine baroque monuments.

THE HIGH RENAISSANCE RELIEF

THE story of the High Renaissance relief is governed by the fact that no mature relief was
carved by Michelangelo. Both the Julius monument and the façade of San Lorenzo were
to include narrative scenes, but none of them was sketched out, and the only thoughts
that he committed to relief were contained in the Battle of the Centaurs and the Madonna
of the Steps, preserved in his studio and therefore inaccessible, and the Pitti and Taddei
tondi, which, as their names denote, remained in private hands. Had either of these last two
works been finished, it would have inspired many secondary reliefs, but because they were
unfinished, they were almost without influence. The word 'almost' is made necessary by a
single work, a circular marble relief carved by Rustici, now in the Bargello (Fig. 8). It is not

Fig. 75. Giovanni Bologna: THE SALVIATI CHAPEL. S. Marco, Florence.

Fig. 76. Dosio: THE NICCOLINI CHAPEL. S. Croce, Florence.

Fig. 77. THE CAPPELLA DEI PRINCIPI. S. Lorenzo, Florence.

a relief of great distinction – Rustici was a modeller rather than a carver, and his grasp of form in marble sculpture was insecure – but it shows that he was fascinated (as we might expect other sculptors to have been) by the organisation of the Taddei tondo and by Michelangelo's approach to the circular relief. Rustici's Virgin, like Michelangelo's, is seated with her forward leg outstretched across a segment at the base of the relief. The beautiful movement of the Taddei Child he does not attempt to emulate, but at the left a genuflecting figure of the Baptist on a rear plane proves that the spatial lesson of Michelangelo's design has been partly understood.

Where we might suppose that the two tondi would be reflected is in the circular Madonnas built into wall monuments. On Andrea Sansovino, however, they had not the smallest influence, and since he left Florence in 1505 it is even doubtful whether he had studied them. The lunette of his Sforza monument in Santa Maria del Popolo includes a Virgin in three-quarter length in profile to the left holding the Child in benediction in her arms (Fig. 57). The figure is carved in exceptionally deep relief, and is conceived illusionistically, with the head protruding from the frame and the moulding at the base hidden by cloud, but its style is fundamentally traditional. In his Basso monument in the same church (Fig. 58) the composition is more ambitious; the Virgin is relatively flatly carved, while the Child, in great depth, strides forward through the sky. Possibly this is the earliest surviving work by Jacopo Sansovino. Certainly the Madonna of the Basso monument marks an intervening stage between Andrea's tondo on the Sforza tomb and the lunette carved by Jacopo fifteen years later for the Sant' Angelo monument in San Marcello (Fig. 62), where the containing circle is dispensed with, and the Virgin is depicted frontally in a mandorla of cloud. In the years between Raphael had painted all of his mature Madonnas, and this is reflected in San Marcello in a scheme based on the same principles as the Madonna di Foligno.

From the beginning relief played a greater part in the work of Andrea Sansovino than in that of any other sculptor of his time. One of his earliest works in Florence, the Corbinelli altar in Santo Spirito (Fig. 82), was planned primarily in relief; it included a lunette relief of the Coronation of the Virgin, two tondi of the Annunciation, a relief predella and an antependium relief with the Lamentation over the dead Christ. It was not exceptional in this, for reliefs also occur in the altarpieces which Andrea Ferrucci was carving in Florence at a rather earlier date. What distinguishes it is the thought that was devoted to each of its constituent scenes. Where, for example, the Annunciatory Angel and Virgin Annunciate in Ferrucci's altar at Fiesole are depicted as simple relief figures silhouetted against a dark ground, in the Corbinelli altar the reliefs are planned spatially. The two figures are depicted in front of a perspective of receding columns, and the angle of vision is so adventurous, and the space illusion so complete, that the reliefs make the effect of two holes punched in the altarpiece.

In Rome Sansovino became involved in the greatest relief commission of the High Renaissance, the casing of the Holy House in the basilica at Loreto (Fig. 78). Designed by Bramante, probably in 1510, the casing is an oblong structure with two long sides and two narrow ends.

Each end is flanked by superposed niches between heavy columns, and is filled with wide narrative reliefs, while each of the long sides is punctuated by three superposed niches, with doorways in the intervening wall surfaces, above each of which is a relief. The sculpture of the Holy House comprises in all twenty figures in niches and nine exceptionally large reliefs. The form of the niches resembles those on the Sforza and Basso tombs, and Bramante must have intended that they should be filled with classicising statuettes like the Virtues on Andrea Sansovino's monuments. None of them was executed, and the seated and standing figures in the niches were carved in the fifteen-forties in an altogether different style. Projecting from their niches, they disturb the harmony of the whole scheme. The reliefs, on the other hand, seem to have been begun before Bramante's death (1514), and are conceived in a single style. Bramante's original intention was that the sculptures should be entrusted to Gian Cristoforo Romano, who had experience of a comparable commission in the Visconti monument in the Certosa at Pavia. This was agreed to in 1511, after Julius II had paid a visit to Loreto to inspect the progress of work on the shrine and the new church. But a year later Gian Cristoforo Romano died, and in 1513 he was succeeded by Andrea Sansovino. Among artists the Loreto project was specially unpopular – 'quanto tiene il tempio, bestialissimo quanto si può dire,' declared Gian Cristoforo Romano. Bandinelli, who was responsible for one of the reliefs, rapidly abandoned Loreto for the comfort of Ancona, and Sansovino, in an effort to escape from his purgatory in the Marches, opened negotiations with Michelangelo, offering to work in a subordinate capacity in Florence. His overtures were unsuccessful, and Loreto remained the main scene of his activity until the Sack of Rome brought work there to a temporary halt.

Two of the large reliefs were carved by Sansovino between 1518 and 1524. The less enterprising of them represents the Adoration of the Shepherds (Fig. 81, Plate 46). The scene takes place in front of a Bramante-like structure set at an angle to the relief plane. Beneath a thatched roof thrown out from the central archway is the kneeling Virgin who displays the Child to St. Joseph and the shepherds. All five figures are confined to the front of the relief, and the interest of the scene centres upon two illusionistic expedients. The first, on the right, is a block of masonry covered by a vine, which conceals the moulded border of the scene and thus introduces an element of spatial ambiguity. The second is a row of flying angels which cuts the border along the top of the relief. These figures seem to have been inspired by Raphael's angels in Santa Maria della Pace. The subject of the more enterprising scene is the Annunciation (Fig. 80, Plate 47). Divided into two unequal parts, it recedes backwards from right to left across the whole width of the relief. In the foreground on the right is the Virgin's house, demarcated by two receding walls, between which is the Virgin seated beside her bed. The left side of the scene takes place before a long arcade. In the foreground the annunciatory angel advances towards the Virgin, behind him are two further angels, one in the act of alighting from the sky, and above is God the Father despatching the dove towards the Virgin down a long line of cloud. The head of the Virgin is the only classical feature in this extraordinary work. Owing to the exceptional size of the Loreto reliefs, each of them was made of two slabs of marble. We know from documents that Andrea Sansovino's two reliefs were both carved simultaneously, one slab or quadro from each scene between 1518 and 1520 and the second slab or quadro between 1520 and 1524. The right sides of the reliefs are more advanced in style than the corresponding sections on the left, and the spatial expedients employed in them have a close contemporary parallel in the paintings of Giulio Romano.

By the summer of 1527 Sansovino had partially completed the left-hand section of a third relief, the Marriage of the Virgin, where he carved the beautiful figures of the High Priest, the Virgin and St. Joseph and three attendants to the left. Work on this carving was interrupted by the Sack of Rome, and in 1533 the left side was finished and the whole of the right side carved by Tribolo. In the figures which he added to the left side Tribolo imitated Sansovino's style with great fidelity, but on the right five of the six figures are shown in poses inspired by Michelangelo. Sansovino may also have been responsible for the design of the Birth of the Virgin, begun by Baccio Bandinelli in 1524–5 and completed in 1533 by Raffaello da Montelupo. The scenes that were designed and executed after Sansovino's death are less coherent, and neither Raffaello da Montelupo's puerile Adoration of the Magi, nor the Translation of the Holy House, carved partly by Tribolo and partly by Francesco da Sangallo, approaches the quality of the earlier reliefs.

The problem of the classical relief was also threshed out in Rome, where Raphael designed two bronze roundels for the Chigi Chapel in Santa Maria della Pace, and is traditionally supposed to have made drawings for the relief of Christ and the Woman taken in Adultery now on the altar of the Chigi Chapel in Santa Maria del Popolo (Fig. 79, Plate 41). Unluckily his chosen instrument was not Jacopo Sansovino (who could so well have translated his conceptions into plastic terms), but Lorenzetto. Though the Santa Maria del Popolo relief is strongly Raphaelesque – its scheme recalls that of the tapestry cartoon of Christ's Charge to the Apostles – the whole scene is weak and without emphasis.

In Naples the High Renaissance relief was developed by the Spaniard Ordoñez along very different lines. By training and inclination Ordoñez was a relief artist, and the altar of the Caracciolo di Vico chapel in San Giovanni a Carbonara is, save for two statuettes of Saints, carried out wholly in relief; in front is an antependium relief of the Dead Christ, above it is a predella with St. George and the Dragon flanked by two Prophets, and above this again is a large relief of the Adoration of the Magi, which forms the body of the altarpiece. Not only do reliefs preponderate, but the reliefs are of a rather special kind, in which the surface is fluid and the forms are imperfectly defined. Giovanni da Nola was nothing if not an Italian artist, but in the latest and largest of his reliefs, the great Deposition altar in Santa Maria delle Grazie a Caponapoli (Plate 54), though the composition is Raphaelesque, the relief style into which it is translated is that of the Spanish sculptors among whom he had been reared.

The concern with action which is so incongruous a feature of Tribolo's Marriage of the Virgin at Loreto found a more appropriate outlet in the large relief of the Assumption of the

Virgin which he completed for the Madonna di Galliera at Bologna in 1537 (Fig. 83, Plate 60). The Assumption belongs to a class of composition that was initiated by Raphael in the Transfiguration, and not even the putti in the upper part, which were added in stucco in the eighteenth century, can impair the effect of the small figure of the Virgin isolated in the sky, and the ring of apostles far beneath her gesticulating as they peer into the tomb.

The implications of the Sistine ceiling were no less great for sculpture than for painting, and it was natural that sculptors in the middle of the sixteenth century should assume the task from which Michelangelo abstained, of transcribing this painted style into relief. This was the aim of Pierino da Vinci when, on his return from Rome in 1549, he carved a marble relief of Cosimo I as patron of Pisa, now in the Vatican (Plate 61). Pierino, alone of his contemporaries, worked in limited relief. Like Desiderio before him, he attached supreme importance to continuity of surface, but though his technique must have been based upon the study of quattrocento carvings, the use to which it was applied was an entirely different one. He was concerned neither with space nor atmosphere. His sole interest was the human form, and the human form under one aspect, as silhouette. In his relief there is no space illusion other than that created by a distant ship and by two little demons in the upper corners, and the relative position of the figures is indicated solely by their scale. Vasari tells us that in Rome Pierino made a wax reduction of the Moses of Michelangelo, and in this relief it was the ceiling of the Sistine Chapel that supplied him not with motifs, but with a vision of the beauty and coherence of the human figure that he re-translated into sculpture.

The characteristics of this relief are urbanity and elegance, two qualities that are conspicuously lacking in the reliefs of Bandinelli. Like Pierino, Bandinelli was cognisant of fifteenth-century reliefs, and especially of Donatello, but in the narrative reliefs on his two papal tombs and on the plinth of the statue of Giovanni dalle Bande Nere which he carved immediately afterwards, he relapsed into a type of coarse classicising carving which has few elements of interest. As a relief sculptor Bandinelli is none the less a far from negligible artist. In 1547 when planning the new high altar of the Cathedral in Florence, he surrounded it on eight sides with a balustrade composed of panels with figures in relief (Fig. 87). The conception is academic – each of the panels is surrounded by a moulded frame and shows a single figure posturing on a flat ground – but the figures (Plate 66) speak the language of conviction, and the attitude to Michelangelo reflected in the male nudes in particular is not wholly unlike that revealed by the nudes in Pierino's relief. The two artists are divided not by their approach to style but by their attitude to sculpture, for the tight forms and carefully worked surface of Pierino were alien to Bandinelli, even in these, his most completely realised works.

It was suggested that Cellini should execute a cycle of bronze reliefs for Bandinelli's choir screen, and one relief, an Adam and Eve, was modelled in wax; but the commission came to nothing, partly because Cellini was unwilling to work under Bandinelli, and partly because Bandinelli, as he confesses in a letter, thought that the strength of Cellini's reliefs lay in their chasing, not in their design. Most of what we know of Cellini as a sculptor in relief derives

Fig. 78. THE HOLY HOUSE. Basilica della Santa Casa, Loreto.

Fig. 79. Lorenzetto: CHRIST AND THE WOMAN TAKEN IN ADULTERY. S. Maria del Popolo, Rome.

Fig. 80. Andrea Sansovino: THE ANNUNCIATION. Basilica della Santa Casa, Loreto.

Fig. 81. Andrea Sansovino: THE ADORATION OF THE SHEPHERDS. Basilica della Santa Casa, Loreto.

from a single work, the bronze relief on the base of the Perseus. Cellini's experience of relief when he began work on it was in the main limited to seals. The most elaborate of these, the seal of Ippolito d'Este, was made in 1540 in Rome. Because the Cardinal had a double title, its face is divided down the middle by a pier, with St. Ambrose chastising the Arians on one side and the Preaching of the Baptist on the other. Faced with the rectangular field of the Perseus and Andromeda (Fig. 84), Cellini treated it in the same way; at the top is the arrival of Perseus at the palace of Cepheus, in the centre is Perseus chiding Andromeda's parents, and at the left is Perseus slaying the Sea Monster. This system of multiple narration is a surprising phenomenon in the middle of the sixteenth century, and the reason for it may have been Cellini's professed admiration for the Porta del Paradiso. Like Ghiberti, he was a goldsmith, and his profession leaves its stamp on the beautiful figures of the flying Perseus in the upper left corner and of Andromeda in the centre of the relief.

The three surviving bronze reliefs by Vincenzo Danti, a Deposition in the National Gallery of Art in Washington, a safe door made for Cosimo I, now in the Bargello, and a large relief of Moses and the Brazen Serpent in the same museum (Fig. 85), are bolder and more sculptural. Danti set little store by finish; his three reliefs are chased, but not so extensively as to impair the freshness of the wax models from which they were cast. The modelling throughout is confident and diversified; the foreground figures are almost in the round while the rear figures are little more than scratches in the surface of the bronze. Like Pierino's, Danti's conception of the human figure was derived from Michelangelo, though in the Brazen Serpent his exemplar is not the early frescoes on the Sistine ceiling but the late pendentive of the same scene. In an environment in which results were habitually obtained through reason, there is something deeply disquieting in Danti's use of relief style as a revelation of his own interior vision, buttressed by the emotions but unsupported by rational thought processes.

With Giovanni Bologna reason is reintroduced. Once the subject of the Rape in the Loggia dei Lanzi had been decided on, it became necessary to define it, and with this in mind the sculptor made for its base a bronze relief (corresponding with the relief beneath Cellini's Perseus), which could only depict the Rape of the Sabines and would thus remove all ambiguity. In style the relief (Plate 86) conforms to the great group above. Giovanni Bologna was a clear-headed artist, and to him Danti's solution of an active composition peopled with figures through its whole width and depth must have appeared unworkable. He avoided it by two original expedients, increasing the depth of the relief and breaking up the figures into lucid, self-consistent units, each with a drama of its own. The foreground figures are consequently modelled almost in the round – it is as though rejected models for the statue were soldered on to the relief – and each of the four main groups into which the figures are divided is planned with astonishing resilience and resource.

Giovanni Bologna was not a prolific relief artist, but in two of his religious commissions relief plays an important part. The first of these, the Grimaldi Chapel in San Francesco di

Castelletto at Genoa, included six reliefs of Passion scenes. The Grimaldi Chapel has been destroyed, but we know that its programme, six bronze statues of Virtues and six Passion scenes, was basically Flemish – precedents for it occur in the alabaster carvings of Flemish rood-screens – and nowhere is the Flemish origin of the whole scheme more clearly apparent than in the iconography of the reliefs. Giovanni Bologna's attitude to religious imagery had been formed in the studio of Dubroeucq at Mons long before he was familiar with Italian sculptures, and it has parallels in the work of his contemporaries in Flanders. If, for example, we juxtapose the Ecce Homo at Genoa (Plate 87) with the same scene on Cornelis Floris' rood-screen at Tournai, the similarity of narrative method is self-evident. This is a case of two artists trained in the same tradition and working from the same postulates, and it has implications both for the imagery of the scene and for its style. The Christ stands a little to the right of centre, supported by a soldier and a priest. To his left and right are two caesuras, and at the edges of the scene are two groups of gesticulating figures massed together with their raised hands outlined against the flat wall surfaces.

We might guess that Giovanni Bologna was personally involved with the emotional content of these scenes. The evidence that that was so is supplied by three sketch-models in wax, which were made when the compositions of the scenes had been determined and were in large part immutable. None the less there are changes between the models and the finished works, and these are matters of interpretation rather than of form. In the wax model of the Christ before Pilate, Christ, his body bent and his head bowed, is hustled like a malefactor from the presence chamber, while Pilate gazes after him with an expression of remorse or compassion on his face. In the bronze both figures are modified; Christ's head and body are erect, and Pilate now leans forward intent upon the act of hand-washing. These are small changes, but they are tantamount to a psychological re-thinking of the scene, and the imaginative processes that lie behind them are responsible for the communicative power of the reliefs.

The sculptures for the Grimaldi Chapel were finished by 1585, and before they were complete Giovanni Bologna was caught up in a second undertaking of the same kind. This was for the decoration of the Salviati Chapel in San Marco which included six bronze reliefs of scenes from the life of S. Antonino. The Salviati reliefs (Fig. 88) are three times as large as the reliefs at Genoa, and are higher than they are wide. The relief system used at Genoa had therefore to be abandoned, since the action could no longer be restricted to a frontal plane. Instead of being spread across an oblong field the figures penetrate a narrow one, and Giovanni Bologna accordingly returns to the old Florentine tradition of figures in projected space. The physical recession of the figures is correspondingly reduced. This tendency towards a flattened relief style reaches its climax in a convex relief of Cosimo I summoned by the Signoria to the Government of Florence (Fig. 89) on the base of Giovanni Bologna's equestrian monument of Cosimo I in the Piazza della Signoria, where the figures and the setting are reconciled with marvellous subtlety.

Fig. 83. Tribolo: THE ASSUMPTION OF THE VIRGIN. S. Petronio, Bologna.

Fig. 82. Andrea Sansovino: THE CORBINELLI ALTAR. S. Spirito, Florence.

Fig. 84. Cellini: PERSEUS FREEING ANDROMEDA. Museo Nazionale, Florence.

Fig. 85. Danti: MOSES AND THE BRAZEN SERPENT. Museo Nazionale, Florence.

Fig. 86. Bandinelli: UDIENZA. Palazzo Vecchio, Florence.

Fig. 87. Bandinelli: CHOIR. Duomo, Florence.

Fig. 89. Giovanni Bologna: COSIMO I RECEIVING HOMAGE.
Piazza della Signoria, Florence.

Fig. 88. Giovanni Bologna: MIRACLE OF ST. ANTONINUS.
S. Marco, Florence.

In 1595 the bronze doors at the west end of the Cathedral at Pisa were destroyed by fire. Three new pairs of doors were at once designed by the grand-ducal architect, Raffaello Pagni, and these provided for a total of twenty narrative reliefs. Through 1595 and the early months of 1596 attempts were made to induce Giovanni Bologna first to supervise the making of the doors, and then to undertake six of the reliefs. He was engaged, however, with the Hercules and the Centaur virtually to the exclusion of all other work, and was unwilling, he declared, to turn his hand to other artists' projects. The reliefs were therefore commissioned from individual members of his studio, Francavilla and Tacca among them, from Giovanni Caccini and from other artists. All three doors (Figs. 90, 91) were finished by 1604. In the fifteenth century work on the Porta del Paradiso had consumed twenty-seven years, and to complete three large doors in the space of nine years was a remarkable feat. But it was purchased at the cost of distinction in the overall design and of uniformity in the narrative reliefs. The Porta del Paradiso is fundamental for the Pisa doors, though the central door is not constructed like Ghiberti's with seven square panels in each wing, but with four scenes in each wing divided into pairs by wide strips of decoration with Saints and Prophets which are repeated at the top and bottom of the door. The reliefs are framed in foliated strips inspired by the jambs of the bronze doors of the Baptistry. This foliated decoration recurs in the two lateral doors, each wing of which contains one oblong and two upright scenes. The sense of organic structure throughout the doors is comparatively weak, and the border is so constructed that it repeatedly breaks in on the containing rectangles of the reliefs.

The obsession of the Deputati of the Cathedral with speed is reflected in a low degree of finish in the individual scenes. None the less the doors have some importance as an anthology of Tuscan relief style in the last years of the sixteenth century. In the Visitation on the central door Francavilla makes use of an open receding composition filled with loosely articulated figures for which there is no precedent in Giovanni Bologna's work, while in the Baptism of Christ on the left door and the Arrest of Christ and Christ carrying the Cross on the right, he falls back on loose, picturesque designs which reveal a fundamental lack of sympathy with Giovanni Bologna's constructive processes. By far the most distinguished of the reliefs are the five on the central door by Giovanni Caccini (Plate 93), whose relief style depends not from Giovanni Bologna, but from the marble reliefs carved by Giovanni Bandini about 1575 for the Gaddi Chapel in Santa Maria Novella, and thus, at one remove, from Bandinelli. The anarchical reliefs at Pisa signify the breakdown of an old order, not the creation of a new, and their main interest is as proof that in the field of the relief the style of Giovanni Bologna was not assimilated by local artists.

THE FLORENTINE FOUNTAIN

FOUNTAINS figure from time to time in the history of Gothic and Early Renaissance sculpture – the Fontana Maggiore of Nicola Pisano at Perugia and the Fonte Gaia of Jacopo della

Quercia at Siena are two of the most notable – but only in the sixteenth century did the fountain come to be accepted as an art form in its own right. In the early Renaissance all the great Florentine fountains were commissioned by the Medici. On the most famous of them, in the courtyard or garden of the Palazzo Medici, stood Donatello's Judith pouring water from the corners of a cushion into the basin beneath; in the second courtyard of the palace there was a fountain by Antonio Rossellino, showing putti and dolphins, in which the water spurted from the dolphins' mouths; and in the garden of Lorenzo de' Medici's villa at Careggi was another celebrated fountain for which Verrocchio cast his Putto with a Fish. The expulsion of the Medici in 1494 brought fountain building to a temporary halt, but after their return in 1512 work began again. The Medici Palace had, in the interval, been deprived of Donatello's Judith. The next fountain figure we hear of represented 'a naked Mercury about a braccio high, in the act of flight, standing on a ball,' and in its hands was a rotating instrument 'resembling a butterfly' with four blades set in motion by a jet of water from the mouth. The figure was commissioned by Cardinal Giulio de' Medici, the future Pope Clement VII, and was executed by a pupil of Verrocchio, Giovanni Francesco Rustici. Rustici must have completed the great bronze group of the Preaching of the Baptist when he started work on it, and the figure of Mercury (Plate 40), poised on one leg with head turned upwards and distended cheeks, is modelled with the same liveliness and individuality.

At the beginning of 1537 Alessandro de' Medici was murdered, and his cousin Cosimo I succeeded him. At this point the story of the High Renaissance fountain begins. From his father Cosimo had inherited a villa at Castello, and he continued to live there after he was Duke. But his change of status was reflected in his way of life, and owing to a blessed strain of hedonism in his rather aloof character, the aspect of the villa on which he concentrated was the garden. We have an accurate record of its lay-out sixty years later, in a painting of 1599. In the foreground is the villa, with two pools of water in front of it, and behind, on a higher level and sloping slightly upwards, is a formal garden closed at the back by a wall. Above the wall is a second garden with a rectangular pool. The main features of the garden lie on the axis of the villa. Nearest to the house is a fountain with two basins: a little farther off is a second smaller fountain; and in the pool in the upper garden is a statue of a mountain god. Both garden and fountains sprang from the brain of a single artist, Tribolo. Years later, in 1556 a painting was made by Vasari of Cosimo I surrounded by the artists he employed, and there we see at the Duke's left hand Tribolo, holding a model of the fountains for the lower garden at Castello.

Of all kinds of sculpture, fountains might appear to be some of the most stable. Not only are they unwieldy, but they are technically tethered to the place on which they stand. In Florence, however, as taste changed in the seventeenth and eighteenth centuries, a fashion grew up for moving them about, and as a result of this the smaller and earlier of the Castello fountains, the Fountain of the Labyrinth, was moved to the terrace of the Medici villa of Petraia only a short walk away (Fig. 93). Its effect is made by contrasts. The first is a contrast of form between the outer basin and the pedestal, which are both octagonal, and the inner basin and upper elements, which are both circular. The second is a contrast in plastic emphasis, for all the figure sculpture is in marble and in relief except the topmost figure, which is free-standing and in bronze. Tribolo was a disciple of Jacopo Sansovino, and he brought to the Castello garden sculpture many of the classicising predilections that Sansovino in his turn had brought to the Bacchus in the Gualfonda garden a quarter of a century before. Moreover at Loreto he had been involved in the decoration of Bramante's Holy House, and that exper-ience too is distilled in the Fountain of the Labyrinth. The form of the upper part is classical – Lomazzo, the Milanese theorist, explains that fountains of this type were based on antique candelabra – and so is its imagery, from the marine nymphs at the bottom to the figure at the top. Such fountains were also made in the Quattrocento, but the proportions of Tribolo's fountain are those of its time. This can be seen in the much heightened stem above the basin, which ensured that the water descended from the upper to the lower basin in the long, thin, mannerist jets that were found specially appealing in the sixteenth century. The model that Tribolo holds in the painting in the Palazzo Vecchio shows a figure of Florence on top of the fountain, and the design for this must have been Tribolo's, though it was only realised after his death by Giovanni Bologna, who gave it a genre character more Flemish than Italian. But at one point he left Tribolo's design alone. The figure is represented wringing water from her hair, and when the fountain is turned on, it is from the damp tress of hair that the water springs.

The second and larger of Tribolo's fountains, the Fountain of Hercules (Fig. 92), still stands in the garden at Castello, and here too the upper part was left unfinished in 1550 when Tribolo died. But in this case also he prepared a model for the group, which was carried out in 1559 by Ammanati. Once more its principal distinction is a conceit, for when this fountain is turned on the water is precipitated from the mouth of the Antaeus in a single jet straight into the air. The main advance in the Fountain of Hercules is not in the conception of the fountain as an organism, but in the part that sculpture plays in it. In the Fountain of the Labyrinth all the marble sculpture is in relief; in the Fountain of Hercules much of it is carved fully in the round, or in such deep relief that it registers as free-standing sculpture. This is an extremely significant change, for Tribolo here develops an animate relationship between the jets of water and the sculpture, which opens the path to the fountains of Bernini. At the top are four little putti pouring water into the small basin below; round the stem between the basins are two more pairs of putti, again pouring water; at the base of the four main descending jets, on the lip of the basin, are four bronze bathing putti, and round the lower support are seven marble putti sheltering from the curtain of water that tumbles into the big pool beneath. These devices contained the seed of a whole new development.

Sculpturally the four putti with geese round the stem (Plate 59) are by far the finest feature of the fountain. They are fused in a continuous circular design, and though they depend from classical naturalistic sculptures, their limbs are opposed and combined and interlaced in such a way that they create an intricate harmony of form. In these figures Tribolo is working out in sculpture ideas that were explored in painting by Pontormo twenty years before. It is as though Pontormo's putti were invested with a third dimension, and diluted in the brain of an artist whose temperament was more objective and more classical. The four bronze putti on the edge of the basin are said by Vasari to have been cast from models by Pierino da Vinci, and they are handled in a rather different way. It is not just that the modelling is tighter than Tribolo's, but that the figures themselves are conceived more naturalistically. Tribolo's putti are a compromise between children as we know they are and a theory of form that has been applied to them. With Pierino's putti the formal element is less pronounced, and if we imagine real children scrambling about on the rim of the basin, we can conceive that they might possibly get into poses somewhat like these. What the bronze figures lack in sculptural impact is made up in human spontaneity.

From private fountains the Duke's mind moved, slowly and logically as it habitually did, to a project for a public fountain in the Piazza della Signoria. Not one major public fountain was built in Florence in the whole fifteenth century. But in the sixteenth century public fountains were constructed in other towns, above all at Messina, and the Messina fountains served as a stimulus for the fountain in Florence. There was every reason why they should do so, because their sculptor was a Florentine, Montorsoli. The earlier of his fountains (Fig. 97) was building in 1550, and was substantially complete in 1551, and it must have seemed a specially exciting work on a number of counts. One of them was its size. When it was erected, it was by far the tallest fountain in Italy, and by far the largest in extent. Another reason was its unprecedentedly elaborate ground-plan; it was dodecagonal, and four of its faces were scooped away to make room for subsidiary basins into which water was poured by reclining River Gods. The central element has the same two basins that we find in Tribolo's fountains at Castello, but the part played by the figure sculpture is entirely different. At Castello the architectural forms are carefully articulated, and the figure sculpture is subordinate to the whole design. At Messina, on the other hand, the figure sculptures conceal the architectural forms, and establish visual tensions of their own. The cause of this is that Montorsoli was influenced, to the depth of his creative being, by Michelangelo, and that the figure sculpture on his fountain lives its own independent life, just as, on a higher plane, does the sculpture of the two Medici tombs.

The evidence of a connection between this fountain and the fountain in Florence is supplied by a letter written in 1550 by Baccio Bandinelli to the secretary of Cosimo I. 'Pray tell your master,' this letter reads, 'that to comply with his wishes I have carefully investigated the masters who have worked on the fountains at Messina, and I find they are magnificent. I promise His Excellency that, if my plans please him, I will make him a fountain which will not only surpass any that exist on earth, but I vow that the Greeks and Romans never had such a fountain.' Bandinelli then adds a sentence that casts a little shaft of light on Cosimo's principal limitation as a patron, his cupidity. 'If other lords have spent ten,' says Bandinelli, 'I will give such concise instructions that his Excellency will not spend five.' The fountain

Fig. 91. Pagni: BRONZE DOOR. Duomo, Pisa.

Fig. 90. Pagni: BRONZE DOOR. Duomo, Pisa.

Fig. 93. Tribolo: FOUNTAIN OF THE LABYRINTH. Villa della Petraia.

Fig. 92. Tribolo: FOUNTAIN OF HERCULES. Villa di Castello.

Fig. 95. Giovanni Bologna: FOUNTAIN OF OCEANUS. Boboli Gardens, Florence.

Fig. 94. Giovanni Bologna: FOUNTAIN OF NEPTUNE. Piazza Nettuno, Bologna.

Fig. 96. Montorsoli: FOUNTAIN OF NEPTUNE. Messina.

Fig. 97. Montorsoli: FOUNTAIN OF ORION. Messina.

required a flow of water, and laboriously pipes were laid from the Porta San Niccolò to the Piazza della Signoria. The completion of this task was commemorated by a medal with the head of Cosimo I on one side, and on the other a figure of Neptune drawn by sea-horses raising his trident. This is the first evidence that the subject of the fountain, the Fountain of Neptune, had been laid down. At this point there was a delay in Florence but not at Messina, where Montorsoli in 1557 completed a second fountain, the Fountain of Neptune (Fig. 96). It was smaller than the earlier fountain, and was entirely different in plan. It was dominated by a large marble figure of Neptune presiding over two smaller figures of Scylla (Plate 57) and Charybdis. Rumours of this fountain too must have reached Bandinelli, and very welcome they would have been, since his strength, in his own view, lay in the carving of colossal marble figures. Chance played into his hands, for in 1558 there was excavated at Carrara a block of marble more than ten braccia high, which was eventually purchased by Cosimo I. Marble blocks of exceptional size were some of the most sought-after artistic commodities in the sixteenth century. In an extremely practical fashion they represented opportunity. For this reason, as soon as it was known that the block at Carrara had been bought by the Duke, trouble began. It was caused by Cellini and Ammanati, who insisted that the commission for the fountain figure should be opened to a limited competition in which they and Bandinelli would take part. The Duke agreed, not because he felt any hesitation about Bandinelli's suitability for the commission, but because he hoped that rivalry would spur him on. This was a miscalculation. Bandinelli was old and defensive and irascible, and though he had had an extremely successful career, he was dogged by lack of the only currency he valued, the currency of popular acclaim. He was an hysteric, and when he learned about the competition, he hurried to Carrara and defaced the marble block. His intention was to make his rivals' task more difficult, and he succeeded in that to this extent, that it was no longer possible to show the Neptune with the right arm raised. Though he should properly have been disqualified, he would still have been awarded the commission but for an unforeseen eventuality, his death. The immediate result was that in 1560 the closed competition for the statue became an open one. Giovanni Bologna, who had arrived in Florence three years earlier, started to prepare a model, and so did four other sculptors. But as a foregone conclusion the victor of the competition was Ammanati, who was a highly experienced marble sculptor, and who had in his hand the most powerful string that any artist of the time could pull, the support of Michelangelo.

From written accounts the competition seems to have related only to the central figure. Designs for the fountain proper had been submitted ten years earlier by Bandinelli to the Duke, and the presumption is that these, in a modified form, are represented by the fountain as it stands today (Fig. 98). Its unsatisfactory appearance is indeed due to a central dichotomy between the arid open scheme of Bandinelli and the proclivities of the much more considerable sculptor by whom it was adapted and carried out. It is likely that Ammanati, when he won the competition and took charge of the fountain, was confronted by two irreversible facts. The first was a ground plan the size and form of which had been decided between Bandinelli and the Duke. The second was a block of marble which ensured that the central figure should be far too large for the basin in which it stood. The Neptune stands across the way from Bandinelli's Hercules and Cacus, and simply because both statues are white and overpowering, they tend to be associated in our minds. But it is planned in quite a different way from Bandinelli's group; it is posed more simply, and though it is free-standing, it is conceived with a flat front and back. Ammanati's taste and style were formed in Venice in the studio of Sansovino, and the closest parallel for the Neptune is to be found in the colossal sculptures for the Scala dei Giganti of the Palazzo Ducale on which Sansovino was working at this time. In one respect, however, the Neptune is a product of its place and time, in that its pedantic programme is characteristically Florentine. On the wheels of the chariot are the signs of the zodiac, and round the head is an incongruous wreath of metal fir-cones, introduced because the pine used for building ships was sacred to Neptune and a crown of fir-cones was proffered to the victors of the Isthmian Games. The meaning of the figures on the basin has not been deciphered, and all we know is that two of them represent the nymphs Thetis and Doris, while two of them are marine gods. These figures were made after the Neptune, between 1571 and 1575.

Visually the use of bronze in the supporting figures was a mistake, since bronze figures tend from a distance to look smaller than they are, and the disparity of scale between the perimeter figures and the Gigante in the centre was thereby accentuated. But as works of art the bronze figures on the corners are the most satisfactory features of the fountain. The best of them, and the only one that can be ascribed with confidence to Ammanati himself, is a bearded Marine God (Plate 74), which has something of the elevation and solidity of the Del Monte effigies. Very different is the schematic Nymph with a Shell, where the whole figure, instead of resting obliquely on its plinth, is aligned on the front plane of the base. At each side of the reclining figures are bronze fauns and satyrs, which sit on little ledges projecting from the basin as though they were (what they may actually have been) additions made to reinforce the angle figures.

The laborious process by which this fountain was evolved is in marked contrast to the single creative act that threw up the Fountain of Neptune at Bologna (Fig. 94). The decision to build the Bologna fountain was made in 1563, just after the fountain in Florence had been begun, and the design for it was prepared by the architect Tommaso Laureti. Laureti's scheme, however, was transformed and vivified by Giovanni Bologna. To Bologna he carried the trunk-load of ideas that he had salvaged from his rejected scheme for the Fountain of Neptune in Florence, and among them may have been a small clay model loosely based on Montorsoli's Neptune in Messina. In this the action of the arms has been reversed, but the weight still rests where it rests in the Messina Neptune, on the right leg. The effect is elegant but insecure, and is corrected in the next model, in bronze, where the right foot is retracted and the weight rests on the left. The head in this model is based on the Moses of Michel-

Fig. 98. Ammanati: FOUNTAIN OF NEPTUNE. Piazza della Signoria, Florence.

Fig. 99. Giovanni Bologna: MODEL FOR A RIVER GOD. Victoria & Albert Museum, London.

Fig. 100. Giovanni Bologna: APPENINE. Villa Demidoff, Pratolino.

angelo. But even so the figure must have appeared insufficiently substantial for a full-scale statue, and in the final version the head was changed once more, the swinging movement was checked, the right arm was brought in closer to the body and the left arm was moved forwards, so that the figure became heavier, more monumental and more compact. By the standard of the last large figure cast by a Florentine sculptor, Cellini's Perseus, the Bologna Neptune (Plate 81) must have looked even more vital and compelling than it does to-day.

Ammanati's fountain in Florence has upwards of seventy jets, but most of them are dissociated from the figure sculpture. In the Bologna fountain each figure is functionally justified, and the Neptune apart, there are no sculptures that do not contribute directly to the water pattern. In this respect Giovanni Bologna's fountain attains a level of sophistication that made it, when it was completed in 1566, the most advanced fountain in the whole of Italy.

In 1569 Giovanni Bologna completed in Florence a small fountain for the Casino Mediceo on which his Samson and a Philistine was set, and immediately after he received the commission for another fountain, this time for the garden behind the Palazzo Pitti. It was a commission from the Grand-Duke, and it had the rather intractable character of all of Cosimo I's artistic projects. As usual it hinged on something that was extraneous to the fountain as a work of art, a colossal granite basin which had been found by Tribolo on Elba in 1550 and in 1567 with great labour was brought to Florence. As we look at the fountain to-day (Fig. 95), we can only wonder that Giovanni Bologna reconciled himself to using it at all. He did so with great ingenuity. Obviously no figure sculpture could be placed beneath the basin unless it too was of colossal size. The fountain was therefore planned as an antithesis between a lower part in which the basin rested on a simple central support and the architectural forms were unadorned, and an upper part in which the architectural forms were concealed by figure sculpture. On the fountain the central figure of Oceanus has been replaced by a copy, and the original is now in the Bargello. By the standard of the Bologna Neptune it is a nerveless hulk carved in the studio from a model by the sculptor. But its design gives an intimation of circularity, a suggestion of potential movement, to which Ammanati on the Fountain of Neptune in Florence did not aspire. More vivid and more lively are the three River Gods (Plate 83), who pour water from their pitchers into the great basin below.

Once the Fountain of Oceanus had been installed outside the Palazzo Pitti, we should expect it to have remained there. But in the early seventeenth century taste in garden design changed, and work began on the construction of the so-called Isolotto in the Boboli Gardens, a flat circular island in the centre of a small lake surrounded by a balustrade with decorative sculptures. As planned by its architect Giulio Parigi, the Isolotto had in the centre a little temple of greenery. If it looks featureless now, it must have looked more featureless when it was new, and in 1618 this was redressed by the costly expedient of uprooting the Fountain of Oceanus from the setting for which it had been planned, and planting it in the centre of the island. As a result we see it now from a greater distance than Giovanni Bologna intended, and in an open position for which it was not designed. More important, it was originally surrounded by a hexagonal balustrade, with figures on the corners facing inwards from whose mouths water poured into the pool. The balustrade was an integral part of the fountain, and the seated figures formed a visual complement to the outward facing River Gods.

The role of sculpture in a natural setting differs from that of sculpture in a street or square or church. It is surrounded by the living organisms of trees and plants, and from them it takes on a vicarious life, as though it too had grown organically where it stands. The first sculptor to sense that was Tribolo, in the beautiful figure of a River God in the Villa Corsini, which is compounded of every artifice known to sculptors in the second quarter of the cinquecento, but none the less has the timelessness of a natural phenomenon. But the sculptor who exploited this vein most fully was Giovanni Bologna, and the first work in which we are aware of it is the Fountain of Oceanus, where the age-old River Gods survey the world about them with immemorial detachment and maturity. This romantic quality was not something imposed upon the figures in their final phase, but was implicit in them from the start, as can be seen clearly enough in Giovanni Bologna's clay models for fountain statuary. In 1570 work began on the most famous of the Medici villas, Pratolino, which has as its dominant feature a giant figure carved from the living rock. At first the figure, which presides over a pool, was to show a River God, and the earlier of Giovanni Bologna's two clay models, that in London (Fig. 99), was made in preparation for this work. But the configuration of the ground at Pratolino was hilly, so almost at once the River God was set aside, and was replaced by a mountain God, the Appenine. The classical River Gods on which the first model was made had no applicability to the new theme, and Giovanni Bologna therefore prepared a second model, preserving the style and ethos and handling of the earlier sketch, but changing its whole form. This sketch, now in the Bargello, was copied faithfully in the colossal statue (Fig. 100). Giovanni Bologna is a Janus-faced artist, and when we look at his austere sculptures in Florence, it is important to remember their opposite, this deliquescent, richly imaginative work.

VENETIAN HIGH RENAISSANCE SCULPTURE

ONE of the consequences of the Sack of Rome was that the artists at the papal court dispersed through the peninsula. By accident rather than design the greatest of them arrived in Venice. Before the Sack forced him to flee, Jacopo Sansovino 'already had Rome in his hands', and when he came to Venice he was on his way to France. But as soon as he arrived his presence was brought to the notice of the Doge by Cardinal Grimani, to whom his work was known, and he was invited to report on the structure of St. Mark's. Sansovino was a proficient architect – in Rome he had designed the church of San Marcello, and had won the competition for the church of San Giovanni dei Fiorentini – and in 1529 he was appointed Protomagister of St. Mark's. Possibly he was influenced in his decision to remain in Venice by

Fig. 101. Jacopo Sansovino: LOGGETTA. Piazza San Marco, Venice.

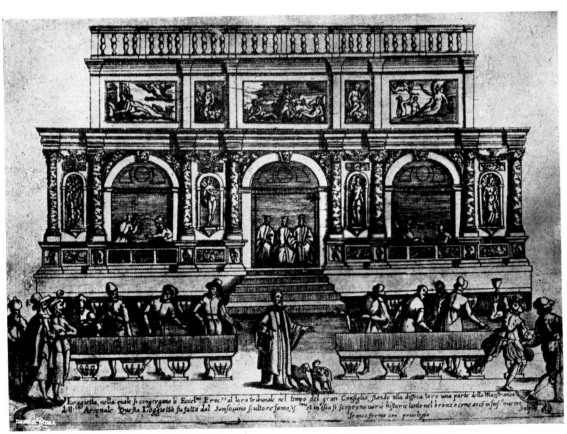

Fig. 102. Giacomo Franco: ENGRAVING OF THE LOGGETTA.

Fig. 103. Jacopo Sansovino: ALLEGORY OF VENICE. Loggetta, Venice.

Fig. 104. Danese Cattaneo: VENUS CYPRICA. Loggetta, Venice.

Fig. 105. Jacopo Sansovino: THE VENIER MONUMENT. S. Salvatore, Venice.
Fig. 106. Danese Cattaneo: THE FREGOSO ALTAR. S. Anastasia, Verona.

Fig. 107. Jacopo Sansovino: MARS. Palazzo Ducale, Venice.
Fig. 108. Danese Cattaneo: THE BEMBO MONUMENT. S. Antonio, Padua.

Fig. 109. Vittoria: ALTAR.
S. Francesco della Vigna, Venice.

Fig. 110. Vittoria: ALTAR OF THE LUGANEGHERI.
S. Salvatore, Venice.

Fig. 111. Rusconi: ALTAR OF THE SACRAMENT.
S. Giuliano, Venice.

Fig. 112. Grapiglia: THE LOREDANO MONUMENT.
SS. Giovanni e Paolo, Venice.

the poet Pietro Aretino, for whom he made a stucco copy of the Laocoon. Certainly it was Aretino who, a decade later, dissuaded him from returning to the papal court. 'The conceptions which spring from the heights of your genius,' wrote Aretino at this time, 'have added to the splendours of the liberal city we have chosen for our home.... Good has sprung from the evil of the Sack of Rome, in that in Venice, this place of God, you carve your sculptures and construct your buildings. It does not surprise me that cardinals and priests should pester you with invitations to return to Rome, but I should be astonished if you traded safety for insecurity, and abandoned the Venetian senators for servile priests.'

When he arrived in Venice, Sansovino was at once adopted as a member of what would now be known as the Establishment. He became a friend of Titian – we have an account of Sansovino and the humanist Priscianese looking out from Titian's garden at the boats thronging the lagoon towards Murano – he patronised Florentine artists when they came to Venice – Cellini describes a dinner at which 'he never stopped chattering about his great achievements, abusing Michelangelo and the rest of his fellow sculptors, while he bragged and vaunted himself to the skies' – and when in 1566, four years before his death, he became a fellow of the Florentine Academy, his portrait was painted by Tintoretto.

As an architect Sansovino changed the face of his adopted home. Vasari gives a careful list of his Venetian buildings – the Libreria, the Zecca, the Loggetta, the Scuola della Misericordia and many more – but devotes only a brief paragraph to his Venetian sculptures. Yet the importance of the sculptures was very great, and all the greater in that in Venice Sansovino stepped into a void. In 1525, when Tullio Lombardo delivered the second of his great marble reliefs for the Chapel of St. Anthony at Padua (Vol. II, Plate 142), Venetian sculpture was grinding to a halt. There was little possibility that Tullio at the close of his career would embark on a third narrative relief, and before 1528, when the Deputati invoked Sansovino's aid, it must have seemed that the decoration of the chapel would be completed by carvers of proved incapacity. In the circumstances any competent sculptor would have been assured of a warm welcome, but a special welcome was extended to an artist whose background, whose aesthetic convictions and the whole fabric of whose style marked him out as the natural heir of the Lombardi.

To Venice he brought the classical ideal of integrated sculptural and architectural forms which had been sketched out by Raphael in the painted sculptures of the School of Athens, and which, had Raphael lived, would have been realised in the Chigi Chapel. The work in which this message is most clearly to be read is the Loggetta beneath the Campanile (Fig. 101, 102). Begun in 1537, it was completed in three years, and in 1545 the four bronze statues destined for the niches on the front were put in place. The figures represent Pallas, Apollo (Plate 109), Mercury and Peace (Plate 108), and were intended by the sculptor as an allegory of the government of Venice. Pallas, he explained, was depicted as alert and fully armed because the wisdom of the Venetian senators was without peer. Mercury symbolised eloquence, and the part it played in the Venetian state. Apollo represented the freedom of the Venetian constitution, and, through the analogy of music, the harmony with which it was administered, while Peace was the condition which had transformed the city into the metropolis of Italy. Such a programme would have been inconceivable in Medicean Florence, and so would the style of the sculptures through which it is expressed. The Sansovino of the Loggetta was the same lyrical, romantic artist who had carved the Bacchus for Giovanni Bartolini thirty years before. His opposition to Michelangelo was as firm as it had been when he started work on the St. James in Florence, and his admiration for Raphael as fervent as when he carved the Madonna del Parto in Rome. All this can be seen in his four statues. They were niche figures, and Sansovino's first concern was the integrity of the four silhouettes. A classical model was employed for the Apollo, but it was translated into terms of line. No less important was the placing of each figure in its niche. To Sansovino the rigid frontality of the statuettes beneath Cellini's Perseus would have seemed awkward and primitive, and on the Loggetta he paid close attention to the recession of the planes. The figures were, moreover, planned as a coherent plastic scheme, with the Apollo and Mercury orientated on the entrance, and the Pallas and Peace turning their backs on the two archways at the sides. More than any other works these statues determined the form of the bronze statuettes that were turned out in Venice in the later sixteenth century.

In the Venier tomb in San Salvatore (Fig. 105) the principles of the Loggetta are applied to the sepulchral monument. With its high triumphal arch housing the effigy, it derives from the Vendramin tomb of Tullio Lombardo, but the rich display of figure sculpture on the earlier monument is reduced to two marble figures of Hope and Charity in tabernacles at the sides. Were they less fine in quality, it might be felt that the quantity of figure sculpture was insufficient, but so moving is their imagery and so concentrated is their form, that their significance within the tomb is out of all proportion to their size. In the Hope, as later in a figure of St. John the Baptist in the Frari (Plate 114), Sansovino transmits to sculpture an inwardness and spiritual repose akin to Titian's.

The style of these figures and of the Loggetta statues is fundamental for the two colossal figures carved by Sansovino for the Ducal Palace (Plate 113, Fig. 107). Commissioned in 1554, they were described by Vasari when still incomplete as 'two most beautiful marble statues in the form of giants, each seven braccia high, a Neptune and a Mars, symbolising the power of the Republic by sea and land'. Thirteen years later they were installed on the stairway of the Palace. Nowadays both figures are weathered, and there is a temptation to look at them as though their function were merely decorative, but their flat, generalised forms give scarcely the least indication of the effect Sansovino intended to produce. The distinction between the figures he conceived and the figures that confront us now can be measured by means of certain protected areas at the back of Mars, where the original surface and modelling are preserved, and by the later of the two reliefs which Sansovino carved for the Chapel of St. Anthony at Padua (Plate 112). From the bearded figure on the left of this relief we can form some impression of how the Mars and Neptune were meant to look. Though they are

Fig. 113. Jacopo Sansovino: SACRISTY DOOR. St. Mark's, Venice.

Fig. 114. Jacopo Sansovino: THE MIRACLE OF THE MAIDEN CARILLA. S. Antonio, Padua.

Fig. 115. Campagna: THE RAISING OF THE YOUTH AT LISBON. S. Antonio, Padua.

free-standing, each of them postulates a single viewpoint as decisively as though it were en-closed inside a niche, and their dramatic silhouettes are impaired by the indeterminate archi-tectural setting against which they are shown. Tintoretto regarded them as the supreme Venetian sculptures.

The classical synthesis of the Loggetta and the Venier monument was personal to Sanso-vino. His style was an expression of his temperament, and though his supremacy was never challenged during the forty-three years he worked in Venice, the pattern of Venetian sculpture in the later sixteenth century is that of a reaction against his principles and personality. Initially this is apparent in the work of his pupil, Danese Cattaneo, whose Fregoso altar in Sant' Anastasia at Verona (Fig. 106) was completed in 1565. Supported by fluted columns taken over from the architectural repertory of Sanmicheli, its central and lateral sections are uniform in height, and since all three of them are narrow, the result is an exaggerated emphasis on vertical-ity. Throughout the altar the figure sculpture is conceived in opposition to the architectural frame. In the centre a black rectangle of stone is used to throw into relief a figure of the suffering Christ (Plate 121), while at the sides the statues are raised on plinths two-thirds of their own height. As with Sansovino, coloured marble is extensively employed, but it is used to point a contrast between the figure sculpture and the delicate pink ground. The altar differs from the Venier tomb not only in its form but in the ideas it illustrates; it is constructed to an abstruse literary scheme, with statues of Jano Fregoso and Military Virtue, reliefs of Minerva and Victory, spandrels with the instruments of the Passion, and at the top statues of Eternity standing on a globe and Fame taking off in flight. Were this programme not recorded with approval by Vasari, we should, from the statues alone, gain no impression of the meaning of the tomb.

Simultaneously in Venice another Sansovino pupil, Vittoria, was experimenting along somewhat the same lines. His altar in San Francesco della Vigna (Fig. 109), begun in 1561 and finished three years later, is more modest than the Fregoso altar, but it reveals the same concern with height. Its two lateral sections consist of orthodox shell niches filled with statues, but in the centre the shell is raised above the cornice so that the niche is a third higher than those at the sides. This ratio is repeated in the statue of St. Anthony the Abbot in the centre of the altar. The niches are treated as a background, and the statues, thrown forward on little consoles, stand in opposition to the architectural forms. Again the sculptor invokes the aid of colour, this time in the contrast between the white marble of the statues and their grey stone ground.

With the abandonment of Sansovino's principle of integrated sculpture and architec-ture, the way lay open to a type of tomb in which the designer and the sculptor were different artists. This is the case with the colossal Loredano monument in the choir of Santi Giovanni e Paolo (Fig. 112), where the portentous structure is due to the architect Grapiglia and the sculpture (Plate 120) is largely by Cattaneo. Cattaneo's powers were failing when he began work on this tomb, but even a sculptor in his prime might have quailed before

Grapiglia's awkward elevation and monstrous upper register. On a smaller scale, the design of Gian Antonio Rusconi's Altar of the Sacrament in San Giuliano (Fig. 111) offers the same hazards. In this case, however, they were successfully surmounted by Cattaneo's pupil, Girolamo Campagna, who filled the niches at the sides with figures in bronzed terracotta and for the centre carved a relief of the Dead Christ with Angels which recalls the work of Veronese.

The principle of opposition between the architecture and the figure sculpture, established by Cattaneo at Verona and by Vittoria in Venice, culminates in two great works. One is Vittoria's Altar of the Luganegheri in San Salvatore (Fig. 110), which is flanked by columns, two in a front and two in a rear plane. The only figure sculptures are two statues of Saints Sebastian and Roch, which are set against the outer columns and posed in so free and overtly emotional a fashion that for the first time we are justified in speaking of the liberation of the sculpture from architectural restraint. The second work is the high altar of San Giorgio Maggiore (Plate 123), executed by Campagna between 1591 and 1595 from a design by the painter Vassillacchi. In this case the construction of a conventional sculptured altarpiece was ruled out, since at the back there ran a double colonnade, and it was unthinkable that an alien architectural unit should block the view through this to Palladio's choir. The solution adopted by Vassillacchi was to employ the columns at the back as visual constituents in his scheme, and to fill the space in front of them with a pyramid of figure sculpture. What resulted was the central part of the high altar as it exists to-day, a globe supported by the four Evangelists, with on its face the Holy Ghost plunging down towards the crucified Christ and at its summit God the Father in benediction. The credit for its success must go in large part to Campagna, who translated this pictorial conception into bronze, modelling the four Atlas figures, weighed down by the great copper globe, with a vehemence worthy of Tintoretto.

These changes in the form of tomb and altar are reflected in the figure sculpture. The emphasis on verticality throughout the Fregoso altar affects the proportions of Cattaneo's suffering Christ, and the same proportions are preserved in the statues of the Loredano monument. Vittoria's St. Anthony the Abbot in San Francesco della Vigna is also, by the classical canon of Sansovino, unjustifiably attenuated. But paradoxically it was Vittoria who rescued Venetian sculpture from the arid mannerism of these works. Born in Trent, Vittoria came to Venice in 1543, joining the workshop of Sansovino. After nine years the two sculptors parted company, and though in 1561 they collaborated on the Venier monument, they continued to view each other with suspicion and mistrust. The rift was caused by Sansovino's disapproval of Vittoria's style. A fluent, sometimes facile artist, Vittoria was from the first incapable of the slow act of concentration, the close reasoning and self-criticism of Sansovino. He was inventive and impetuous, and his concern lay with appearances rather than with intrinsic quality. By temperament he was a modeller not a carver – his technique in marble sculpture was no more than adequate – and the large stucco statues he made for the Cappella del Rosario in Santi Giovanni e Paolo and for San Giorgio Maggiore are some of his most vivid works. Above all, he was attracted to the sculptures of Michelangelo. He represented, therefore, all those tendencies against which Sansovino protested early in the century, and which during his years in Venice he continued to oppose.

The first statue in which Vittoria employed motifs from Michelangelo is the St. Sebastian on the altar in San Francesco della Vigna (Plate 126). His model was the Dying Slave, which was despatched to France in 1544, and which he can have known only through a cast or statuette. His acquaintance with Michelangelo at this time was shallow, and this led him to modify, among many other features, the elevation of the left elbow and the position of the head. Oblivious of the weaknesses of this strange statue, Vittoria reproduced it twice as a bronze statuette. At this or at a rather later time he must also have obtained a copy of the Rebellious Slave, and when he carved a statue of St. Jerome for the Frari (Plate 128), he had studied it so thoroughly that he could invest his figure with a continuity of movement that is truly Michelangelesque. The two Slaves were not the only works by Michelangelo Vittoria knew – he was certainly familiar with the Rachel of the Julius monument which he used as the basis of statues of SS. Daniel and Catherine of Alexandria in San Giuliano, and also with the Dawn and Evening, which he adapted in two allegorical figures in the Palazzo Ducale – but he viewed the Slaves with an obsessive interest. In 1576, in a statue of St. Jerome in Santi Giovanni e Paolo (Plate 129), he returned to the Rebellious Slave once more, transcribing it this time from the end, and reproducing the torso, shoulders and right leg. Finally, in about 1600, he reverted to the Dying Slave, which inspired his most successful statue, the St. Sebastian in San Salvatore (Plate 127), where the magnificently modelled torso alone rests on the front plane of the block, the slack legs are threaded backwards round the tree-trunk, and the ecstatic head is shown upturned. These four statues mark Vittoria's progress from a schematic, external view of Michelangelo to a more profound understanding of his style.

From the time that he arrived in Venice a large part of Sansovino's sculptural thinking was devoted to relief. His first task was to complete an unfinished relief by Antonio Minelli for the chapel of St. Anthony at Padua, and this in turn was followed by six bronze reliefs for the tribunes of St. Mark's, the marble reliefs on the Loggetta, the sacristy door of St. Mark's, and a second relief for Padua. His links with painting were especially intimate. In Rome he was acquainted with Raphael and prepared a model for Perugino; in Florence he assisted Andrea del Sarto on the Scalzi frescoes; and in Venice he became the friend of Lotto, Titian and Tintoretto. He did not disdain to learn from painting and sometimes he translated pictorial motifs into relief, but he exercised a reciprocal influence on painters through the medium of his reliefs. In the six tribune reliefs Sansovino's task was to perform in Venice for the legend of St. Mark what Donatello had done in Padua for the legend of St. Anthony, and each of the six stories is told with an impetus and passion that stem from Donatello. But they are built up with strong diagonal accents in depth which Sansovino must have learned from Raphael's tapestries in Rome, and the visual expedients that are employed in the St. Mark casting out Demons (Plate 111), with its mass of violently activated figures, and the Miracle of the Slave, where the figure of the Saint flies forward through the whole depth of the scene, explain much that would otherwise be puzzling in the early style of Tintoretto.

The second of Sansovino's relief commissions for St. Mark's, the bronze sacristy door to the left of the high altar (Fig. 113), was modelled in 1546 and assembled in 1569, but was not installed till 1572. Based on Ghiberti, the door constitutes a sixteenth-century critique of the Porta del Paradiso; the only features that have no precedent in Ghiberti are its concave shape, the pairs of classicising putti beside the Prophets and over the Evangelists, and the strips of decoration by which it is broken up. It has been contended that the second of Ghiberti's doors is inferior to the first in that its structure is sacrificed to figurated ornament. In Sansovino's door structure is reasserted by a framework of emphatic vertical and horizontal ribs. It has also been claimed that Ghiberti's relief system is ambiguous. With Sansovino, not only are the frame figures modelled in greater depth than the reliefs, but they gaze at one another across the door as though commenting on the two scenes. These scenes are the Entombment and the Resurrection. In the former Sansovino's thoughts went back to the Entombment of Raphael; none of the figures is exactly reproduced, but the tensions within the composition are those of Raphael's altarpiece. Raphael too lies at the heart of the companion scene (Plate 110). With its banner behind the central Christ and its ring of gesticulating soldiers, it proceeds from the world of the Stanza dell'Incendio. The intellectual context of these and of the six tribune reliefs is supplied by Dolce's *Dialogue on Painting* (1557), where Pietro Aretino praises Donatello as the greatest sculptor before Michelangelo, and exalts the genius of Raphael. Both to Aretino and to Sansovino the issues involved in the antagonism between Michelangelo and Raphael in the second decade of the century were still alive, and in 1550 the Raphaelesque style in which the Entombment and the Resurrection are composed had an almost polemical significance.

The style of the reliefs in the Chapel of St. Anthony at Padua was laid down by the Lombardi, but the second of the scenes carved for the chapel by Sansovino, the Miracle of the Maiden Carilla (Plate 112, Fig. 114), recalls the Resurrection in St. Mark's in so far as it takes place before a semi-circle of spectators with an onlooker in deep relief at either side. Commissioned in 1536, but carved in the main after 1557 and completed only in 1562, it is the unchallenged masterpiece of High Renaissance relief sculpture. In the earlier of his reliefs for Padua, Sansovino was hampered by the fact that Minelli had already carved almost two thirds of the scene, in the later he was his own master. The relief is carved with greater authority and confidence – such a figure as the mother kneeling over the drowned girl was beyond the reach of any sixteenth century Italian sculptor save Michelangelo – and is conceived with an epic nobility that raises it as narrative to the level of the finest Venetian subject paintings.

The most important of the marble sculptures on the Loggetta are three oblong allegorical reliefs. Two of them are by Sansovino's pupils Danese Cattaneo and Tiziano Minio, but in that in the middle (Fig. 103) the subtle gradations of the surface, the ambivalent movement of the central figure, and the pure classical forms of the reclining nudes all reveal Sansovino's hand. Cattaneo's less weighty personality is reflected in a more artificial relief style (Fig. 104) and when, freed from his master's tutelage, he came to model the bronze allegorical reliefs for the Loredano monument (Plate 117), he rephrased Sansovino's relief on the Loggetta in the mannered language of Tintoretto. Before he died in 1573, he had prepared a model for the last of the reliefs for the Chapel of St. Anthony at Padua, St. Anthony resuscitating a dead Youth, and on his death the contract was transferred to his pupil Girolamo Campagna in the belief that he would imitate his master's manner and would carry out the work 'with more care and affection than any other artist.' The design of the relief (Fig. 115) must be Cattaneo's, and its affinities are once more with Tintoretto; the heads project abruptly from the relief plane, and the figure in the centre is first cousin to the plague-stricken youth on the left of the Ministration of St. Roch. Left to his own devices, Campagna proved a sensitive, rather placid relief sculptor, both in marble in the Dead Christ tended by Angels in San Giuliano (Fig. 111), and in bronze in the beautiful Annunciation designed for the Palazzo del Consiglio at Verona (Fig. 118), where the Angel (Plate 122), floating languidly to earth, and the attenuated Virgin at her lectern are disposed on the long diagonals that are familiar from Veronese's altarpieces. Vittoria, on the other hand, was blind to the possibilities of relief as an art form. To Sansovino's Venier monument he contributed a lunette with, in the centre, a coarse pastiche of the St. Peter's Pietà (Fig. 105), and in a later work, the Birth of the Virgin in San Giuliano, he debases himself to the level of a Venetian Bandinelli.

The story of the Venetian High Renaissance relief is brought to a close by two makers of bronze statuettes, Tiziano Aspetti and Roccatagliata. Aspetti (who was responsible for the Altar of St. Anthony at Padua and for two unadventurous bronze statues on Palladio's façade of San Francesco della Vigna) produced three reliefs, two in the Duomo at Padua (Fig. 135) and one in Santa Trinita in Florence. Unlike the tribune reliefs of Sansovino, they do not employ a consistent relief style, but are conceived as groups of statuettes attached to a flat ground. The treatment of the intermediate planes is lifeless, and even the figures in the round are stamped with a fatal flaccidity. Roccatagliata, a more varied and ambitious artist, modelled one major relief, the bronze antependium of the altar in the sacristy of San Moisè in Venice (1633). Containing an Allegory of Redemption (Fig. 136) with a dead Christ surrounded by exuberant putti, this marks the first tentative advance of a Venetian relief sculptor into the territory of baroque.

LOMBARD HIGH RENAISSANCE SCULPTURE

IN Lombardy the principal High Renaissance sculptor was an intruder. Of Aretine stock Leone Leoni was trained as a goldsmith and medallist, and when he came to Milan in 1542 it was as an engraver at the imperial mint. He had behind him a period at the papal mint in Rome, where he had come into collision with Cellini. Leoni's character was violent, vindictive and ungenerous, and though he was Cellini's intellectual superior – his letters reach an extremely high level of articulacy, and throughout his whole career he was on terms of friendship with Pietro Aretino, Annibale Caro and other humanists – he was almost totally devoid of the disinterested artistic aspirations which supplied Cellini with his passport to immortality. What the two artists shared was an ambition to advance beyond the medal to sculpture in larger forms. The first evidence of this occurs in 1546, when the writer Muzio presses Leoni's claim to design the monument of Alfonso d'Avalos. Leoni's wish, writes Muzio, is to leave behind him one of those memorials through which other artists have made their names eternal. Everything that he has read or heard or seen of ancient and modern sculpture encourages him in the wish to emulate those on whom fortune conferred the boon of an occasion to display their gifts. Leoni possessed Cellini's pertinacity as well as his hot temper, and a few months later he turned to a new project. The emperors of antiquity, he explains in a letter to his patron Ferrante Gonzaga, had the foresight to order equestrian statues of themselves while they were still alive. If the present emperor should decide to follow their example, he would be ready to make a life-size horse with a figure fully armed, on a Doric pedestal with reliefs showing the emperor's victories. This plan for a bronze equestrian statue came to nothing – for one thing there was no reason to suppose that Leoni was capable of modelling a full-scale horse – but from it there grew the statue of Charles V restraining Fury (Fig. 141) in Madrid. The problem that confronted Leoni in this work was akin to that with which Cellini was confronted in the Perseus, and he solved it in the same manner, by using for the vanquished figure a motif from Donatello. But by nature he was a less heroic artist than Cellini, and his group is artificial and confused, a table-ornament expanded to a needlessly large size. Experience, however, brought him confidence, and between 1556 and 1564 he carried out a more successful work, the two-figure bronze group of Ferrante Gonzaga triumphant over Envy (Fig. 142) at Guastalla. On this occasion guidance came from Cellini (whose Perseus was installed in 1554), and the pose of the Medusa was adapted for the Satyr in Leoni's monument.

The statue of Ferrante Gonzaga was planned as an allegory of Gonzaga's triumph over the malign envy of his foes. This vision of life as an unremitting contest was central to Leoni's thought, and was elaborated by him in his most personal and most impressive work, the decoration of his house in Milan. Inspired by the house which Giulio Romano had built for himself at Mantua, it was decorated not with classicising paintings but with the artist's sculptures and with casts after the antique. In the middle of the courtyard, on a base supported by four columns, stood a cast of the Marcus Aurelius, and for the façade Leoni carved six prisoners in three-quarter length (Plate 105), each representing a barbarian tribe over which Marcus Aurelius had been victorious. The statue inside has disappeared, but the prisoners survive. An amalgam of the male herms on the pilasters of the Julius tomb and the standing figures on the Arch of Constantine, they are works of extraordinary imaginative force. Not a little of their effect is due to the fact that in each case the head is free of the wall surface, while beneath, instead of merging with the pilaster, the figure is severed at the knees, so that it reads as the body of a legless giant suspended on the surface of the house. The reliefs in the courtyard include representations of the visual arts, and among them is the wheel of fortune revolved by the sculptor's eponymous emblem, the lion. Above the central window is the most remarkable feature of the building, a relief of two lions, again emblematic of the sculptor, devouring a satyr, again symbolic of envy or malignity (Plate 104). The fascination of this relief is not only that it is unashamedly autobiographical, but that the satyr is represented falling forwards out of the relief, convulsively clutching with one hand the pediment of the window beneath. This is the single case in the entire Renaissance in which the language of Giulio Romano's Sala dei Giganti at Mantua is translated into sculpture. Leoni's house was planned as the dwelling-place of a successful artist, but it is also the record of a tragedy, a proof that, had he in his other sculptures been less servile, less conventional, and less ambitious, and allowed his style to well up from the depths of his own temperament, he could have become one of the greatest sculptors of his day.

In 1567, two years after Leoni had secured possession of his house in the Via Moroni, Pellegrino Tibaldi (1527–96) was appointed architect of Milan Cathedral. A painter, designer and architect of exceptional distinction, his direct impact on sculpture was made through more than a hundred reliefs in the Cathedral, in which his essentially pictorial cartoons were carried out in marble, wood and stucco by other hands. Indirectly his influence was fundamental for the style of the most distinguished Milanese sculptor of the third quarter of the century, Annibale Fontana, and for its most distinguished sculptural complex, the façade of Santa Maria presso San Celso (Fig. 144). Completed in 1572, the façade made provision for a central relief over the main entrance, lateral reliefs over the two doorways at the sides, four figures in superimposed niche at the sides, and four small reliefs in the upper register, as well as for two sibyls on the pediment above the entrance and an Annunciation group above. Beside the lateral doorway were statues of Adam and Eve.

The first thought of the church authorities was to entrust the sculpture to a Tuscan artist, Stoldo Lorenzi. The Adam which Lorenzi delivered in 1575 is an elegant variation on the Adam carved by Bandinelli for the high altar of the Duomo in Florence, while the Annunciation, completed three years later, though free of the taint of Bandinelli, is again redolent of Florentine academism. Early in 1582 the sculptor returned to Tuscany. One of the factors in his resignation or dismissal was that he had been working since 1574 in competition with Fontana, who a year after the delivery of the Adam completed two statues of Prophets for the uppermost of the four niches, which conformed to the stylistic preconceptions of Tibaldi and to the tradition of Lombard sculpture. It must from the first have been apparent that there was a fundamental difference between the figures of Lorenzi – self-contained units that resulted from the cerebration of an undistinguished mind – and these freer, more adventurous statues. In his last work, a group of the Virgin of the Assumption with two Angels (Plate 102) inside the church, completed in 1586, a year before his death, Fontana advanced further along this path, achieving an image of transitory ecstasy which looks forward to the sculptures of Bernini.

The main scene of activity of Lombard sculptors in the later sixteenth century, however, was not Milan but Rome, where the period of Florentine supremacy came to an end soon after 1550 with Ammanati's Del Monte tombs, and taste thenceforth was formed by Lombard artists. The turning of the tide is marked by the rise, in or before 1546, of a sculptor of genius, Guglielmo della Porta. Employed at first on the repair or reproductions of antiques – his earliest Roman commission was for a head of Antoninus Pius – Guglielmo della Porta in 1547 succeeded the painter Sebastiano del Piombo in the sinecure office of Keeper of the Apostolic Seal, and in 1549 was entrusted with the most important commission awarded since the Julius monument, the tomb of Paul III.

Trained in Milan in the classicising circle of Bambaia, Guglielmo della Porta is first heard of in 1534 in Genoa, where he was engaged with his uncle, Gian Giacomo della Porta, and another sculptor, Niccolò da Corte, on the funerary chapel of Giuliano Cibo, Bishop of Girgenti, in the Cathedral. The seven figures on the Cibo altar (Fig. 143) are conceived as a dramatic unity. In a narrow central niche are St. Peter and St. Paul, with, between them, the Redeemer blessing the effigy, which originally projected at the front. At the sides, between paired columns, are figures of St. Jerome and St. John the Baptist, each crouching in a low niche, and at the outer edges, in front of the paired columns, are Abraham, pointing rhetorically backwards to the central niche, and Moses with the tablets of the law. The sculptures are unequal – like most works of their kind in Liguria and Lombardy they are collaborative – but one of them, the Abraham (Plate 98), is more powerful and more resilient than the rest, and this is due to Guglielmo della Porta.

In Genoa Guglielmo came in contact with the painter Perino del Vaga, and he was associated with Perino when he first arrived in Rome. But there a fresh experience awaited him, that of Michelangelo. He recognised that his debt to Michelangelo was very great: 'I too,' he wrote, 'believe that I should be numbered among his pupils.' The debt was personal, stylistic and technical. It was personal in that his success in Rome was due to Michelangelo's encouragement, stylistic in that his first scheme for the tomb of Paul III included eight reclining figures inspired by the allegories in the Medici Chapel, and technical in that his statues were produced in the same way as Michelangelo's. 'He does not work from models like other sculptors,' wrote Annibale Caro, as he watched the carving of the Justice for the papal tomb, 'but continues to uncover the complete limbs, so that the figure looks like a naked woman emerging from the snow.' Caro's influence is reflected in the classicising imagery of the tomb. If Justice was to be portrayed, she must be represented as the virgin daughter of Jupiter and Thetis, proud-eyed and formidable and with a certain melancholy dignity. If Abundance, she must be depicted as the classical Annona or, following a coin of Antoninus Pius, the goddess Ceres, and if Peace, she must be accompanied by Pluto, the god of riches, in the likeness of a blind child holding a purse.

Before his death at the end of 1549, the Pope bought from Guglielmo della Porta a bronze and marble base made for another tomb, and chose the classical sarcophagus in which his

Fig. 116. Jacopo Sansovino: MONUMENT OF TOMMASO RANGONE. S. Giuliano, Venice.
Fig. 117. Vittoria: DOGE NICCOLO DA PONTE. Seminario, Venice.

Fig. 118. Campagna: ANNUNCIATION. Palazzo del Consiglio, Verona (formerly).

Fig. 119. Francesco da Sangallo: GIOVANNI DALLE BANDE NERE. Museo Nazionale, Florence.
Fig. 120. Bandinelli: GIOVANNI DALLE BANDE NERE. Piazza San Lorenzo, Florence.

Fig. 121. Cellini: COSIMO I. Museo Nazionale, Florence.
Fig. 122. Cellini: BINDO ALTOVITI. Gardner Museum, Boston.

Fig. 123. Poggini: FRANCESCO DE' MEDICI. Museo Nazionale, Florence.
Fig. 124. Poggini: VIRGINIA PUCCI RIDOLFI. Museo Nazionale, Florence.

Fig. 125. Leone Leoni: THE EMPEROR CHARLES V. Prado, Madrid.
Fig. 126. Roman, second century A.D.: COMMODUS. Palazzo dei Conservatori, Rome.

Fig. 127. Leonardo da Vinci (after): MOUNTED WARRIOR. Szepmuveszetimuseum, Budapest.

Fig. 128. Pierino da Vinci (?): SAMSON AND TWO PHILISTINES. Louvre, Paris.
Fig. 129. Bandinelli: HERCULES. Museo Nazionale, Florence.
Fig. 130. Giovanni Bologna: ARCHITECTURE. Kunsthistorisches Museum, Vienna.

body was to rest. Less than a year later a wooden model was prepared, and in this Guglielmo della Porta returned to an idea with which Michelangelo had experimented in the early stages of the Julius tomb, that of a free-standing monument. The model was supported by eight terms, inside its chapel-like interior was the sarcophagus, on top was a seated life figure of the Pope, and round the sides were eight reclining statues, two on each face. Guglielmo's son, Teodoro della Porta, boasted that 'never since antiquity had a larger structure of this type been planned,' and the vicissitudes of the monument stemmed from that very fact. Their source was Michelangelo, who concluded that the tomb would violate the space and symmetry of the new church. He accordingly proposed that the free-standing tomb should be abandoned, and that the bronze statue of the Pope should be placed in a niche 'so that it should look like a judge on the Campidoglio.' The new Pope, Julius III, was sympathetic to his arguments, and in 1553 it was decided that the tomb should be replanned as a wall monument. This was frustrated by the sculptor, who was wedded to his free-standing scheme. The death of Michelangelo removed the main impediment to the completion of the tomb, and Guglielmo della Porta, with the support of Pope Gregory XIII, arranged for it to be set up in the right aisle of the church. Its form was simpler than in the model – the conception of a funerary chapel was abandoned, and the eight terms and four of the allegories were eliminated – and in its new guise it consisted only of the sculptures which were already finished, the bronze statue of the Pope on its marble and bronze base above a marble plinth with paired reclining allegories at the front and back. The artist's amour propre was satisfied, but the effect, to judge from a drawing made of the tomb at about this time, was thoroughly unsatisfactory, not least because its crowning feature, the statue of the Pope (Plate 100), was planned as a flat silhouette. For this reason in 1587 it was treated as Michelangelo had recommended, and installed as a wall monument in one of the niches in the piers beneath the cupola, with two allegories in front and two more at the top sliding off the pediment. Forty years later it was moved to its final position in the tribune (Fig. 145), and the allegories from the pediment were transferred to the Palazzo Farnese. Our knowledge of it therefore is restricted to its constituent sculptures, the idealised statue of the Pope, the Justice (Plate 99), which in 1595 was covered with metal drapery, the aged Prudence, the loosely posed Abundance and the lyrical Peace.

Both in the tomb of Paul III and in two later monuments made for Giacomo della Porta's Cesi Chapel in Santa Maria Maggiore (Fig. 146), Guglielmo della Porta shows a North Italian bias towards polychromy. This was taken over and developed by another Lombard artist, Domenico Fontana, when in 1574 he started work on the tomb of Pope Nicholas IV (Fig. 148). Fontana was an architect, and the tomb of Nicholas IV is an architectural unit in which sculpture plays a secondary part. The interest of the tomb rests in its sensuous colour rather than in its three constricted statues by Leonardo da Sarzana; the veined white marble of the base merges with rosso antico and alabaster in the register above, and the portasanta columns and pilasters are offset by the lining of the niches and the austere black epitaph. Nicholas IV

(d. 1292) was a Franciscan, and his tomb was the first significant commission of a Franciscan cardinal, Felice Peretti, who in 1585 became Pope Sixtus V. Before he was elected Pope, Peretti commissioned from Fontana a second, more important work, the Cappella Sistina or Cappella del Presepio in the right transept of the church, and after his elevation to the papacy it was decided that two tombs should be constructed in this chapel, one for the Pope himself (Fig. 149) and the other for his predecessor, Pope Pius V (Fig. 150).

The papal tombs in the Cappella Sistina are far larger and more splendid than the tomb of Nicholas IV. They fill the whole width of the lateral walls to the full height of the piers, and form the principal decoration of the chapel. In each the main register is punctuated by four huge coloured marble columns, and has an arched niche in the centre and two rectangular spaces at the sides; above it is a deep cornice supporting an attic punctuated by four herms. More sculpture was naturally required than in the earlier tomb, and the rectangular spaces in the main register and the three spaces in the attic were therefore filled with narrative reliefs. The way to this solution had been pointed out by Bandinelli in the tombs of Leo X and Clement VII in Santa Maria sopra Minerva, where the upper register also contained three narrative scenes. Fontana, when he adopted it, must have been actuated by two considerations. One was iconographical, that in this way it was possible to enhance the commemorative character of the whole tomb, and the other was structural, that the use of a uniform system of relief emphasised the flat plane of the chapel wall. But in shape and style the reliefs are totally unlike those of Bandinelli. Though executed in the main by Flemish artists, they are late sixteenth-century revivals of Lombard narrative reliefs like those which had been carved for the Certosa at Pavia ninety years before. The reliefs on the tomb of Pius V illustrate historical events, while those on the Sixtus V tomb are largely allegorical, and the programmes are completed by figures in niches at right angles to the monuments, two Dominican saints beside the tomb of Pius V and two Franciscan saints beside that of his successor. Of the two portrait statues one, the Pius V by Leonardo da Sarzana, is timid and constrained; the other, the Sixtus V (Plate 135), is less conventional. Carved by a Lombard sculptor, Valsoldo, it shows the Pope kneeling in prayer before the Presepio in the centre of the chapel, and it was hoisted into place in the Pope's presence in the summer of 1589.

The pendant to the Cappella Sistina, the Cappella Paolina on the opposite side of the church, was founded by Pope Paul V three months after his election in 1605. Its structure was substantially complete by 1611, and the altar was finished two years later. The architect chosen by the Pope was a Milanese, Flaminio Ponzio, and the scheme that he adopted derived directly from the earlier chapel. The effect of Ponzio's chapel is more opulent and sensuous than Fontana's. In the seventeenth century opinion was divided as to their respective merits; Bellori, who praised architecture in the ratio of its restraint, admitted that the Pauline Chapel was the richer of the two, but thought it inferior in order and design, while Baglione considered that it far surpassed the earlier chapel. To Evelyn it seemed 'beyond all imagination glorious and beyond description,' and in the richness of its orchestration it remained unchallenged through the whole lifetime of Bernini.

In the Pauline Chapel the lateral walls are again filled with tombs, on the right that of Clement VIII (Fig. 151) and on the left that of Paul V (Fig. 152). Architecturally speaking, Ponzio's tombs are faithful reproductions of Fontana's, but the effect they make upon the eye is rather different. The garlands above the reliefs in the main register are elaborated and enriched with cherub heads, and in the section above the staid herms of the earlier monuments are replaced by full-length caryatids with crossed feet and raised arms, which are shown in movement against the flat plane of the tomb. Similarly the reliefs are carved in greater depth, and are designed with stronger visual emphasis. The meaning of this change can best be judged if we compare the single scene that is common to both chapels, the Coronation relief in the centre of the upper register of all four tombs. Whereas in the tomb of Sixtus V the Pope is represented as a small figure seated slightly to the right of centre at the top of a wide flight of steps, in that of Paul V (Fig. 155) the figure is enlarged and centralised, and the supporting clerics are posed in such a way as to lead the eye towards it. In the tomb of Clement VIII the figure of the Pope is again set centrally (Fig. 156), but the cushion beneath his feet is asymmetrical, and in front three half-length figures in full relief conceal the foreground and protrude beyond the frame. This scene marks a decisive stage in the development of the Baroque relief.

The function of the Sistine Chapel was the display of the Cappella del Presepio in the centre of the chapel, while that of the Pauline Chapel was to house St. Luke's painting of the Virgin, which could be shown only on an altar on the rear wall. This difference of focus is reflected in the tombs. One of the two papal statues, that of Clement VIII, was diverted to the chapel from the Campidoglio, and is therefore posed frontally, but the other, that of Paul V, is turned towards the altar wall, as though participating in the Mass. This change of axis is also a Baroque device.

All the main sculptors active in Rome in the first decade of the seventeenth century are represented in the Pauline Chapel. Four of them are of particular importance. The first, Camillo Mariani, a native of Vicenza, had been trained in Venice in the workshop of Vittoria. A modeller rather than a carver, he brought to his figures of the two Saints John beside the altar recollections of Vittoria's stucco statues. The second, a Lombard, Stefano Maderno, modelled a bronze relief above the altar and carved on the tomb of Paul V the larger scene of Cardinal Serra leading the papal troops against the Turks. Maderno did a trade in terracotta statuettes after the antique, and in the relief he appears in his true colours as a listless, pedantic classicist. A few years earlier, however, he had been responsible for one of the most celebrated statues of his time, the St. Cecilia in Santa Cecilia in Trastevere (Plate 159), which commemorated the discovery of the Saint's body by Cardinal Sfondrato in 1599. The body was small – it measured only five and a half palms in length – and, according to Bosio's *History of the Passion of St. Cecilia*, lay on its right side, with the head turned towards the ground as if in sleep. Charged with the task of representing it, Maderno returned to the antique, basing the pose on a Hellenistic statue of a dead Persian, in which the figure was also shown on its right side, with one leg contracted beneath the other and the left arm outstretched. Placed under the high altar in a black marble recess which reads as a sarcophagus or burial chamber, his statue was prophetic of the future, but the credit for it properly belongs to Cardinal Sfondrato, who laid down the terms of the commission, and not to the timid classicising sculptor by whom it was carried out.

The third sculptor, Niccolò Cordieri, was a native of Lorraine, who had scored his first considerable success with the effigies of the parents of Pope Clement VIII in the Aldobrandini chapel in Santa Maria sopra Minerva (Fig. 147). Cordieri was a restorer of antiques – two of his restitutions are still in the Borghese gallery – but through his make-up there ran a vein of Northern naturalism which prevented him from lapsing into the artifices of Maderno. He was a resilient marble sculptor, and his four statues in the Pauline Chapel (Plate 136) break new ground, in that they make use of open poses, and are not, like the statues in the chapel opposite, circumscribed by a containing silhouette. A generation later Cordieri's figures proved a fertile source of inspiration for Algardi.

The fourth sculptor is Pietro Bernini, the author of the caryatids and of the scene of the Coronation of the Pope (Fig. 156) on the Clement VIII monument. Pietro Bernini is an enigmatic artist, not because his sculptures are particularly rare or his style is particularly recondite, but because his importance for the art of sculpture was out of all proportion to the merits of the works he actually produced. His sculptures were adversely criticised; towards the end of his life an attempt was made to expel the best of them, a figure of St. John the Baptist, from the Barberini Chapel in Sant' Andrea della Valle (Plate 137), and the first version of the Coronation of Pope Clement VIII was rejected and replaced by the relief we know to-day. In the eyes of his contemporaries he was remarkable above all else for technical facility. One day in Naples Baglione watched him mark a block, and without further preparation carve three fountain figures. 'It was astonishing to watch him,' he writes, 'and if he had had more design, he would have made great progress.' A Florentine, Bernini was trained in his native town, but guided by the hope of personal advancement he moved first to Rome and then to Naples, where he carved a quantity of hesitant classicising statues. In 1594, however, he returned to Tuscany, collaborating with Caccini on a relief on the façade of Santa Trinita in Florence. Caccini's statues left a deep impression on his mind, which was reflected in the most important of the works he carved when he moved back to Naples, the statues of the Ruffo Chapel in the Gerolomini and two figures of Security and Charity (Fig. 154) on the Monte di Pietà. His feeling for tactility was more restricted than Caccini's, and he invariably planned his figures as though they were reliefs. But he possessed a lively imagination, and when in 1606 he returned to Rome, the first commission he received there, for a marble relief of the Assumption of the Virgin for Santa Maria Maggiore (Plate 138), gave full scope to this aspect of his work. Inspired by Lodovico Carracci, it portrays a variety of emotions that no sculptor had attempted to depict before, and is carved with unusual enterprise, in that the forward figures are undercut and the surface textures differentiated. This emotive attitude to sculpture, this empirical approach to style, and this remarkable technical facility were among the gifts he handed on to his son Gian Lorenzo Bernini.

THE HIGH RENAISSANCE PORTRAIT

THE High Renaissance was a period of great portraiture. In painting it produced a host of portraitists of the first rank, for whom the problem of the portrait was not, as it had been for their predecessors in the fifteenth century, that of recording a specific physiognomy, but rather of projecting on to canvas the thoughts, the aspirations and the fears hidden within the mind. Throughout the fifteenth century the painted portrait lagged behind the portrait bust; in the sixteenth century the position was reversed. One reason was that no portrait sculptor in Florence was an artist of the stature of Pontormo or Bronzino, and that no sculptor in Venice was an artist of the magnitude of Titian. In Florence Cellini, and Cellini alone, was capable of the imaginative act that forms the prerequisite of living portraiture, but in this field as in others his opportunities were too restricted to enable him to realise all of his potentialities. Another reason was the nature of the High Renaissance portrait. The Early Renaissance portrait bust, Rossellino's Antonio Chellini or Benedetto da Majano's Pietro Mellini, is the confidential record of a private individual. The High Renaissance sculptured portrait, on the other hand, is more often than not a public affirmation, the portrayal of an office-holder not as he was but as he wished to be. This view of the portrait as an icon was entertained with particular rigidity in Medicean Florence, and was deeply incompatible with serious portraiture.

On two occasions Andrea Sansovino, in a rather simple-minded fashion, embarked on portrait sculptures. Jacopo Sansovino, who later emerged as a great portraitist, seems not to have made any portraits before he moved to Venice, but in Florence his contemporary Francesco da Sangallo was intermittently concerned with portraiture from 1522 until his death in 1576. His medium was the medal, but the medal in deep relief treated in a manner which leaves us in no doubt that it could only have been modelled by a large-scale sculptor. Sangallo was a heavy, insensitive artist, and when his image was enlarged, it lost in life-likeness and in intensity. The most striking of his portraits occurs on the Marzi monument in the Annunziata (1546), where the effigy (Plate 55) is built up from enumerative detail, and is treated with the same pathetic emphasis as figures in paintings by Pontormo. Pontormo's portraits also supply a point of reference for Francesco da Sangallo's portrait bust of Giovanni dalle Bande Nere in the Bargello (Fig. 119). Representing its subject in half-length with the arms severed at the elbows, it belongs to a class of bust initiated by Verrocchio's Lady with the Primroses (Vol. II, Pl. 77).

Sangallo's bust offers a criterion of judgement for Bandinelli's Medicean portraits. Bandinelli was not a realistic portraitist; for him the portrait was an ideal image, which preserved only the general aspect of the sitter's face. The head of his statue of Giovanni dalle Bande Nere in Piazza San Lorenzo (Fig. 120) is, for example, several degrees further from reality than Sangallo's bust. The originator of the ideal portrait was Michelangelo. Writing in 1544, Niccolò Martelli declared that Michelangelo did not depict Giuliano and Lorenzo de' Medici 'as Nature had portrayed and composed them, but rather gave them a size, proportion and beauty . . . which he thought would bring them greater praise.' This theory was fundamental for the portrait sculptures of Bandinelli. When Cosimo I moved to the Palazzo Vecchio in 1540, he was urged by Bandinelli to perpetuate the memory of himself and of his forebears in sculpture, as had been the custom in antiquity. The result was the so-called Udienza (Fig. 86), a raised platform for public audiences at one end of the Sala Grande, with niches containing statues of Pope Leo X, Alessandro de' Medici, Giovanni dalle Bande Nere, and the reigning Duke. The secular figures wear classical armour, and are represented as historical abstractions not as living individuals. This was acceptable enough for the figures which belonged to history, but the inadequacy of the head of Cosimo I was apparent even to the members of his court; it did not, they protested, resemble the Duke in any way, and eventually the sculptor cut it off, with the intention of replacing it. Vasari tells us that when he was criticised for his incompetence, he defended himself by referring to the excellence of an earlier portrait he had made of Cosimo I. Ironically enough this earlier bust (Plate 68), which is now in the Bargello, also looks like a head cut from a statue; the cuirass terminates abruptly below the chest, and the arms are cut off below the shoulders, the left arm being slightly raised, so that if it were continued it would project like the left arms of the statues in the Udienza and the left arm of Francesco da Sangallo's Giovanni dalle Bande Nere. Where the bust differs from the statues is that Bandinelli carved it with greater pains; it forms indeed the high-water mark of his achievement as a marble sculptor. In particular the structure of the jaw and cheek-bone is rendered with great subtlety. But the notion that the portrait should reflect the living man would have struck the sculptor as heretical, and his bust, for all its skill, evades the challenge of the sculptured portrait.

Cellini's bust of Cosimo I (Fig. 121, Plate 69) illustrates not merely a different style, but a different notion of the role of portraiture. Writing after the bust was exiled to Portoferraio, he tells us that it was modelled in clay in the goldsmiths' workshop of the Palazzo Vecchio, and adds the deprecatory sentence: 'My sole object in making it was to obtain experience of clays suitable for bronze casting.' But if ever there was a portrait in which the sculptor's interest and imagination were wholeheartedly engaged, it is this bust. Cellini was a court artist whose self-realisation was contingent upon patronage, and a great part of his *Life* deals with his relations with his patrons, those semi-divine beings whose disfavour spelt frustration and whose favour represented opportunity. At the time that he left France he was planning a colossal apotheosis of Francis I as Mars on a fountain at Fontainebleau, and the first task that occupied him after he reached Florence was a bust of his new master, not quite so large but still on an appropriately over life-size scale.

One distinctive feature of Cellini's bust is the treatment of the base. Its form is roughly semi-circular, and it is not finished off symmetrically, like Bandinelli's, but is handled in a way that suggests a body, and a body in movement, beneath. This effect is due in part to the cloak, which falls over the Duke's left shoulder and is caught up on his right arm. Bandinelli makes use of a conventional classical corselet of the type used by Michelangelo for the Giuliano de' Medici. Cellini, on the other hand, clothes the Duke in fantastic armour, decorated with a Medusa head. The neck of the corselet is circular; in this it recalls the suits in which Cosimo I is depicted by Bronzino, but with the close-fitting neck piece removed. This was an aesthetic device, designed to obviate the flatness of Bandinelli's bust. The keynote of the head is action. The locks of hair are not trained forwards and down, as they are by Bandinelli, but are swept back as though by movement, and the knitted brows, drilled eyes and tightened lips give an effect of ferocious momentary concentration that is far removed from the petulant, rather feminine expression captured by Bandinelli. That this proceeds from Cellini's conception of the portrait can be seen from a letter he addressed to Cosimo I in 1548, in which he declares that the bust meant more to him than did the Perseus, and that 'in accordance with the noble fashion of the ancients, there is given to it the bold movement of life'.

The only other bust that Cellini produced is a portrait of Bindo Altivoti in Boston (Fig. 122), which was made in Florence a few years after that of Cosimo I. To judge from a medal of Altoviti struck about the middle of the century this was a speaking likeness, and an effect of actuality is arrived at by precisely the same means as in the earlier bust. Again the base is asymmetrical, again a cloak is used to indicate the volume of the body and its continuance beneath the bust, and again the head is represented in arrested movement, as though interrupted in the act of speech. The tremulous beard and parted lips reveal the same aspirations as the blood spurting from the severed neck of Medusa in the Perseus. The bust makes its impact through the vitality of its detail, and this was observed by Michelangelo. 'My dear Benvenuto,' he wrote when he had seen it, 'I must tell you that Messer Bindo Altoviti took me to see his bust in bronze, and informed me that you had made it. I was greatly pleased with the work, but it annoyed me to notice that it was placed in a bad light; for if it were suitably illuminated, it would show itself to be the fine performance that it is.' Cellini was always an unlucky artist, and nowadays at Fenway Court the bust is even less well lit than when it stood in Bindo Altoviti's house.

This search for liveliness impaired Cellini's value as a court portraitist. Brilliant as was his bust of Cosimo I, it was not how the Duke wished to look. Better the impassive mask clamped on to his features by Bandinelli and Bronzino, better the porphyry reliefs of Tadda than this extravagant, ebullient portraiture. If Poggini, who likewise was a goldsmith and medallist, felt called to follow in Cellini's footsteps when he carved the portrait of Francesco de' Medici in 1564 (Fig. 123), he resisted the temptation, conforming instead to the frigid idiom of Bandinelli, but replacing the classicising corselet with contemporary military costume. The employment of contemporary dress as a means of imposing a linear pattern on this portrait and on the charming bust of Virginia Pucci Ridolfi in the Bargello (Fig. 124) reflects the influence of Bronzino, though the heads are, by Bronzino's standard, relatively inarticulate.

Giovanni Bologna seems to have felt little interest in the portrait bust. He had, as is proved by the equestrian statue of Cosimo I, a gift for portraiture, but the idealist trend in his artistic make-up invariably led him in the completed work to deprive the life image of its authenticity. This occurred with the bust of Francesco I de' Medici carved from his model for the Palazzo Corsi, with the marble bust of Ferdinand I over the door of his own house in the Borgo Pinti, and most signally with the bronze bust of Ferdinand I in the Bargello, which must have been modelled at about the same time as the far more vivid head of the equestrian monument in the Piazza dell' Annunziata (Fig. 137). The bulk of the portrait commissions in the last quarter of the century went instead to Bandinelli's pupil, Giovanni Bandini, who carved the statue of Francesco Maria della Rovere in the Palazzo Ducale in Venice as well as a number of Medicean portraits, and to Giovanni Caccini, who produced a statue of Francesco I de' Medici in the Palazzo Vecchio and a quantity of stolid private busts. Fundamentally both sculptors remained faithful to the generalised portrait style of Bandinelli. The heads of Pietro Tacca's two statues in the Cappella dei Principi (Plate 97), on the other hand, are modelled with disconcerting individuality, and they suggest that Tacca, had he curbed a journalistic tendency to over-statement, might have become a major portrait sculptor.

By far the most prolific and experienced Tuscan portrait sculptor of the High Renaissance was Leone Leoni. His introduction to portraiture was through the medal, and in 1537 in Padua he completed an engraved portrait of Bembo, which was judged by Aretino, Sansovino and Titian to be much superior to the medal of Bembo by Cellini. 'I shall never believe,' wrote Aretino to Leoni, 'that Bembo is insufficiently clear-sighted to discern the difference.' In Milan the vision of imperial portrait sculptures that had long dangled before Leoni's eyes was translated into fact. In 1549 during a short visit to Brussels, he prepared life-size busts of the Emperor and of his sisters, Mary of Hungary and Eleanora of France, and these were later cast in Italy. From the portrait bust it was an easy transition to the portrait statue, and by the middle of September he had agreed to make for Mary of Hungary 'effigies entières de bronze'. In 1551, at Augsburg, he again for a few months rejoined the imperial court. Back in Milan, Leoni assiduously worked up the portraits he had taken during these brief visits, and by 1555 these resulted in the full-length statues of Charles V restraining Fury (Fig. 141), Philip II of Spain, the Empress Isabella, and Queen Mary of Hungary (Plate 106) which are now in the Prado in Madrid. All these statues resulted from life study except that of the Empress Isabella, which was based on a posthumous painting by Titian, and they form an equivalent in sculpture for Titian's imperial portraits. But the portrait statue was a cult image, and not simply a likeness, and when we compare Leoni's figure of Philip II of Spain with

Fig. 131. Ammanati: OPS.
Palazzo Vecchio, Florence.

Fig. 132. Poggini: PLUTO,
Palazzo Vecchio, Florence.

Fig. 133. Stoldo Lorenzi: AMPHITRITE.
Palazzo Vecchio, Florence.

Fig. 134. Bandini: JUNO,
Palazzo Vecchio, Florence.

Fig. 135. Aspetti: MARTYRDOM OF ST. DANIEL. Duomo, Padua.

Fig. 136. Roccatagliata: ALTAR FRONTAL. S. Moisè, Venice.

the great portrait in the Prado which Titian executed at precisely the same time, we find that it is lacking in all the psychological refinements that Titian commands with such success. This was not due to incapacity, for the medal of Martin de Hanna, the friend of Titian, is there to confirm Aretino's and Titian's confidence in Leoni's talent as a portraitist. It resulted rather from the deliberate suppression of some of the legitimate objectives of portraiture. The most impressive of the statues as a work of art is the Mary of Hungary, which is treated more naturalistically than the rest and relies for its effect on a strongly characterised pose, not on elaborate chiselling. There is nothing in these statues to suggest Leoni's deep and constant interest in the antique. He appears, however, to have had a special interest in Roman busts of the type of the Commodus in the Palazzo dei Conservatori (Fig. 126), which is cut off at the waist, and is raised on an allegorical base with two small figures of provinces. From this or from some similar bust he evolved the half-length portraits of Charles V (Fig. 125) and Philip II in Madrid, which also taper down to figurated plinths.

On two other occasions the giant personality of Titian impinged upon the sculptured portrait. On the first the sculptor was Guglielmo della Porta and the subject was Pope Paul III, a patron who had no predisposition towards conventionalised portraiture. The earlier of the two busts of the Pope carved by Guglielmo della Porta (Plate 101) seems to date from 1546-7, and when he made it he was almost certainly familiar with the portrait of the Pope which Titian had painted at Bologna in 1543. Titian's painting could not be translated into terms of sculpture, but it provided an interpretative standard which Guglielmo della Porta successfully imposed upon his bust. A profoundly truthful head, formulated like the head in Titian's painting, is framed in a great yellow cope inlaid with allegorical reliefs. What resulted is one of the noblest sculptured portraits of the sixteenth century. The Pope's family, and perhaps the Pope himself, were sensitive to the frailty of his appearance in the last years of his life – Titian's portrait group of 1546 was apparently left incomplete on that account – and when the sculptor came to model a seated figure for the Pope's tomb, he invested it with a synthetic animation that diminishes its value as a portrait. In Rome Guglielmo della Porta's successor was Bastiano Torrigiani, whose three bronze busts of Pope Sixtus V (Plate 134) are the most penetrating portrait sculptures produced in Rome between the death of Paul III and the advent of Bernini.

Guglielmo della Porta can have encountered Titian no more than briefly in 1546, but in Venice from 1527 on Titian's infinitely rich and complex style supplied a background to the sculptures of Sansovino. In the portrait his indebtedness to Titian is particularly marked. Initially it can be traced in the six heads projecting from the border of the bronze door in St. Mark's (Fig. 113), which include portraits of Titian and Aretino and a self-portrait of the sculptor, built up impressionistically with a minimum of surface working. Only once did Sansovino experiment with a life-size portrait in the same style (Plate 116). Modelled in 1554, it forms part of the Rangone monument (Fig. 116), where, among the properties from a Venetian painting, a table and tablecloth, books, reading-desk and astrolabe, there is set the greatest and most elevated High Renaissance sculptured portrait.

Sansovino's pupil Cattaneo, though an efficient portrait sculptor, was lacking in interpretative weight. The finest of his portraits is the marble bust of Bembo, carved in 1547 as the central feature of Sanmicheli's Bembo monument (Fig. 108). Girolamo Campagna was a conventional portrait sculptor, and from the fifteen-sixties on the world of portraiture was dominated by Vittoria. Vittoria's extrovert bronze portrait of Rangone in the Ateneo Veneto (Plate 124) is very different from Sansovino's. Whereas in Sansovino's statue the planes are rendered smoothly and merge as they do in life, in Vittoria's bust the cheek bones are accentuated, so that they divide the cheek and the area beneath the eye into two sharply differentiated planes, while the treatment of the eyelids gives the eyes an illusory sense of depth, and the dome of the forehead is accentuated by the furrows which confer on so many of Vittoria's sitters an aura of wisdom and maturity.

Vittoria's modelled portraits are much superior to his marble busts. Among Venetian painters his sympathies lay with Palma Giovane, but the artist of whom he most forcibly reminds us in his portrait sculptures is Tintoretto, not only in the vigour with which the externals of character are rendered, but in his repeated recourse to formulae. Vittoria's are in the full sense of the term official portraits; his sitters are shown in their civic character, and on their faces are stamped the virtues they respected, prudence, sagacity and self-control. In Venice there was a vast demand for portrait busts, and Vittoria was nothing if not a prolific sculptor. The secret of his productivity was that the bodies of his busts were almost invariably conventionalised. In a few cases, of which the most notable is the Niccolò da Ponte in the Seminario Arcivescovile (Fig. 117), the majestic head has its corollary in sweeping folds of cloak, but these busts are exceptional, and their quality makes us all the more resentful of the blunted artistic conscience which led so gifted a sculptor to reject the portrait as an integrated work of art.

THE BRONZE STATUETTE

As a boy Michelangelo worked with the bronze sculptor Bertoldo, but neither then nor later did he share Bertoldo's enthusiasm for the making of bronze statuettes. The impediments to his doing so must have been twofold, that the medium of bronze was uncongenial, and that the natural movement of his mind was on a bolder scale. As a result he exercised no direct influence on the growth of the small bronze in the sixteenth century. Instead the deity who presided at its birth was Leonardo da Vinci, whose style is reflected in a number of small bronzes of horses and riding figures (Fig. 127). These bronzes have often been associated with the two equestrian monuments on which he worked in Milan, but their true reference is to the studies for the fresco of the Battle of Anghiari in the Palazzo Vecchio. The insecure stance and splayed rear legs of these little horses occur repeatedly in the drawings for the fresco but never in those for the two monuments, and the conclusion is inescapable that the statuettes were made in Florence about 1508. This was the time when Leonardo was collaborating with Gian Francesco Rustici on the bronze group of the Preaching of the Baptist over the entrance to the Baptistry, and it is possible that the statuettes were a by-product of that work. The poses are fascinating, but the horses are cast models rather than small bronzes in their own right.

The same objection may be raised to the only small bronze based on a sketch by Michelangelo. The sketch was made about 1530 for the projected group of Samson and two Philistines, and the small bronze derived from it is wrongly ascribed to Pierino da Vinci (Fig. 128). How faithfully the model is reflected in the bronze we cannot tell, but for all the ingenuity with which it was adapted, the group that resulted is unmistakably a study for a larger statue and not a genuine bronze statuette. In this it differs from the single authenticated statuette by Tribolo, which dates from 1549. Showing a small figure of Pan seated on a vase (Plate 58), it impresses us at first as a miracle of spontaneity, and only when we look down from the smiling head to the oval base, with the legs disposed diagonally across it in counterpoint to the elbows above, do we notice the hard thinking that has gone into its seemingly innocent scheme. Tribolo after 1534 was working under the heavy shadow of Michelangelo, and there is something truly Michelangelesque in the structure and modelling of this bronze. It is an anti-climax to pass from Tribolo's small tribute to Michelangelo to the protests against his style that were committed to the small bronze by Bandinelli. The principles that Bandinelli advocated in his statuettes (Fig. 129) are the same as he proclaimed in marble on a larger scale. Sometimes the feet of his figures are retracted, sometimes they are advanced, but always the body is set flat across one plane, a linear theorem without physical reality. Bandinelli was a more successful artist on a small scale than on a large, but the concepts he translated into bronze none the less make an under-vitalised impression beside the work of Tribolo and of Cellini.

Our knowledge of Cellini as a maker of bronze statuettes is derived from the base of the Perseus, where there are four niches with bronze figures of Danae, the hero's mother, with the boy Perseus at her side, of his father Jupiter (Fig. 47), and of his benefactors, Athena (Fig. 48) and Mercury. These figures form Cellini's first excursion into this field. In France he was commissioned by the King to make twelve silver statues of Gods and Goddesses, of which four were modelled, and one, a Jupiter, was finished in 1544. The Jupiter beneath the Perseus is treated with the precision of a practised metalworker, and it perhaps reflects the lost Jupiter for Fontainebleau. The same thought may cross our minds with the figure of Athena, where the vacant head and the modelling of the breasts and shoulders closely recall a drawing for the Juno that Cellini made in France. It may indeed have been the wish to utilise the models for the silver figures that led him to the innovation of statuettes let into the Perseus base. In the statue above, his mind turned to Donatello, and in the base it reverted to the prophets in niches on Ghiberti's Gate of Paradise. Ghiberti's figures were reliefs, not statuettes, but from them Cellini learned one valuable trick, the raised arm that links so many of Ghiberti's figures to the rounded surface of the niche. The four statuettes are modelled with extraordinary refinement – above all the Danae, which is one of the most beautiful nude figures of its time – and they carried a message for the future, for when Vasari decided that the Studiolo of the Palazzo Vecchio should be decorated with bronze statuettes, his source of inspiration was Cellini's Perseus base.

Work started on the Studiolo in 1570, a year before Cellini's death. One of a series of apartments planned by Vasari, it was intended to house a collection of precious and semi-precious objects 'such as jewels, medals, engraved gems and crystal, vases, instruments, and other similar things of moderate size, kept in cupboards each according to its kind.' Its programme was referred by Vasari to Vincenzo Borghini, the Prior of the Innocenti, who replied that in his view 'the whole invention should be dedicated to Nature and Science, and should include statues of those who were discoverers or causes, or (as the ancient poets believed) teachers and guides to the treasures of Nature.' The matter used by Nature in its operations consisted of the four elements, and one element should be depicted on each of the four walls. Provision had been made for two niches on each wall, and the four Elements had therefore to be represented by four pairs of statues. The two niches for Earth, declared Borghini, should be filled with 'the statue of Pluto, not the brother of Jupiter but another of the same name, believed by the poets to be the god of Wealth', and with a figure of Earth 'or Ops as she is called'. Water must be represented by two female figures, Venus and Amphitrite, and Air by Juno 'who was considered by the ancients mistress of the air', and Boreas, 'who would be a winged youth with a piece of crystal in his hand, since it solidifies with great cold.' Lastly Fire should be represented by Apollo, 'master of light and warmth, a beautiful youth', and Vulcan 'to stand for the hard metals such as steel and iron, in the working of which fire is a main agent.' Borghini's proposals were approved by Francesco de' Medici, and drawings were then made of the eight figures. They were submitted to Borghini, who protested that the wrong god Pluto was portrayed and that the male representative of Air was now Zephyr and not Boreas. The first of these mistakes was rectified, but the Aeolus or Zephyr was retained – the difficulty of designing a bronze figure holding crystal may well have appeared insurmountable – and Amphitrite was shown not as a mermaid but as a nymph. Where such pains were taken to impose a uniform programme on the figures, it might be supposed that an effort would also have been made to instil a common style. Each sculptor, however, consulted his own preferences. Giovanni Bandini's Juno (Fig. 134) derives from the small bronzes of Bandinelli, and the practice of Bandinelli is reflected once more in the heavy Vulcan of Vincenzo de' Rossi. Stoldo Lorenzi, in the Galatea (Fig. 133), avoids the clumsy frontality of these two figures with a form of elementary contrapposto, and Poggini represents the Pluto (Fig. 132) striding forwards in its niche. As niche figures all these are much inferior to the statuettes beneath the Perseus. Two more considerable sculptors applied their minds to the figures as silhouettes. One was Ammanati, who in the beautiful bronze of Ops (Fig. 131) adapted a classical model that he had previously used for a marble figure intended for the Palazzo Vecchio, and the other was Vincenzo Danti, who brought to his Venus Anadyomene (Plate 78) the sinuous grace of the Salome over the south door of the Baptistry.

The most beautiful of the eight figures is the Apollo (Plate 79), where we are confronted not with an aggregation of mannerisms but with a positive canon of design. On one side, with marvellous ingenuity, a firm vertical is constructed from the tree-trunk, lyre and left forearm, and on the other, opposing it, are the relaxed curves of the human form. The artist of the Apollo is Giovanni Bologna, the supreme exponent of the High Renaissance bronze statuette. As we look at Giovanni Bologna's small bronzes, we have the sense that, after the turmoil and stress of the middle of the century, the ship has come safely into shore. The clouds have dispersed, and the sun pours down on an unashamedly hedonist art. Perhaps the proportions of these ideal figures differ a little from those of figures as we know they are, yet they have an innate lifelikeness, a sensuality that marks them off from Ammanati and Danti, indeed from Cellini himself. Giovanni Bologna's bronzes have no programme; his favourite motif, a woman drying herself with a towel, is almost as uncommitted, as lacking in emotional overtones, as the ballet dancers of Degas. He was the first great advocate in sculpture of the doctrine of significant form, and so well founded was his faith and so consistent was its application that, from the time when they were made, his statuettes have never varied in their appeal. Long after the Renaissance was at an end, copies of his large statues found their way to Wrest Park and to Queluz, and among small bronzes the little Venuses that are not Venuses, the Rapes that are not Rapes, the Mercuries who bear no message, are the best-sellers of all time. For that reason they sometimes look a little tired and stale to us to-day. But there is a vast difference between Giovanni Bologna's ideas as they were realised by his assistants, and Giovanni Bologna's ideas as he presented them himself, and when we look at his few autograph bronzes, we find that at his touch the forms ignite.

Riccio, the great master of the Early Renaissance bronze, was active in Padua until 1532, and had a counterpart in Venice in Camelio, the author of a number of etiolated classicising statuettes. But after 1527 the style of both sculptors was superseded by that of Sansovino. There are not many autograph bronze statuettes by Sansovino. The finest of them, a Jupiter in Vienna (Plate 118), has the same flexibility of pose as the Mercury on the Loggetta, and is modelled with the classical precision of the Christ on the tabernacle door cast for St. Mark's (Plate 115). None the less, Sansovino, through the statues on the Loggetta, dominated the Venetian statuette. Without these figures the small bronzes of Campagna, of Aspetti, and even of Vittoria would have assumed an entirely different form. No less rare than Sansovino's are the small bronzes of Cattaneo, who in the Fortuna in Florence (Plate 119) and the Luna in Vienna develops the figures of the marble relief on the Loggetta and the bronze reliefs on the Loredano monument into free-standing statuettes. Evincing the feeling for material that distinguishes Venetian High Renaissance painting, Cattaneo's bronzes are modelled with a voluptuous warmth that is never met with in the middle of the sixteenth century in Florence.

Bronze sculpture in Venice in the later sixteenth century is dominated by four artists. The first of them, Campagna, produced a quantity of staid, undistinguished statuettes, none of which attains the animation of his monumental sculptures. The second is Tiziano Aspetti, a mellifluous sculptor who devised a hieroglyph for the female figure that found its way on to countless doorknockers and into countless statuettes. Where Campagna was by temperament a large-scale artist, Aspetti was most at ease in works of modest size, and the sculptures he made for the altar of the chapel of St. Anthony at Padua are little more than expanded statuettes (Plate 132). The appeal of his bronzes is due as much to the richness of their facture as to the interest of their design. The third sculptor was the Genoese Roccatagliata, a more complicated and ambitious artist who was admired by Tintoretto. The statuettes of putti by which he is generally known are by no means his best works. His treatment of the human form is less constricted than Aspetti's, and in the ecstatic, swaying figure of St. Stephen in San Giorgio Maggiore (Plate 133) he breaks with the idiom of Sansovino, and reveals a zest for movement that offers a foretaste of baroque.

The fourth sculptor is Vittoria. In the small bronze, as in other fields, Vittoria is an unequal artist. Unlike his master, Sansovino, he had not been trained in the hard school of Florentine makers of free-standing statuary, and the small bronze, which of its very nature was free-standing, brought him face to face with problems he could not evade. He seems to have set special store by the figure of St. Sebastian (Plate 126) which he carved for San Francesco della Vigna in 1563, a small homage to Michelangelo in the Raphael-dominated cosmos of Sansovino. In 1566 he prepared a bronze reduction of this figure, and nine years later, in 1575, he made another, which was preserved in his studio and is mentioned in his will. One of these statuettes is now in the Metropolitan Museum in New York, and in it Vittoria makes a painstaking attempt to transform a statue with one face into a free-standing statuette. The development in his conception of the statue between the early St. Sebastian and the figure of the same saint in San Salvatore (Plate 127) is reflected in turn in the small bronze. Here the main document is the splendid figure of St. John the Baptist on a holy-water basin in San Francesco della Vigna (Plate 130), where the torso is modelled with unwonted energy and the pose is fully circular.

Vittoria made a number of small bronzes at this time, but only in one of them were all his sluggish faculties aroused. It shows Neptune stilling the waters to protect the Trojan fleet (Plate 131), and it has the dynamism of a figure from the Sistine ceiling cast in bronze. Rising not from the circular base that imposes a uniform pattern on so many of Vittoria's small sculptures, but from an oval base formed by a shell floating on the waves, the figure is set lengthwise, one foot in front and one behind, with a sea-horse between its legs. The effect of this design is remarkable enough when the bronze is looked at from the sides, but still more astonishing is its front view, where the heads of Neptune and the sea-horse appear in profile, turned on opposing axes, and the sweeping gesture of the right arm registers to the full. More unambiguously even than the marble St. Sebastian in San Salvatore, this statuette proclaims the imminent emergence of Bernini.

THE EQUESTRIAN STATUE

IN 1496 Verrocchio's Colleoni monument was unveiled in Venice, and ten years later, in Milan, Leonardo started work on the second of his equestrian statues. From these beginnings it might be supposed that the sixteenth century would leave behind it a large number of equestrian monuments, but it did not do this. From time to time we hear of projects for mounted statues – in 1546 Leoni sought permission to make one of the Emperor Charles V – but none was carried through, and the first significant commission for such a monument dates from 1587, ninety-nine years after Verrocchio's death and ninety-one years after the completion of the Colleoni statue.

The motive power behind the earlier equestrian monument was generated in North Italy, but the sculptors were invariably Florentines, and it was in Florence, under Medicean patronage, that the making of equestrian statues was resumed. A sign of interest in the riding commemorative figure occurs in 1539, when Cosimo I de' Medici married Eleanora of Toledo, and the nuptial decorations included a figure of Giovanni dalle Bande Nere on a horse twelve braccia high by Tribolo standing on a base painted by Bronzino. But more than forty years go by before we hear of any scheme for an equestrian monument in bronze. The first mention of it occurs in 1581 in a letter to the Duke of Urbino describing the commissions with which Giovanni Bologna was busy at the time. Giovanni Bologna, says this letter, impelled by a thirst for glory, is carving a three-figure group, the Rape of the Sabines, to be placed near the Judith of Donatello, and is planning, for a position opposite the David, a horse twice the size of the horse on the Campidoglio. The term used to describe this work, *un cavallo Traiano*, is ambiguous, but the reference to the Marcus Aurelius statue suggests that what was contemplated was an equestrian monument, and not just a colossal horse. Presumably the monument was approved by Francesco de' Medici, but it was commissioned only under his successor, Ferdinand I. It was to represent the founder of their dynasty, Cosimo I, and Bernardo Vecchietti, Giovanni Bologna's earliest Florentine patron, was named as supervisor of the work.

The statue of Cosimo I (Plate 90) was the first equestrian monument to be made in Florence, and Giovanni Bologna approached the task with even more than his usual deliberation. Projected in 1581 and commissioned in 1587, it was not unveiled till 1595. As the term *cavallo Traiano*, which is used of the project in its earliest stage, and the nomination of Vecchietti as its supervisor might lead us to expect, the statue derives from the antique. In the fifteen-fifties, when he first came to Rome, Giovanni Bologna had studied the Marcus Aurelius. He was by no means the first sculptor to do that – in the fifteenth century Donatello had studied it before him – but the conditions in which he looked at it were new. It was no longer in its informal setting outside St. John Lateran, but since 1538 stood where Michelangelo had placed it, on the Capitol (Vol. II, Fig. 84). This change of site affected its artistic character. By virtue of its new position in the centre of the Campidoglio it became a symbol of imperial rule, and when in 1565 it was placed on the base that Michelangelo had planned for it almost twenty years before, it was elevated into a great work of art. For Giovanni Bologna, therefore, it was not the paragon of naturalism that it had seemed to Donatello, but a supreme commemorative monument, and when he began his preparations for the statue of Cosimo I, he was at pains to set it on a base that was recognisably related to Michelangelo's, and to maintain the same relationship between the riding figure and the plinth. For that reason, too, his attitude towards his model was more respectful than that of his predecessors in the fifteenth century; his horse's head curves outwards to the right, the right foreleg is raised, and the left rear hoof is suspended above the base. But his horse is not a servile copy of that in Rome. Through countless statuettes he had obtained a thorough understanding of the mechanism of the horse, and in connection with the statue he modelled an écorché bronze horse which is now in the Palazzo Vecchio. The relevance of the riding figure of the Emperor to that of Cosimo I was naturally less close. Giovanni Bologna none the less seized upon one feature of the mounted figure that had been ignored by both his predecessors, the long line of cloak that falls diagonally back on to the rear quarters of the left side of the horse. The cloak worn by Cosimo was necessarily short, but in the statue it is artificially extended by means of the scabbard at his side. The purpose of the statue was to immortalise the virtue and wisdom of the first of the Medici Grand-Dukes, and in its setting in the Piazza della Signoria it has a moral significance that is recognisably related to that of the statue on the Capitol.

The statue has a smoothness and a continuity of line that no equestrian monument had possessed before, and hardly was it finished than it became an archetype. In 1601 Giovanni Bologna started work on a statue of the Grand-Duke Ferdinand I, which was completed in 1608 by his pupil Pietro Tacca and installed in the Piazza dell'Annunziata (Fig. 137). This was an inversion of the earlier statue. In 1604, when this work was still incomplete, came a demand for an equestrian statue of Henry IV of France for the Pont-Neuf in Paris, and this was erected in 1611 by Francavilla, who modelled four bronze prisoners for its base (Plate 95). Two years later, in 1606, there followed a request from Spain, which resulted in 1616 in the statue of Philip III of Spain which was set up by Tacca in the Plaza Mayor in Madrid. The horses of both statues derived from that of Ferdinand I.

From these facts alone it might seem that Giovanni Bologna and his pupils had a monopoly of equestrian monuments, yet when the authorities of Piacenza decided to erect twin statues to the reigning Duke of Parma, Ranuccio Farnese, and to his father, Alessandro, in 1612, they turned not to Tacca or to Francavilla, but to another Tuscan sculptor, Francesco Mochi. The reason for this was that Mochi, as a youth of twenty-three, had attracted the notice of Mario Farnese, Duke of Latera – 'a boy I have had the good fortune to light on,' says Farnese in a letter, 'who seems to me the equal of all the younger artists' – to whom he owed his first important commission, for a marble group of the Annunciation at Orvieto (completed 1609). Mochi's concern lay with the rendering of movement; his Annunciatory Angel

Fig. 137. Giovanni Bologna: STATUE OF FERDINAND I. Piazza Annunziata, Florence.
Fig. 138. Pietro Tacca: STATUE OF PHILIP IV. Madrid.

Fig. 139. Mochi: STATUE OF RANUCCIO FARNESE. Piazza Cavalli, Piacenza.
Fig. 140. Mochi: STATUE OF ALESSANDRO FARNESE. Piazza Cavalli, Piacenza.

Fig. 141. Leone Leoni: CHARLES V RESTRAINING FURY. Prado, Madrid.
Fig. 142. Leone Leoni: FERRANTE GONZAGA TRIUMPHANT OVER ENVY. Piazza Roma, Guastalla.

Fig. 143. Gian Giacomo della Porta: ALTAR OF THE APOSTLES. Duomo, Genoa.

sweeps down to earth, and his Virgin Annunciate shrinks back as though alarmed at the sound of the descent. This concern with movement dictated his attitude to the equestrian monument. Whereas in Giovanni Bologna's movement is no more than implied, in Mochi's Ranuccio Farnese (Fig. 139) it is explicit: the right foreleg of the horse presses down into the void at one end of the plinth, and the head is shown with frothing mouth turned to the right, and is balanced at the back by the huge curving tail. Giovanni Bologna's equestrian monuments are not mentioned in the documents relating to the statue, but in March 1616, after the horse was modelled but before it had been cast, Mochi, with the permission of his patron, visited Padua, to see the Gattamelata monument, and Venice, to study the bronze horses on St. Mark's and Verrocchio's Colleoni statue. What he saw did not affect his horse, but it may have influenced the riding figure which he modelled soon afterwards, in that the Duke is shown like Gattamelata with a baton in his raised right hand, and like Colleoni has his head turned outwards to the left.

This powerful and imposing monument was unveiled in November 1620, to the sound of a salute fired by musketeers, and Mochi thereupon directed his energies to the second statue. The first monument portrayed the living Duke, and was subject to considerations of decorum and life-likeness, but the second (Plates 162, 163, Fig. 140) was posthumous and was accordingly less circumscribed. It was stipulated in the contract that the horses should correspond, and the head of the second horse is for this reason turned to its left not to its right, and the tail sweeps out on the right side. By strict representational standards the horse is a little grotesque, but its long mane blowing in the wind and partially concealing the riding figure is a striking dramatic device, which is enhanced by the treatment of the cloak, folded across the rider's shoulder and blowing out behind, as though the Duke were represented on the battle-field caught up in a storm. The difference in the characterisation of the two figures is borne out by the reliefs beneath; those on the statue of Ranuccio Farnese are allegories of good government and peace, while those on the statue of Alessandro Farnese illustrate military scenes.

Mochi's wild, romantic statues have more than a little in common with the portraits of Rubens, and it was Rubens who was responsible at second hand for the last decisive step in the development of the equestrian monument. The proof of this is contained in a letter written by the Count-Duke of Olivares to the Florentine ambassador in May 1634, expressing a wish to commission a statue of the King, Philip IV, 'conforme a unos retratos de Pedro Pablo Rubens.' In Florence the request was referred to Tacca, who had carried out the statue of Philip III in Madrid, and by 1636 he had completed a small model of the statue and a large terracotta model of a pacing horse. But as soon as news of these reached Spain, it transpired that they were not what the King and the Count-Duke required. Instead they envisaged a horse in the act of galloping or rearing, with both its forelegs off the ground. To Tacca this problem was no novelty. Between 1619 and 1621 he had made a bronze equestrian statuette of Charles Emmanuel of Savoy with its two forelegs free (*con gambe dinanzi alzate in atto di corvettare*). Nothing daunted by the difficulty of translating it to a full scale, Tacca requested that two paintings by Rubens, a small canvas of the King on horseback and a life-size head, should be sent to Florence. Probably the paintings he received were not originals by Rubens (who had left Madrid in 1636), but there can be no doubt from the sources that a painting by Rubens supplied the inspiration of the pose. The horse was cast in the course of 1639, and Tacca then busied himself with the riding figure, which must have been in large part complete by January 1640 when the second portrait of the King, in the light of which the features were to be modelled, arrived in Florence. In September 1640, shortly before Tacca's death, the statue was shipped to Spain, where it was erected in October 1642 by Ferdinando Tacca (Fig. 138). Tacca's biographer, Baldinucci, echoing the opinion of experts in manège, complained that the pose of the horse was ambiguous, but for the skill the sculptor showed in maintaining its equilibrium there was undivided praise, and in the eighteenth century it was this splendid work that inspired the last great equestrian statue, Falconet's Peter the Great at Leningrad.

BERNINI AND THE BAROQUE STATUE

GIAN Lorenzo Bernini was born in Naples in 1598. At that time Giovanni Bologna in Florence was completing his Hercules and the Centaur, and Vittoria in Venice was carving the St. Sebastian in San Salvatore; Campagna's altar in San Giorgio Maggiore in Venice and Fontana's Assumption in Santa Maria presso San Celso in Milan had been in existence for respectively three and thirteen years. In the year of his birth, therefore, in a number of different centres, sculptors whose styles were incompatible and who were not necessarily acquainted with each other's work, as though carried forward by a single impulse, were experimenting with the rendering of the human body in movement in the round. Whether it be Hercules in desperate conflict with the Centaur, or St. Sebastian writhing in agony against the column, or the Evangelists crushed by the imaginary weight of a huge globe, or the Virgin journeying towards heaven, the sculptures depict a transitory state. Bernini was the predestined agent by whom this tendency was welded into a coherent, universal style. Baldinucci, his biographer, describes how, as a boy, he was presented to Pope Paul V. The Pope, Baldinucci tells us, was so much impressed with Gian Lorenzo's promise that he ordered Cardinal Maffeo Barberini to supervise his work. 'Let us hope,' he exclaimed, 'that this youth may become the great Michelangelo of his century.' Bernini did not become a Michelangelo – his talent was more facile, and his spiritual horizon was more limited – but he grew up to exercise a greater influence on the art of his own time than any sculptor had exercised before.

Not since the youth of Michelangelo was the training of a sculptor scrutinised with such expectancy. His technique was learned in his father's studio, but his taste and his ambitions were directed by patrons determined to ensure that the great monuments of contemporary painting were supplied with an equivalent in sculpture. Foremost among them was Cardinal

Fig. 144. THE FAÇADE OF S. MARIA PRESSO S. CELSO. Milan.

Fig. 145. Guglielmo della Porta: TOMB OF POPE PAUL III. St. Peter's, Rome.
Fig. 146. Guglielmo della Porta: TOMB OF CARDINAL PAOLO CESI. S. Maria Maggiore, Rome.

Fig. 147. Giacomo della Porta: TOMB OF LUISA DETI ALDOBRANDINI. S. Maria sopra Minerva, Rome.
Fig. 148. Domenico Fontana: TOMB OF POPE NICHOLAS IV. S. Maria Maggiore, Rome.

Fig. 149. Domenico Fontana: TOMB OF POPE SIXTUS V. S. Maria Maggiore, Rome.
Fig. 150. Domenico Fontana: TOMB OF POPE PIUS V. S. Maria Maggiore, Rome.

Fig. 151. Flaminio Ponzio: TOMB OF POPE CLEMENT VIII. S. Maria Maggiore, Rome.
Fig. 152. Flaminio Ponzio: TOMB OF POPE PAUL V. S. Maria Maggiore, Rome.

Fig. 153. Cordieri: ST. GREGORY THE GREAT. S. Gregorio al Celio, Rome.
Fig. 154. Pietro Bernini: CHARITY. Monte di Pietà, Naples.

Fig. 155. Ippolito Buzio: THE CORONATION OF POPE PAUL V. S. Maria Maggiore, Rome.
Fig. 156. Pietro Bernini: THE CORONATION OF POPE CLEMENT VIII. S. Maria Maggiore, Rome.

Scipione Borghese, whose enlightened taste embraced the work of Reni and Caravaggio and who commissioned Domenichino's Diana at the Chase. Of Bernini's early secular groups one was made for the garden of the Villa Montalto, where it rose above a pool surrounded by Roman statues; three were made for the Villa Borghese, where they stood, as they still do to-day, among antiques; and one was installed in the Villa Ludovisi among the Roman sculptures which are now in the Museo delle Terme. During the time that he was working on them, Bernini was also engaged upon the restoration of antiques – the Borghese Herm-aphrodite and the Ludovisi Ares are two of the works that he restored – and his earliest sculptures are invariably constructed round a classical motif. In the Pluto and Proserpine an antique fragment determined the posture of the Pluto, in the Apollo and Daphne the Apollo was based on the Apollo Belvedere, and in the David, the least successful and most academic of the statues, the stance was inspired by the Borghese Gladiator in the Louvre.

More important than this borrowing of motifs is the fact that Bernini felt strongly drawn towards a type of Hellenistic sculpture represented by the Vanquished Gaul slaying his Wife which forms part of the Ludovisi collection in the Museo delle Terme (Fig. 158). This group is planned with one main and two subsidiary views, and its plinth is not a neutral area, like the plinth of Giovanni Bologna's Rape of the Sabines, but is treated as a stage on which the figures move. As narrative it is incomparably vivid, and appeals directly to the emotional responses of the onlooker. The body of the woman is precariously balanced, about to slump on to the ground, and blood spurts from a self-inflicted wound in the throat of the standing warrior as he looks across his shoulder at an unseen foe. If we pass directly from this group to the Pluto and Proserpine (Plate 140) which Bernini carved for the Villa Ludovisi, we shall find first that it is built up in the same way, second that the plinth is also treated spatially, and third that it makes use of precisely the same narrative device; Proserpine cries vainly to the unseen figure of her mother Ceres as she is lifted from the ground.

Like the antiques from which they were derived, Bernini's early sculptures were intended to be shown against a wall. They are fully finished off behind, but they depend for their effect on the presence of a background, and have a single dominant view. The earliest, the Aeneas leaving Troy (Plate 139), was set on a cylindrical base, the back of which was cut away so that it fitted to the wall. The front face of the statue is the face illustrated in this book. Its two secondary faces, at right angles to the wall, are wider and less compact; one of them shows Aeneas looking across his shoulder with, above him, the statues of the tutelary gods, and the other the profiles of Anchises and of the young Ascanius. With the Rape of Proserpine the dominant aspect is the widest view, and this is enriched by carefully worked out three-quarter views, and by side views from which only one figure can be seen. The Apollo and Daphne (Plate 142) likewise creates its full effect only from the front, the single view from which the long diagonal that runs back from the extended right hand of Apollo to the raised right arm of Daphne registers as the sculptor intended that it should. In the course of preparation of this book, the surprising fact transpired that the sculpture has not been illustrated from this view.

Not only were the groups placed against a wall, but they were shown close to the level of the eye. This set a premium on illusionism. Many years later, in conversation with Chantelou, Bernini touched upon this point. Michelangelo, he declared, was a greater architect than sculptor, because architecture consisted only in design; in sculpture he had never had the power to make his figures look like flesh, and they were beautiful only for their anatomy. The nature of Bernini's aspirations may have been determined by the blood pouring from the throat of the Dying Gaul, but by his early twenties his sleight of hand – as we can see it in the transparent tears coursing down the cheek of Proserpine and Pluto's fingers pressing into the soft surface of her thigh – was more accomplished than that of any Hellenistic artist. By temperament he was an illustrator; the form and subjects of his early groups may vary, but the intention behind all of them is uniform, to provide a visual embodiment of a literary text. Ovid's Pluto, like Bernini's, has been pierced by Cupid's dart, and is inspired by love, not lust. It is Ovid who describes the wind baring the limbs of Daphne and Apollo's hand feeling her pulse beneath the bark, and Ovid who pictures Triton rising from the water to sound his echoing conch as Neptune stills the flood. In the seventeenth century it was popularly held that painting was mute poetry. Bernini transposes this conception to the sister art of sculpture. In France he expressed his admiration for Poussin with the words *O il grande favoleggiatore*, and Poussin alone rivals the mythopoeic faculty, the gift for supremely sensitive narration, evident in his early groups.

The theory behind these groups was applicable also to religious sculpture, and in 1624, when the Apollo and Daphne was still unfinished, Bernini started work on a religious statue (Plate 143). The occasion was supplied by the discovery, in two glass receptacles, of the body of a martyred virgin, Santa Bibiana. The relics were inspected by the Pope – who, as Maffeo Barberini, had watched the carving of Bernini's early groups, and composed a distich for the base of the Apollo and Daphne – and on his instructions a statue of the Saint was commissioned for the church of Santa Bibiana from Bernini. Since the statue was to occupy a niche behind the altar, which was itself only a little higher than the nave (Fig. 162), the differentiated texture of the Borghese groups could be transferred to the new figure. Against the surface of the niche, moreover, contour could enjoy the same supremacy as in the earlier statues. What was lacking in the commission was the element of drama present in the mythologies, and this was rectified by a painted God the Father in the vaulting to which the Saint directs her eyes, and which explains the wondering gesture of her raised right hand.

Bernini might well have continued along the lines laid down by this restrained, subtle and incredibly proficient work. But fate decided otherwise, for the first artistic project that occupied Maffeo Barberini after his election to the papacy was the completion of St. Peter's, and his chosen agent was Bernini. Baldinucci tells the story of a visit paid to St. Peter's by Bernini as a boy in the company of Annibale Carracci. 'Believe me,' said Annibale Carracci

Fig. 158. Hellenistic, second century b.c.:
GAUL KILLING HIS WIFE IN FACE OF AN ENEMY.
Museo delle Terme, Rome.

Fig. 157. Bernini: DAVID. Galleria Borghese, Rome.

Fig. 159. Bernini: LONGINUS. St. Peter's, Rome.

Fig. 160. Bernini: NEPTUNE AND TRITON.
Victoria and Albert Museum, London.

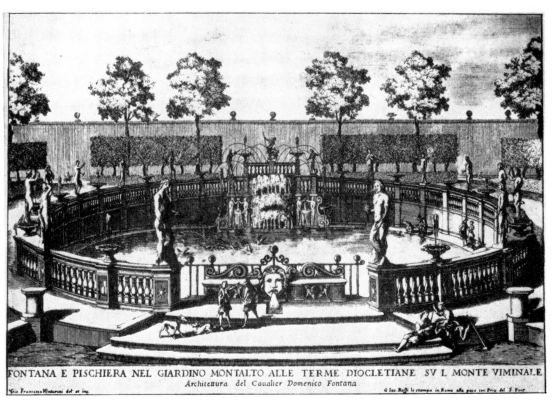

FONTANA E PISCHIERA NEL GIARDINO MONTALTO ALLE TERME DIOCLETIANE SV I. MONTE VIMINALE
Architettura del Caualier Domenico Fontana.

Fig. 161. Venturini: ENGRAVING OF THE PESCHIERA IN THE GARDEN OF THE VILLA MONTALTO.

on this occasion, 'a prodigious genius is still to come who will make, here beneath the cupola and there in the apse, two huge piles proportionate to the dimensions of this church.' To which Bernini replied, like Radamès in the opera *Aida, O fussi pure quello io*. In the summer of 1624 he received his first commission for the church, for a bronze baldacchino to replace the baldacchino set up by Paul V over the high altar, and in 1628, on the Pope's orders, he turned his mind to the piers beneath the cupola. This resulted in the commissioning of the Longinus and three companion figures for the niches in the piers. The significance of Bernini for St. Peter's falls outside the purview of this book. It can be argued that he was the only genius capable of furnishing the spaces of the church as they deserved. It can also be argued that his sympathies with Renaissance art were so restricted, and his creative processes so emotive and unintellectual, that he was temperamentally unfitted for the task. There can be no doubt, however, as to the significance of the commissions for Bernini. They transformed him from a sculptor of human dimensions to a sculptor of superhuman size; they precluded all the subtleties with which his earlier works were filled; and they compelled him to adopt a style which would be legible at a great distance from the eye. In short, they forced him to assume a scenographic attitude towards sculpture.

Of the four colossal statues in the piers beneath the cupola one, the Longinus (Fig. 159), was executed by Bernini, and two were allotted to sculptors with established reputations, the St. Veronica to Mochi (Plate 161) and the St. Andrew to Duquesnoy (Plate 160). The fourth and weakest of the statues is by Bernini's pupil Bolgi. Had the plan been set in motion a few years later, this figure might have been entrusted to Algardi, a Bolognese who had arrived in Rome in 1625, but who was still an unknown quantity in 1628 as far as large-scale sculpture was concerned. Duquesnoy's St. Andrew was the first of the statues to be begun. A Fleming, Duquesnoy was associated throughout the whole of his career in Rome with the rigid classicism of Domenichino and Poussin, and his St. Andrew reads like a figure by Domenichino invested with a third dimension and magnified. According to Bellori, whose sympathies lay with Duquesnoy rather than Bernini, it shows the Saint 'with head raised in the act of gazing up to heaven; behind his shoulders is the cross formed from two tree-trunks. He caresses one of them with his right hand, and stretches out his open left hand in token of divine love in the glory of his martyrdom.'

Mochi's St. Veronica is less placid and less refined. Based on a Niobid figure, it shows the Saint moving forwards, open-mouthed as though announcing the tidings of the miracle, with the veil held out in her excited hands. The most novel feature of the statue is its insecurity of stance, and it was attacked by another classicising critic, Passeri, on that account. Its motion, declared Passeri, was that of running; it was not stable and immobile, as statues ought to be, but showed a passer-by who would not stop. If the noun statue derived from the verb 'stare', argued Passeri, the figure violated one of the essential principles of statuary. Nowadays we would criticise the Veronica not for its movement, but for the haphazard relation between the statue and its niche, and the standard of our criticism would be the

Longinus of Bernini. Owing to their size, none of the statues could be carved from a single marble block. None the less, the Veronica is posed by Mochi in the same constricted fashion he would have adopted had he been carving a smaller figure from one block. The Longinus, on the other hand, is represented in an open pose, with arms outstretched across the niche, gazing up at an imaginary Christ; the drapery no longer clings to the contours of the body but is disposed with great bravura and audacity in a manner that is overtly rhetorical. In both respects the statue marks a break with the Hellenism of Bernini's early groups, and introduces a new view of religious sculpture as drama and of the statue as relief.

The motives which led Bernini in this and later works to explore the dramatic possibilities of sculpture are not difficult to reconstruct. He was a devout man, but his character, so far as we can judge, was free of the least trace of introspection. In his sculptures after the Longinus he remains the inspired illustrator of the mythologies, but the stories he recounts are hagiographical. He retained his interest in illusion, though the emphasis now shifted from surface illusion to illusion of a more far reaching kind. His object was to build up a convincing image not of the real world but of a world of unreality. The point at which this change occurs coincides with the emergence of his interest in the stage. While engaged on the Longinus, he was devising the celebrated sunrise for the comedy *La Marina* and was producing the *Inondazione del Tevere* with its famous depiction of a flood. This theatrical experience reacted on his sculptures, not in the sense that the sculptures became meretricious, but that he tended to invoke theatrical devices to perpetuate transitory effects. The supreme instance of this is the work which he himself regarded as the finest that left his studio, the Ecstasy of St. Teresa (Plates 150, 151, Fig. 163).

For the St. Teresa Bernini built not a simple aedicula flanked by paired columns and pilasters like that in Santa Bibiana, but a protruding polychrome tabernacle containing an elliptical stage. The stage is lit from above, and the daylight directed on the scene is given a celestial character by means of coloured glass, and metal rays which pour down on the vision of the Saint. Stendhal complained that the language of the group was that of profane love, and the relation between the Saint and Angel is indeed almost embarrassingly physical. But the analogy with profane love is implicit in the Saint's own narrative, and in their coloured marble tabernacle against a rich brown ground Bernini's figures take on a visionary quality that is perfectly consistent with the Saint's account of her own mystical experience. Just as the early groups mark the ne plus ultra of mythological narration, so the St. Teresa represents the climax of Baroque religious narrative.

In 1646, while the chapel for which the St. Teresa was designed was being built, but before the two figures were begun, Bernini embarked on a secular counterpart, an allegorical two-figure group. It represented Truth unveiled by Time, and only one of the two figures, the Truth (Plate 152), was carved. Most of what we know of Bernini's intentions for the Time derives from a conversation that he had in France. He proposed, he said, to depict Time flying through the air, and underneath to illustrate the consequences of its passage, in the form of mausoleums and broken columns. Without these supports, he added jokingly, his Time would never fly, even though it were supplied with wings. Drawings prove that the figure of Time would have been shown in profile, holding a scythe, and that the drapery veiling the Truth would have been caught up in his right hand. As we see it in the Borghese Gallery to-day, the Truth is difficult to read. Her drapery, which would have been suspended from the second figure, stands up stiffly like an obelisk, and with her left hand she makes a gesture of surprise which becomes meaningful only when we remember that her naked form has been unexpectedly disclosed, and that her face is turned towards her deliverer. Had it been completed, the allegory would have corresponded exactly with the St. Teresa; its subject is momentary action, it has the character of a relief, and once more it is planned with a single view. Bernini intended the group for his own house. There is no evidence as to how he proposed that it should be displayed, but he may have intended to supply it with an architectural setting, and with its own illumination, in this case a window on the right.

Lest we should feel disposed, as from time to time we may, to question the validity of these devices, it is as well to examine the predicament of sculptors who rejected them. The most notable of them was Bernini's rival Algardi, who under Innocent X enjoyed a brief period of preferment at the papal court. The first works that Algardi carried out in Rome, two stucco statues in San Silvestro al Quirinale, are carefully meditated figures, the style of one of which derives from the Santa Bibiana of Bernini. But thereafter the two sculptors parted company. Algardi was an earnest, rather convention-ridden artist, who felt no temptation to break down the accepted categories of statue and relief. Of the two altars for which he was responsible one, in St. Peter's (Plate 167, Fig. 165), is executed in relief, and the other, at Bologna (Plate 168), is composed of two free-standing statues. In both cases transitory action forms the subject of the scene. At Bologna the figures of St. Paul and his executioner are placed beneath an open tabernacle, and can be inspected from the back and sides as well as from the front. The kneeling figure of St. Paul represents Algardi's work at its impressive best, but the executioner, shown with sword raised above his shoulder, fails to transmit the tension which the artist intended to convey. Algardi's second altar, which shows Attila cowering beneath the vision of St. Peter and St. Paul, was a substitute for an unfinished painting, and is one of the very largest reliefs that has ever been produced. The forward figures are carved almost in the round, but their effect is irretrievably impaired by static figures in the background, and only when we look at the altar across the whole width of the transept are we aware of the effect Algardi was endeavouring to create. Just as the nerveless figures of the Bologna altar explain why Bernini concentrated on a single viewing point and disregarded the conventional free-standing statue, so the altar in St. Peter's explains why he turned his back on the conventional relief.

The supreme achievement of Bernini the magician is the second of the two colossal works he executed for St. Peter's, the Cathedra (Fig. 166, Plates 154, 155). This project grew from comparatively simple origins. Under Urban VIII a new installation was devised for the relic of St. Peter's Chair, and throughout the reign of his successor this was preserved. But no sooner was Bernini's patron Fabio Chigi elected to the papacy than it was decided to move the relic to the apse. The case for this change was a double one; it was doctrinal in so far as the relic formed a natural climax to the relics housed beneath the cupola and to St. Peter's tomb, and it was visual in so far as it offered an excuse for a monumental structure in the apse, the need for which Annibale Carracci had pointed out half a century before. The site selected was the central niche, which was flanked by the tombs of Pope Urban VIII and Pope Paul III. According to Bernini's initial plan (Fig. 167), the relic was to be installed inside the niche behind an altar, and was to be physically supported by four statues of the Doctors of the Church. This scheme was thought out in relation to the papal tombs, and the architecture of the niche therefore remained intact. But the niche was visible through the baldacchino, and by 1658 the logical inference was drawn, that the Cathedra must be conceived in relation to the baldacchino, not the tombs. The altar was accordingly brought forward, so that the foremost Doctors of the Church stood free of the flanking columns; the throne was represented as though mystically suspended in the air and was surmounted by two putti bearing the tiara; and the architecture of the upper part was neutralised by a pair of kneeling angels above the capitals and by a glory of rays between them. From this plan there emerged the Cathedra as we know it now. The whole structure, and not merely the forward figures, was set free of the columns, was broadened out, so that the niche became invisible, and was raised, so that the glory at the top penetrated to the level of the capitals of the great pilasters in the apse. This final change was achieved in two stages, not one, for when in 1660 a wooden model of the structure was set up, it was found to be too small, and the sketches which had been made for the angels beside the chair and for the Doctors of the Church had thereafter to be enlarged. Throughout this last phase in the evolution of the scheme, scenographic considerations were dominant, and the work was thought of as what it still remains to-day, the culminating feature of the church.

As Bernini's ambition swelled, the Cathedra outgrew not simply its architectural setting, but the accepted categories of design. It contained, in the foremost Doctors of the Church, figure sculpture of great distinction, and on the throne were three reliefs, but in its totality sculptural considerations played a secondary part. The glory of angels, part bronze, part stucco, belongs in the realm of theatrical production, not of sculpture, and the device of the dove on an oval of amber-coloured glass, striking as it must have seemed when it was planned, has no enduring significance. Bernini's temperament and his imagination, his facility and his ability to improvise, offered a constant temptation to expand beyond the scale fitted even to his own gigantic talents, and for all its brilliance and originality the Cathedra is, as design, fatally diffuse. There can be no question of the seriousness with which Bernini approached his task, but what resulted is something less than a great work of art.

In the Cathedra Bernini the sculptor is temporarily obscured by Bernini the magician, but as he aged it was the sculptor who came once more to the fore. Work on the Cathedra was no more than begun when his attention was diverted to a second papal project, the Chigi Chapel in the Duomo at Siena. This work was carried out by the same assistants as the Cathedra – it was supervised by the painter Giovanni Paolo Schor, its bronzes were cast by Artusi, and two of its four marble sculptures were by Raggi and Ercole Ferrata – but Bernini made the models for two statues and himself carved one of them, a St. Jerome. Of the four niches in the chapel two beside the altar are visible from the body of the church, while two beside the entrance can be seen only from inside. It might have been expected that the artist of the Cathedra would reserve the altar niches for his own statues, but he chose instead to fill the niches on the entrance wall. In his youth he had looked upon the niche as a containing frame, but by the sixteen-fifties he considered it a background and nothing more. The implications of this change are already evident in the Chigi Chapel in Santa Maria del Popolo, where he filled the pre-existing niches with obstreper-ous figures of Daniel and Habakkuk that bulge out of their setting and violate the architectural scheme. In Siena there were no alien elements. The devout figure of St. Jerome (Plate 156) emerges from its niche as though from the entrance to a cave, and the architecture is twice broken on the right by the Saint's fluttering drapery and his extended hand.

In one subsequent commission this pattern recurs. In 1667 Alexander VII's successor in the papacy, Clement IX, intent upon leaving his own mark on the Roman scene, chose as his sphere of operation the principal bridge across the Tiber, the Ponte Sant'Angelo. His plan was to provide it with a balustrade, to remove the classicising stucco figures of Raffaello da Montelupo which had been placed there by Paul III, and to instal instead ten marble angels holding the instruments of the Passion. Bernini was the stage director of this enterprise, and the individual figures were allotted to sculptors in his orbit, but as at Siena he retained control over two statues. In 1669 the Pope inspected them, and gave instructions that copies should be substituted for them on the bridge, and to this we owe their preservation in Sant'Andrea della Fratte. Baldinucci describes how Bernini in old age, whenever he was not engaged in architectural projects, would work tirelessly till seven in the evening on his marble sculptures, with a boy beside him to ensure that in a moment of abstraction he did not tumble off the scaffolding. 'Let me be, I am in love,' he would reply when he was asked to rest, and such was his concentration that he seemed to be in ecstasy. It appeared, says Baldinucci, that the force to animate the marble was projected from his eyes. Before the Angels in Sant'Andrea delle Fratte all this is credible. One of them, the Angel with the Superscription (Plate 157), is fully autograph, while the other, the Angel with the Crown of Thorns, is in part by the same hand as the Magdalen at Siena, but both spring from a single impulse, and they speak to us, not with the boisterous egotism of the dramatist and the designer, but with the humble voice of the dedicated marble sculptor.

In these works the tide of drama which had carried forward so many of Bernini's earlier sculptures ebbs, and when in 1671 he began work on his last great sculpture, the Death of the Beata Lodovica Albertoni (Plate 158), he rejected the flamboyant idiom of the St. Teresa, and cast it in a more restrained, more tranquil style. The scene is again set above the altar, and is again supplied with its own source of light, but the setting is now relatively simple, and at the back there is a painted altarpiece. Bernini's subject, the moment when the Saint's soul leaves her body, has more in common with the *Metamorphoses* illustrations of his youth than with the sculptures of his middle years, and the fact that the statue was intended to be shown almost at eye level enabled him to treat the surface with a softness and delicacy that recall the early groups. No longer was it necessary to force the figure forward on to a single plane, and instead it could be planned, like the Borghese groups, as an image that was fully in the round. Bernini himself set no store by the concept of 'style of old age'. Confronted in France with a late work by Poussin, his only comment was that 'at a certain age one must stop work-ing.' But the Beata Lodovica Albertoni, which was carved when he was almost eighty, is treated with a mellowness and a disdain of ostentation that would have been unthinkable at any earlier time. It is on this sublime figure rather than on the St. Teresa that his claim to be accepted as the peer of the very greatest Italian artists must ultimately rest.

BERNINI AND THE PAPAL TOMB

AFTER the rebuilding of St. Peter's only two papal monuments were set up in the church. The first and more remarkable was Guglielmo della Porta's tomb of Paul III, which was moved in 1587 to the south-east niche beneath the cupola. The second, the tomb of Gregory XIII by Prospero Antichi, was demolished in the eighteenth century. A much less distinguished work, it conformed to Guglielmo della Porta's tomb in so far as its main feature was a seated statue of the Pope with two reclining figures on volutes at his feet. These tombs were joined in 1621 by Pollajuolo's monument of Innocent VIII (Vol. II, Fig. 71), reconstituted in accordance with the dictates of contemporary taste, with the seated statue of the Pope set over the sarcophagus.

In 1627, when it was decided to fill the niches beneath the cupola with statues, it became necessary to move the tomb of Paul III, and this roused in the reigning Pope an interest in his own tomb. The Sistine and Pauline Chapels in Santa Maria Maggiore had been erected as funerary chapels during the lifetimes of the Popes from whom they derived their names, and it was natural that Urban VIII, who had contributed so much to the interior of St. Peter's, should be commemorated there. At first the two projects were distinct; it was proposed to install the tomb of Paul III in a niche on the right side of the tribune opposite the papal throne, and to build a monument for Urban VIII between the tribune and the altar of St. Leo nearby. But before long they merged, and it was ruled that the tomb of Paul III should be installed in a niche on the left of the tribune, not the right (the reason for this was that the seated figure would otherwise have looked into the apse), and that the tomb of Urban VIII should fill the right-hand niche. Bernini was the instrument by whom this change was brought about.

Bernini seems to have modified the tomb of Paul III (Fig. 145) in two respects; he increased its height, so that the head and shoulders of the effigy projected above the cornice of the niche, and he increased its width, so that the two allegories, instead of being close together in the centre of the base, were opened out. The effect of these changes was to transform the tomb into a triangle or pyramid, and this form was in turn imposed on the tomb opposite. If the two monuments were to correspond, the mediums used by Guglielmo della Porta – bronze for the statue of the Pope and marble for the supporting figures – must also be employed in the new tomb. The style of Guglielmo della Porta's figure sculptures was uncongenial, and for his papal portrait type Bernini turned back to the tomb of Gregory XIII. A drawing made before this tomb was destroyed proves that it showed the Pope with right hand raised and his left arm extended beneath his cope, in a pose that forms a precedent for that adopted by Bernini. The allegories on the tomb of Gregory XIII were set on volutes like those of Guglielmo della Porta, but their bodies were shown erect above the hips. From such figures it was only a short step to the standing Virtues of Bernini's tomb. If, however, the Virtues were to be shown standing, it was necessary to fill the space between them, and this led Bernini to introduce a feature that was present in neither of the earlier tombs, a sarcophagus in the form of an ornamented variant of the tomb-chests in the Medici Chapel. This had the advantage that the allegories could be shown leaning against its ends, so that their bodies fell along the sides of the notional triangle round which the tomb was planned.

It is wrong, however, to think of the tomb of Pope Urban VIII (Plate 146) as the outcome of a single inspiration. It was commissioned in 1627, was still unfinished when the Pope died in 1644, and was not completed till 1647, twenty years after it had been begun. The magnificently virile figure of the Pope was cast in 1631. The group of Charity, though blocked out in 1634, was not carved till after 1639, and work on the Justice did not start till 1644. While therefore the statue of the Pope dates from the period of the baldacchino, the two Virtues stand on the threshold of the Truth Unveiled and of the St. Teresa. The Justice is a relaxed figure, animated only by its profuse drapery, but the Charity (and in this it is typical of the time at which it was produced) is planned as a dramatic group, in which the attention of the female figure is momentarily caught by a child clutching at her skirt. A wooden model for the sarcophagus was prepared in 1630, but the form of the epitaph was not decided on till 1639, so that this also belongs to the dramatic world of Bernini's middle age; it shows a bronze skeleton inscribing the Pope's name in a book placed asymmetrically on the plinth. From this time too date the Barberini bees climbing up the base.

It was one thing to decide that St. Peter's should be adorned with tombs, another to discover persons who could be suitably commemorated in this way. One such was the Countess Matilda, the eleventh-century benefactress of the Holy See, and in 1633 the Pope sent to Mantua for her bones. Bernini's tomb of the Countess Matilda (Fig. 164) is a perfunctory work. In a statement of 1644 he claimed to have made models for all the figures, and to have carved certain of the marbles, but his models were in the main entrusted to assistants, and the tomb is lifeless in handling and relatively undistinguished in design. It includes one innovation of importance, a trapezoidal relief on the sarcophagus. Hardly was it begun than this feature was taken over in the second supererogatory monument put up in the church, the tomb of Pope Leo XI who had reigned for just under a month in 1605. The Leo XI monument (Plate 166) is the first important work by Alessandro Algardi. Algardi approached his task in a less imaginative spirit than Bernini. He resisted the use of coloured marble and the mixed mediums of the Urban VIII tomb. The niche in which his monument is set is faced in white, and the tomb itself consists of three white marble figures and a white marble sarcophagus. He rejected the buoyant visual rhythms of Bernini's Virtues. His own figures of Majesty and Liberality stand erect against the edges of the niche, and one of them is based on a classical Athena in the Museo delle Terme for whose restoration he had been responsible. To the classical theorists of the Seicento Algardi seemed superior to Bernini because he was more orthodox, but the tomb of Leo XI is in fact a sadly uninventive work. None the less its influence was very great, for like all academic art it could be imitated, and its effects were felt as late as the middle of the eighteenth century in the tomb of Pope Benedict XIII.

Not till the last years of the reign of Alexander VII was Bernini again engaged upon a papal monument. He was almost seventy at the time, and Domenico Bernini tells us that he agreed to undertake the tomb 'on account of his gratitude to the memory of this prince . . . notwithstanding his age and the decline of his strength which made him daily less capable of such work.' Where the Urban VIII monument belongs to a traditional tomb type, the monument of Pope Alexander VII (Plate 147) is conceived as an apotheosis. In its early stages there was some doubt as to the destination of the tomb. At first it was intended for St. Peter's, but the architectural aspirations of Alexander VII's successor, Clement IX, centred upon Santa Maria Maggiore, and he devised a plan for reconstructing the choir of the basilica and installing in it his own and his predecessor's monuments. Fortunately he died before this barbarous scheme was realised, and his successor, Clement X, transferred the tomb once more to St. Peter's where it was completed in 1678 shortly before the sculptor's death. Unlike the Urban VIII tomb, which is contained within the framework of its niche, the tomb of Alexander VII has no specifically architectural character. When he designed it, Bernini had the experience of the Cathedra behind him, and to it he brought the same preconceptions. The area of the niche is treated like a stage, and the four supporting allegories are disposed in depth, like the Doctors of the Church below the Cathedra, with Charity and Truth in front and Justice and Prudence in half-length at the back. In the centre of the stage on a high plinth is the statue of the Pope, represented not in a conventional seated posture as a temporal ruler, but kneeling in an attitude of prayer. Praying statues were adopted in Santa Maria Maggiore for the tombs of Sixtus V and Paul V, and the decision to portray Alexander VII in the same way is a survival from the time when his monument was destined for this church. Over the front of the stage falls a Sicilian jasper shroud; Bernini intended that the Truth in the right foreground be shown naked enveloped in its folds. At the back of the niche was a door, which was brought forward and incorporated in the tomb, and from it there emerges a bronze skeleton placed immediately above in the centre of the shroud.

Fig. 163. Bernini: THE CORNARO CHAPEL. S. Maria della Vittoria, Rome.

Fig. 162. Bernini: HIGH ALTAR. S. Bibiana, Rome.

Fig. 164. Bernini: MONUMENT OF THE COUNTESS MATILDA. St. Peter's, Rome.
Fig. 165. Algardi: THE MEETING OF ATTILA AND POPE LEO THE GREAT. St. Peter's, Rome.

Fig. 166. Bernini: THE CHAIR OF ST. PETER. St. Peter's, Rome.
Fig. 167. Studio of Bernini: DRAWING FOR THE CHAIR OF ST. PETER. H.M. The Queen, Windsor Castle.

The conception of the tomb is incomparably vivid, and might have given rise to one of the very greatest sepulchral monuments. But the merit of Bernini's sculptures is inseparable from the work he did on them himself, and though he made small models for the figures – two of them survive – he left their execution to other hands. The only areas in which he may himself have intervened are in the hands and forehead of the Pope. The statue of the Pope was entrusted to Michele Maglia assisted by two other sculptors; the Charity, the least insensitive of the supporting figures, was allotted to the Sienese Mazzuoli; the Truth was begun by Lazzaro Morelli and the Prudence by Giuseppe Baratta, and both were finished by Giulio Cartari, who also carved the Justice. It would be unreasonable in these circumstances to expect the sculptures to attain a significant level of expressiveness, and there remains a gulf between the monument as a celestial idea and the monument as earth-bound fact.

BERNINI AND THE BAROQUE FOUNTAIN

THROUGH the later sixteenth century the influence of Florentine fountain design spread southwards. In Sicily, where Montorsoli's fountains at Messina were already a familiar sight, a third Florentine fountain (Fig. 168) was installed in 1573. It had been commissioned in 1550 by Don Pedro da Toledo, the father of Eleanora of Toledo and the father-in-law of Cosimo I, for his villa outside Florence. Owing to the death of Tribolo it was entrusted to a minor sculptor, Camilliani. Two years after it had been begun, Don Pedro da Toledo himself died, and work was suspended till 1570, when the six hundred and fifty odd pieces of the fountain were bought from Don Garzia da Toledo by the city council of Palermo for use in the Piazza Pretorio. The fountain was added to in 1573, and there is some doubt as to which pieces formed part of the original, but one of them certainly was the central element, a shapely but uninspired derivative from the Tribolo fountains at Castello.

In Rome fountain design was the preserve of architects, not sculptors, and fountains were thought of mainly in architectural terms. Even the beautiful fountain at Loreto was originally planned (1604) by Fontana and Maderno without figure sculpture. In a few exceptional fountains a sculptural component was envisaged from the start. This was the case with the Fountain of the Tortoises (Fig. 169), the most distinguished Roman fountain of its time, which resulted from collaboration (1585) between Giacomo della Porta and the Florentine sculptor Landini. It is a work of great elegance and charm, in which the architecture and the figure sculpture coexist but are not satisfactorily merged. In the most elaborate of the fountains of Domenico Fontana, the Fountain of Neptune which was planned for a position near the Arsenale in Naples and is now in Piazza Bovio, the figure sculpture is again ancillary to the design. Among the artists who worked on this fountain was Pietro Bernini (1600–1). Gian Lorenzo Bernini undertook no fountain sculpture before the early sixteen-twenties, but by some strange coincidence his earliest fountain group was imposed upon a setting by Fontana, an oval pool known as the Peschiera or Peschierone designed in 1579–81 for the garden of the Villa Montalto (Fig. 161). Built on the Viminal, the pool was cut into the hill, and was surrounded by a balustrade with a row of antique statues. The statues were a rather heterogeneous company – they included two Mercuries, an Apollo, two Roman emperors and some fauns – and had little in common save their psychological detachment from the pool. It was for this setting that Cardinal Montalto, the nephew of Pope Sixtus V, commissioned the Neptune and Triton in London (Fig. 160). For Bernini, fresh from the Borghese David, the commission offered an occasion to plan a figure which would perform an active role in relation to its site. He was working at the time on the group of Apollo and Daphne, which was drawn from the *Metamorphoses*, and a passage from the *Metamorphoses* supplied him with the inspiration for his fountain group. It describes how, after the flood, Jupiter orders the sea to be recalled. 'Then Neptune,' writes Ovid, 'called to the sea-god Triton, who rose from the deep . . . (and) bade him blow on his echoing conch-shell, and recall waves and rivers by his signal. He lifted his hollow trumpet, a coiling instrument which broadens out in circling spirals from its base. When he blows upon it in mid-ocean, its notes fill the furthest shores of east and west. So now too the god put it to his lips . . . and blew it, sending forth the signal for retreat as he had been bidden. The sound was heard by all the waters that covered earth and sea, and all the waves which heard it were checked in their course.' The water entered the pool from the high ground at the further end, and there, on a rocky plinth, Bernini depicted Triton blowing his conch-shell at Neptune's bidding, and the sea-god thrusting his trident downwards as he controlled the waves.

At only one place was the Roman fountain in the sixteenth century freed from the pedantic pattern imposed on it by Lombard architects. This was the Villa d'Este at Tivoli, where Ippolito II d'Este, before his death in 1572, planned or commissioned a whole series of fantastic fountains. The most widely publicised, the Water Organ, was begun in 1568, and in 1572 played to the delighted ears of Pope Gregory XIII. Its counterpart at the opposite end of the terrace, a Fountain of Neptune, in which Neptune was to be depicted driving a chariot with four sea-horses across the water, was never built, but in 1567 work started on the Fountain of Rome, which had as its centrepiece a reconstruction of the ancient city by Ligorio, and in 1569 there was built the Lane of the Hundred Fountains, adorned with stucco reliefs from the *Metamorphoses* and twenty-two stone boats. The fountains at Tivoli supply the background to the first independent fountains designed by Bernini. The most remarkable of these, the Fontana dell'Aquila in the Villa Mattei (1629), has been destroyed, but we know from engravings that it was set against a cliff, and consisted of a shallow, shell-like basin supported by three dolphins. In the basin stood three upright scallop shells, and above them, as though alighting on the rock, was a colossal eagle with outstretched wings. Another fountain in the same garden showed a Triton in a round basin, and this prepared the way, in the mid-thirties, for a more ambitious work of the same kind, the Fontana del Tritone (Fig. 170). In the Neptune and Triton for the Villa Montalto sculpture and water were still treated, as they had been through the sixteenth century, as opposing elements. But in the Fontana del Tritone the barrier between them is broken down, and the whole body of the fountain becomes a natural form rising mysteriously from the water and liable once more to be submerged. The notion of architecture is abandoned, and the basin is a shell raised above the water by the united efforts of four dolphins, with, in its centre, a sea-god blowing on his conch. The effect of this change was to liberate not only the sculpture of the fountain but the water too. In a drawing at Windsor for the Fontana del Tritone (Fig. 171) we see an ideal water pattern for this fountain, with three powerful jets issuing from the conch, one thrown high into the air and the others pouring down in curtains of water at the sides. Water had a recurring attraction for Bernini. Years later in Paris, watching the water swirling under the Pont-Neuf, he complained of the meanness of the fountains at Saint-Cloud, and through his whole life he was fascinated by the possibility of using water to enhance the simulated movement of the sculpture with which it was juxtaposed.

The credit for harnessing Bernini's energies to a great public fountain belongs to Pope Innocent X, who after his election to the papacy in 1644 determined to improve the amenities of the Piazza Navona in which the palace of his family was set. In the centre of the square was a marble trough installed by Pope Gregory XIII, and the first thought of the Pope was to replace it with a fountain. For this purpose water was fed from the Acqua Vergine into the square. The designated architect of the new fountain was Borromini, who had been entrusted with the reconstruction of St. John Lateran in the preceding year. Meanwhile an event occurred which determined the form the new fountain would assume. This was the discovery near San Sebastiano of a colossal obelisk. One Thursday afternoon in April 1647 the Pope visited the obelisk, and decided to install it in the square. Contemporaries had no doubt of his motives in doing this; he was, they said, following in the footsteps of Pope Sixtus V, whose architect, Fontana, had erected the obelisk outside St. Peter's. From this visit there sprang the plan for a fountain crowned by an obelisk.

Bernini, as a Barberini protégé, was in disfavour with the Pope, and at first his name did not come into question for the commission. But at the suggestion of Prince Niccolò Ludovisi, a nephew by marriage of Innocent X, he made a model which was shown by a stratagem to the Pope. This model gained him the contract for the fountain, and re-established his relations with the papal court. If it was identical with an early model for the fountain that still survives, it showed the obelisk set on a rocky base, with pairs of seated figures lifting up the papal arms. In a drawing at Windsor (Fig. 173) which is probably a little later than this model the lifting motif is abandoned, and two seated figures are shown holding the papal shield with their arms lowered. But Bernini evidently felt that the function of the figures as supporters restricted the design. So in the final version (Fig. 174) the shields and figures were divorced, and the figures were shown lying down. This new scheme had two advantages; the figures could be set in a seemingly arbitrary fashion on the plinth, leaning outwards from the surface of the rock, and they could also be posed in such a way as to establish the circular horizontal rhythm that the base of so high a structure required. From the very first Bernini intended to pierce the rocky base. The transverse views of the piazza in which this resulted were of no consequence, and the significance of the device was rather in relation to the obelisk, which must seem to have no proper support and to be poised precariously on the rock. The four figures contribute to this illusion, above all the Rio della Plata, which is shown staring in wonder at the obelisk balanced above.

The programme of the fountain was constant from the first, for the four seated figures in the model, like the reclining figures which succeeded them, represent the four great rivers of the world. As they were eventually carved, they show the Danube, with a lion, the Nile (Plate 153), with its head covered by a cloth denoting the obscurity which for so long covered the continent of Africa, the Ganges, with an oar indicating the extent of its navigable waters, and the Rio della Plata, accompanied by coins symbolising the riches of America. Bernini did not work extensively on any of these figures, and for that reason they are not uniform in style. The Rio della Plata (which was entrusted to Francesco Baratta, who had worked with Bernini in the Raimondi Chapel in San Pietro in Montorio) and the Nile (which was entrusted to another Italian assistant of the master, Giacomo Antonio Fancelli) show a close understanding of Bernini's intentions, whereas in the Ganges (which was carried out by Claude Poussin) Bernini's model is assimilated to the static norm of French academism. Once the programme of the fountain was established, it was natural that the figures of the rivers should become the source from which the water springs. But here too Bernini's solution was a novel one, for the water gushes out irregularly from the rocks beneath the figures in broad streams which widen and enlarge the base, and play a structural part in the design.

After the Fountain of the Four Rivers was unveiled, attention veered towards the smaller fountain at the south end of the square. Designed in the late sixteenth century by Giacomo della Porta, it was roughly octagonal in form, with semi-circular projections filled by sculptured tritons on the four main sides. By the standard of the new fountain, its ground-plan was complicated, static and inert. We learn from a drawing that Bernini at one time considered reshaping it with a circular basin like that of the large fountain, and resiting the four tritons so that they corresponded with the four Rivers and were no longer set axially to the square. But for a variety of reasons, of which the most important was economy, this scheme was not proceeded with, and Bernini was allowed to do no more than supply the existing fountain with a new central element. The first proposal was for the papal insignia elevated in the centre of the fountain on a shell, but before long this was replaced by a design derived from the Fontana del Tritone, which showed a large shell raised vertically on the intertwined tails of three dolphins, with water cascading from the top. This design was carried out in marble – there is a payment of 1652 for *la Lumaca di Marmo retta da tre pesci* – and the shell was placed in the centre of the fountain. To the Pope's eyes it appeared too small, and Bernini was instructed to substitute a statue. He thereupon worked up a new scheme, recorded both in a drawing and a terracotta model, in which the fish from the base of the earlier design were supported on the shoulders of two tritons with their tails waving in the air. But this too failed to

Fig. 168. Camilliani: FOUNTAIN. Piazza Pretorio, Palermo.

Fig. 169. Giacomo della Porta and Landini: FONTANA DELLE TARTARUGHE. Piazza Mattei, Rome.

Fig. 170. Bernini: FONTANA DEL TRITONE. Piazza Barberini, Rome.
Fig. 171. Bernini: DRAWING FOR THE FONTANA DEL TRITONE. H.M. The Queen, Windsor Castle.

Fig. 172. Bernini: FONTANA DEL MORO. Piazza Navona, Rome.

Fig. 173. Bernini: DRAWING FOR THE FOUNTAIN OF THE FOUR RIVERS.
H.M. The Queen, Windsor Castle.

Fig. 174. Bernini: FOUNTAIN OF THE FOUR RIVERS. Piazza Navona, Rome.

Fig. 175. Bernini: POPE PAUL V.
Galleria Borghese, Rome.

Fig. 176. Bernini: COSTANZA BUONARELLI.
Museo Nazionale, Florence.

Fig. 177. Bernini: POPE URBAN VIII.
Prince Urbano Barberini, Rome.

Fig. 178. Bernini: CARDINAL SCIPIONE BORGHESE.
Galleria Borghese, Rome.

meet the Pope's requirements, and was replaced by a plan for a flat shell raised on dolphins with a large Neptune standing on the top. The objection to this solution was that it did nothing to correct, and may even have tended to exaggerate, the rigid symmetry of Della Porta's scheme. This danger was eliminated in the fourth design (Fig. 172), where a shell developed from the second project forms a platform for the central figure, which is posed in such a way as to invest the static basin with the illusion of circularity. A conceit from the third scheme is preserved in the fish writhing between the triton's legs and ejaculating water from its mouth. Bernini's concern is once more with instability, communicated in this case by the precarious balance of the shell, the fish lifted from the waters of the pool, and the animated figure of the sea-god revolving on its own axis with superhuman force.

BERNINI AND THE BAROQUE BUST

It might be supposed that Counter-Reformation Rome would offer a rich field for portraiture. Yet in practice there is no Roman equivalent for Vittoria's portrait busts, and little evidence of any wish to perpetuate the features of living individuals. Under Pope Sixtus V the continuing tradition of the papal portrait recaptured some of its vitality, but papal portraiture apart, the Roman sculptured portrait in the later sixteenth century is confined to faces peering down from circular or oval apertures in sepulchral slabs. Sometimes the faces are more lifelike and sometimes less, but scarcely ever do they achieve the status of a work of art.

The first sign of impending change occurred in 1605, when a portrait relief by a boy of seven was shown by his father to the new Pope, Paul V. Bernini a year before, had carved his father's portrait, and his interest in portraiture must have been coterminous with his awakening interest in sculpture. About 1617 he made his first independent sculptured portrait, a bust of Paul V in the Borghese Gallery (Fig. 175). Because of its small size – it is little larger than a statuette – the first impression of it is modest and undemonstrative. But as soon as we bend over it, we discover that it marks a break with the convention of the Roman portrait. The structure of the head is perceived with preternatural clarity, and below, the rumpled collar of the alb and the irregular edges of the cope invest it with a sense of movement that no bust carved in Rome had ever had before.

We know something of Bernini's theory of the portrait. If, he declared, a candle were placed so that it threw the silhouette of any person in shadow on the wall, the shadow could be identified, since in no two men was the head set on the shoulders in precisely the same way. The first task of the portrait sculptor was to seize this image (*le général de la personne*, as Chantelou transcribed it when he took this conversation down), and only later should he study his sitter in detail. The force of this doctrine can be seen in Bernini's caricature drawings, where the sitter's character is established by distortion of the silhouette. In the sculptured portrait, Bernini argued, faithful imitation would not alone produce a natural effect. The portrait sculptor was compelled, by his own terms of reference, to transpose a coloured model into monochrome, and just as a human face which had been whitewashed would be unrecognisable, so would his bust lack individuality unless he were sufficiently resourceful to redress the colourlessness of his medium by means of an empirical technique. To create an illusion of colour on the diversified white surface was therefore one of his prime tasks. When Bernini started work in Paris on the bust of Louis XIV, he observed that one side of the King's mouth was different from the other, and that there were differences also between his eyes and cheeks. The King's eyes, he commented, were lustreless, though that was no great disadvantage in sculpture, but his mouth was exceptionally mobile, and this made it necessary to study his head carefully, so as to seize the moment at which the features appeared at their most favourable. The point at which the features should be caught, he added, was when the lips tightened before speaking or relaxed from speech.

Bernini's conception of mobility was not restricted to the face. His son, Domenico, tells us that when he was engaged upon a portrait, 'he did not require that his sitter should stay still, but preferred that he should move and talk in his customary way, since in that fashion it was possible to see all of his qualities, and to depict him as he was. If he were motionless, he was less true to himself than if he moved, because movement revealed all those qualities which were peculiar to him and not to others, and which give authenticity to portraits.' A member of the French court who saw the King's bust when it was almost finished observed that though it had no arms or legs, it seemed to move, and Bernini certainly spared himself no pains to produce precisely this effect. In the lower part of his life busts movement is invariably implied.

In Rome Bernini's only rival as a portrait sculptor was Algardi, and if Algardi had discussed the theory and practice of the portrait, he would have expressed himself in an entirely different way. He was an advocate of static portraiture, and even in the finest of his life busts, the splendid portrait of Cardinal Laudivio Zacchia in Berlin (Plate 164), what he is representing is a man seated in a chair. The head is rendered with great sensibility, without distortion and in meticulous detail, yet there is an almost total lack of the immediacy and the directness through which, in Bernini's busts, the essence of the individual is isolated. Seldom has the human face been represented more delicately or more faithfully than in Algardi's busts, but when we translate them into flesh and blood we rapidly become aware of their deficiencies. In their own lifetimes, none the less, the two ranked equally as portrait sculptors. In 1650 the Duke of Modena, anxious to commission busts of himself and his brother Cardinal Rinaldo d'Este, proposed that Bernini and Algardi should each execute a bust. 'I say frankly,' he wrote, 'I am indifferent whether Bernini makes my bust or that of your Eminence,' adding that if Bernini's price were unwarrantably high, he would entrust Algardi with both busts.

Not all busts in Seicento Rome were necessarily life portraits. Soon after the accession of Urban VIII in 1623, Bernini was commissioned to carve portraits of the new Pope's parents, his uncle Monsignor Francesco Barberini (Plate 144), who had died when Bernini was a child, and the founder of the fortunes of the family, Antonio Barberini. Algardi, in particular, was a specialist in the carving of such portraits; one of the finest of them is the bust of Roberto Frangipane in San Marcello, and at the extreme end of his life he was engaged upon a bust of Laudivio Zacchia's brother, Paolo Emilio Zacchia, who had died in 1605 and whose features he was reconstructing from two paintings supplied by Zacchia's niece, Marchesa Rondanini. In the posthumous portraits of Algardi, the meticulous reproduction of detail comes to a sudden end, the features are generalised, and the body is handled with the freedom of figures in the Attila relief. Bernini's posthumous portraits, on the other hand, suffer from what can only be construed as loss. Marvellous as is the plastic continuity of the head of Francesco Barberini, and beautiful as is the contrast between the crumpled alb and the flat planes of the cassock that is worn over it, the bust lacks the intimation of direct experience that is the lifeblood of Bernini's portraiture.

There is another class of bust of which the subjects were indeed alive, but which were made without life sittings. The most celebrated of them is the lost bust of Charles I made from a portrait by Van Dyck, and they include the busts of Richelieu, probably after Philippe de Champaigne, and of Francesco I d'Este, after Sustermans (Plate 149). Bernini himself complained bitterly of the labour which these busts entailed. In one respect, however, they conferred on him a freedom he did not possess with the life portrait, the occasion to elaborate the meagre image offered by the painting with the free invention that was permissible in sculptures in other forms. The bust of Charles I (which for all its interest cannot have been one of Bernini's most significant achievements) was filled out with a scarf tied on the right shoulder and falling across the chest, while the superb bust of Francesco d'Este at Modena is enriched with drapery planned like that of St. Teresa, from which it takes on an adventitious emotive character. Indeed we may suspect that the long period of fourteen months which Bernini dedicated to the Este bust was not the outcome of necessity, but resulted from a disinterested fascination with the problems – the *recherche de particularités et délicatesses* in the face and flowing hair – that this extraordinary work involved.

Bernini's supreme achievements as a portrait sculptor none the less are his life busts, the Costanza Buonarelli in the Museo Nazionale in Florence, the twin busts of Cardinal Scipione Borghese, and the portraits of his first and greatest patron, Pope Urban VIII. These portraits are so direct, convey so strong a sense of speed in execution, and in one case, that of the second bust of Cardinal Scipione Borghese (Fig. 178), were indeed carved so rapidly, that they have sometimes been discussed as though they were the work of an inspired journalist. Not only is this view incorrect, but it may even be doubted whether there are any sculptured portraits in which the relation of the sculptor to his sitter is more intimate or more complete. Costanza Buonarelli (Fig. 176), Bernini's mistress for some years before his marriage in 1639, is a Latin sister of Saskia and Hélène Fourment. Cardinal Borghese was Bernini's patron for fifteen years before the portrait busts were carved, and Urban VIII, as Maffeo Barberini, had held the mirror for the self-portrait which Bernini introduced into his David, and impressed himself more strongly than any other individual on the sculptor's consciousness. The expression of the sitter may be evanescent, and the action in which he is presented may be transitory, but neither was an arbitrary choice, and each bust presupposes a close knowledge not of the features only but of the mind behind the mask. By contrast the bust of Thomas Baker in London – an occasional portrait carved during the sixteen-thirties when Bernini was working on the bust of Charles I – does not transcend the level of excellent reporting.

The two busts of Cardinal Borghese seem to have been carved in 1632, and have their closest parallel in the statue of Charity on the Urban VIII monument which Bernini was cogitating at the time. The sitter's head is turned slightly to his right, so that on the right-hand side the corpulent neck projects beyond the level of the jaw, the biretta is set crooked, the lips are parted, and the sockets of the eyes are deeply cut. The sources unfortunately tell us nothing of the stages through which this extraordinary portrait (Plate 148) was evolved, nothing, that is, save that when it was complete a flaw was discovered in the marble across the forehead, and that Bernini thereupon, in fourteen days, produced a second version of the bust (Fig. 178). Not unnaturally the features in the second version are rather less lively than in the first. Where the two busts differ most strikingly is not in the head, but in the lower part, for the sculptor seems to have sensed that in the area of the chest and shoulders the forms were over-animated to the verge of triviality, and since fate offered him a second chance, he decided that they should be restrained and unified. In this sense the second bust constitutes a critique of the first.

Just as the transition from the Apollo and Daphne to the figures on the Urban VIII tomb can be charted in terms of finished statues, so the transition from the Francesco Barberini to the Borghese portraits can be charted in terms of finished busts, and of busts moreover of one sitter, Pope Urban VIII. Within the first week of Bernini's stay in France, Chantelou noted in his journal: *Le pape Urbain VIII, de qui il a été aimé et considéré dès sa plus tendre jeunesse, est cité par lui à tout propos.* Bernini's admiration for his patron found an outlet in eight portraits. Some of these busts are emblematic – a colossal bronze bust of the Pope at Spoleto, for example, conforms to the norm of papal portraiture – and the handling of others is inferior – a marble bust in the Galleria Nazionale in Rome is a case in point. But in the aggregate the psychological significance of this series of busts is very great. It opens in 1623 with a portrait in San Lorenzo in Fonte in Rome, in which the Pope is shown bare-headed and the treatment of the cope is still recognisably related to that of the small bust of Paul V. In the late twenties this is succeeded by a bust now in the collection of Prince Urbano Barberini (Fig. 177), in which the Pope looks outwards to his right with an expression of benign determination, his berrettino pushed back from his intellectual forehead, and his mozzetto cut in a semi-circle through the shoulders and the chest. Finally, about 1635, Bernini summed up his long relationship in a large bust (Plate 145), which is perhaps his finest sculptured portrait. In this the body is treated with extraordinary serenity, and is consolidated by means of an expedient taken over from the second bust of Cardinal Borghese, two horizontal folds running the whole width of the chest. Above rises the majestic yet strangely introverted head, treated with an assurance and restraint, a sympathy and a compassion of which few sculptors have been capable.

For Bernini the art of sculpture was intuitive. In his youth he relived, as a spectator, the stories of classical mythology, and in his maturity he recreated the mystical experiences of the great figures of his age. His approach to portraiture was likewise through the imagination. For him the human personality was vibrant and alive, and could be captured only if the portrait bust were presented as the record of a reciprocal relationship. Each of his great portraits postulates the presence of a second figure, that of the sculptor, in the room. The standard by which his portraits must be judged is set not in Italy but in Spain and in the North by Velazquez and Rubens and Frans Hals, and in this exalted company it may be that Bernini, with his faith in portraiture as drama, was the most truthful portraitist of all.

THE HERITAGE OF BERNINI

BERNINI's death in November 1680 may seem an arbitrary point at which to bring this survey to an end. Why, it may be objected, is Baroque sculpture treated in so cursory a fashion, why are the contemporaries of Bernini not more fully dealt with, why are his followers not discussed? The answer to all three questions is implicit in the nature of Bernini's work. Bernini had a greater influence upon the art of his own time than any sculptor had ever exercised. He created a new type of religious sculpture, and so exactly did it meet the requirements of his age that it became an orthodoxy to which other artists, voluntarily or reluctantly, conformed. But his style, though widely imitated, was inimitable, because it presupposed a unique conjunction of great gifts. It presumed the ability to vitalise a more than life-size statue so that it retained the animation of a clay maquette. It presumed an imagination so vivid that the work, despite its enlarged scale, preserved its original intensity. It presumed the capacity to approach each commission freshly, and without reference to a preconceived repertory of forms. None of his contemporaries or followers measured up to these requirements. The most resourceful of them, Melchiore Caffà, in the Ecstasy of St. Catherine of Siena in Santa Caterina a Magnanapoli in Rome, explores no world of feeling that Bernini had not explored before. Ercole Ferrata, whose small models prove him to have been an artist of great inventiveness and sensibility, was unable, on the scale on which he was condemned to work, to invest his altars and sepulchral monuments with the least semblance of vivacity. In Naples Finelli relapsed on empty paraphrases of Bernini's style, and it was Bernini's idiom, shorn of its sensibility, that was carried to Florence by Foggini and to Venice by Parodi. The standard for criticism of these artists is supplied by the French sculptor, Puget, who, in the works he carved during a short residence in Genoa, evinces a more individual sense of form, a more personal imagination, and a more masterful technique.

Notable sculptures were, of course, produced after Bernini's death. The challenge of

Borromini's tabernacles in the nave of St. John Lateran provoked, in addition to a number of indifferent statues, two figures of exceptional quality, while Legros carved a beautiful relief altarpiece for Sant' Ignazio. But in the aggregate later Baroque sculpture is vapid and mannered and uninteresting. The reason for this is a simple one, that Bernini, who in his youth had created the mythologies of the Villa Borghese, weaned Italian sculptors from their age-old dependence upon the antique. Just as the classicising work of Puget is far superior to that of the native-born sculptors of his time, so the most distinguished statues produced in Rome in the middle of the eighteenth century are also by two Frenchmen, Slodtz and Houdon. Late in the century the breach was healed, when Canova, in Venice, worked out the synthesis we know as Neo-classicism, whereby the antique was once more called upon to play a part in the renewal of contemporary art. Canova was the last of the great artists who by this means brought about a revolution in Italian sculpture, and in that select company he was also the least talented. He was no Nicola Pisano or Donatello, no Michelangelo or Giovanni Bologna or Bernini. But though he was lacking in conviction and was fettered by the shackles of good taste, his historical importance is no less great than theirs. In our own time his work has slowly regained popularity, and in the not far distant future the neo-classic sculptures he inspired – those neglected statues in Italian parks and squares, those smooth, anonymous wall monuments – will be regarded with the same rather uncritical respect with which Baroque sculpture of less than the first rank is looked on now. It is here that the story of Italian sculpture after Bernini's death reaches its end, and the time has not yet come to write this book.